The Bottom Line of Green Is Black

The Bottom Line of Green Is Black

Strategies for Creating Profitable and Environmentally Sound Businesses

**TEDD SAUNDERS AND
LORETTA MCGOVERN**

 HarperSanFrancisco

A Division of HarperCollins*Publishers*

HarperSanFrancisco and the authors, in association with the Rainforest Action Network, will facilitate the planting of two trees for every one tree used in the manufacture of this book.

FIRST EDITION

Library of Congress Cataloging-in-Publication Data

Saunders, Tedd.
    The bottom line of green is black : strategies for creating
profitable and environmentally sound businesses / Tedd Saunders,
Loretta McGovern.
       p.   cm.
    Includes index.
    ISBN 0-06-250752-4 — ISBN 0-06-250753-2 (pbk.)
    1. Pollution—Economic aspects—United States. 2. United States—
Industries—Environmental aspects. 3. Green marketing—United
States. I. McGovern, Loretta. II. Title.
HD69.P6.P6S28   1993
658.4'08—dc20
                                      92-56114
                                           CIP

93 94 95 96 97 HAD 10 9 8 7 6 5 4 3 2 1

This edition is printed on acid-free paper that meets the American National Standards Institute Z39.48 Standard.

I dedicate this book to the many people who have inspired me to make this dream a reality.

To my wonderful family, especially my mother, Nina, my father, Roger, and my twin brother, Todd, for their faith in me and their belief in my passion.

To Liz for her expertise, boundless energy, and willingness to always lend a hand.

To Loretta for her tireless efforts and dedication to this labor of love.

And to all of my friends and colleagues for their total support and encouragement.

TS

This book is dedicated to you, Caitlin, my darling child. Although only six years old, you grasp the plight of the planet with a deep understanding and embrace the concerns of environmentalism with greater conviction and commitment than many adults do. On every page of this book is a silent message addressed to you, and it is simply this: "I love you." I pray we still have enough time to make this a more wholesome world for you and future generations.

LMG

CONTENTS

Acknowledgments

This book could not have been completed without the dedicated help of many friends and colleagues. First, the authors would like to thank Sandi Stricklin, producer of the Monitor Channel's award-winning program "The Good Green Earth," who proved to be an invaluable resource. She guided the organization of the book, prepared written research used throughout the text, and watched over the project like an expectant mother with toddlers still in tow. We thank our associates, writers, and business partners, Liz Kay and Doris Pike, who are always there when we need them. Our agent, Stacey Woolf, is greatly appreciated for her enthusiastic support and efforts on our behalf. And to our editor, Amy Hertz, whose meticulous eye and heavy hand with a number two pencil ensured that this book would be readable, thank you; we know it wasn't always easy.

We are also extremely grateful to the many organizations and individuals who contributed information to the book, especially to INFORM, Inc., New York; Norman Willard, EPA, Boston, Massachusetts; Frank Priznar, founder of the Institute of Environmental Auditing, Alexandria, VA; Paul Sorensen, Camp Dresser & McKee, Inc., Cambridge, Massachusetts; Jackie Ottman, J. Ottman, Inc., New York; Janet Bridges, Gaia Communications, Santa Monica, California; John MacDonald, John MacDonald Associates Ltd., Surrey, England; and attorney Mary Freeley, Rackemann, Sawyer & Brewster, Boston, Massachusetts.

Foreword

Too often we become bound by dominant paradigms and do not have the will or vision to overcome these trends to develop innovative and more positive solutions. Thankfully, there are individuals who are willing to buck the system, to face challenges and develop alternatives that are clearly improvements on the traditional methods of action.

Tedd Saunders is an individual who has expended a tremendous amount of personal energy, and has displayed true conviction and drive, in order to break down those traditional barriers to establish a program that yields tremendous environmental benefits and produces positive economic yields. The program that Tedd has developed at The Boston Park Plaza Hotel restructured established practices to create a new system that proved to be more profitable and undeniably more environmentally beneficial.

Environmental protection has been and still is viewed as the enemy of economic growth rather than an essential prerequisite to growth and the creation of new jobs. Since the inception of environmental laws and regulations, there has been a tension between environmental and business interests. This conflict traditionally pits the interest of corporate profit against the protection of natural resources. Corporations typically argue that complying with regulations costs money and diminishes profit. Environmentalists counter that the regulations exist to protect natural resources shared by all citizens and that the costs to companies are external costs that are minor compared to the long-term costs of neglect. While both arguments are worthy of consideration, the goals are not mutually exclusive and there is common ground. If we are to move beyond this stalemate, as a society and, perhaps most important, as individuals, we must look to those shared interests and common goals in order to move toward necessary solutions.

Tedd Saunders has found that common ground between profit and environmental protection. Through the creation of the program at The Boston Park Plaza Hotel and the writing of this book, Tedd Saunders shows he clearly understands and realizes that we face an impending world crisis of enormous proportions unless traditional norms are radically challenged and changed. The use of finite resources must be reduced. Tedd recognizes this; he also realizes that these changes cannot be forced, but must be fostered and developed in such a way as not to threaten our existing quality of life.

We look around in our own country at the thousands of toxic waste dumps, at the multi-billion-dollar mess at our nuclear arms facilities, at our polluted harbors and closed shellfish beds, and at the sad legacy of acid rain, and we realize that we have all contributed to these overwhelming problems through our "business as usual" approach.

We cannot continue as we are, and we cannot survive if others develop as we have, repeating the mistakes that we have made. For if the developing world grew with the same energy and general consumption habits of the developed world—if, for example, a billion Chinese were to become users of CFC-generating refrigerators powered by a coal-fired utility grid—it would not be long before we would face a global crisis more severe and unyielding than any yet known to humanity.

That's why we have to break through the old assumptions about environmental regulation and its conflict with the bottom line. We must commit ourselves to development and growth that is sustainable—a kind of Green Capitalism—where jobs and profits are linked to new technologies and practices, and where we are able to meet present needs without compromising the ability of our children to meet future needs.

Thankfully, the traditional conflict of businesses versus environmentalists is being challenged more and more. Businesses, consumers, and citizens are becoming increasingly aware that this conflict need not exist and that mutually beneficial solutions are possible. One of the greatest benefits of this book will be to raise this level of awareness so that other executives and consumers will be empowered to create innovative solutions. *The Bottom Line of Green Is Black: Strategies for Creating Profitable and Environmentally Sound Businesses* creates the blueprint so that others may follow these examples. My greatest hope is that the energy, enthusiasm, drive, and commitment that is described in this book and was devoted to crafting this book will inspire others to think creatively and innovatively about enviromental solutions.

SENATOR JOHN F. KERRY

Preface

The journey of a thousand miles begins with a single step.

Chinese proverb

This book was born out of the belief that we can all make a difference and that "Business," in particular, has a unique power to bring about positive environmental change.

It could be argued that all great entrepreneurs have been guided by the number one rule of business, that is, "The customer is always right." The number two rule might be, "If there is ever any doubt, refer to rule number one." Every sector of industry strives to uphold this tradition. But what are the new measurements of quality service?

Certainly two of the most important challenges facing business today are meeting our customers' changing needs and maintaining and improving our quality of service. Corporate environmentalism can serve as a catalyst for both of these objectives.

In contrast to manufacturing, the travel and service industries have always been considered "clean" industries. However, as consumers have become more environmentally aware, they have begun to recognize the wastefulness inherent in the marketplace at large. All facets of industry need to respond to this new consciousness. The long-term viability of any company is directly related to its ability to accommodate customers' changing demands.

Over the last two decades, consumer expectations have risen dramatically. Despite all the trends we have adapted to over the years on behalf of our clientele, improving quality and standards of service are still of the greatest importance. One question remains clear: How do we profitably respond to the constantly changing demands of our customers? The first thing we must do is learn to listen to them carefully. According to a major market survey done by the Michael Peters Group, "9 out of 10 respondents stated that environmental concerns are a top priority." In a Lou Harris poll, 97 percent of those surveyed think business and government are doing an inadequate job of protecting the environment. The message is being voiced loud and clear.

Today some progressive companies have already begun to take this call to action seriously and are implementing environmental initiatives that balance economic viability with ecological responsibility. Based on the variety of programs sponsored by business today, the possibilities for positive change are limited only by imagination and commitment.

Some astounding facts that have shaped our concern are the seemingly invisible effect we all have on our environment. The National Wildlife Federation informs us that "every 20 minutes another species becomes extinct due to global pollution and the unchecked clear cutting of forests . . . ; the effects of so called progress." This current shortsighted approach aimed only at convenience and immediate profit sacrifices any future potential for sustainability or efficient use of our limited resources. Much closer to home, did you know that producing a single pat of butter requires 100 gallons of water? Another shocking statistic is that Americans alone toss out enough paper and plastic cups and utensils every year to circle the equator three hundred times.

In this global economy, it goes without saying that all businesses rely on resources from around the world. Many of the products we use every day are derived from materials produced in faraway and unfamiliar places. Yet we must take into account the effect our purchasing decisions have on these distant lands and look not only at the local impact of our consumption but also at its effect on our global natural resources and indigenous cultures. Business has a unique opportunity to educate its consumers to this double-edged sword and to influence positively the behavior of people everywhere.

Certainly environmental issues can be overwhelming at first glance. How can we as a society that has always seen quantity as synonymous with quality maintain our high standards while lessening the often concealed environmental impact of economic advancement? Contrary to popular belief, environmental action does not mean lower quality of life or a loosening of standards of production. In fact in many cases it presents opportunities to reexamine past practices, rethink product presentation, and reshape consumer perception, ultimately allowing us to offer our customers more.

For three generations, my family has owned and operated hotels in the United States. I was raised in a tradition of hospitality and service that emphasized value and quality. Although we had much, we learned not to take anything for granted and to maintain a healthy respect for the world around us.

A number of years ago, it occurred to me that many of the environmentally responsible changes I had made in my own life were relevant in the larger context of my family's business. Little did I realize then that such a simple idea could unleash such a cataclysm. What appeared to be just a set of practical changes has become, in its simplicity, a model for other companies to follow. No matter how mired your company may be in regulatory demands, there are always opportunities to identify and create solutions that are beneficial for both your business, your customers, and the environment.

I did not, however, grow up with an idealistic view of the world. The constant presence of a family-owned and -operated business affected even my childhood and helped me develop a balanced perspective firmly rooted in the realities of life.

One day in 1989, preparing for my family's weekly executive committee meeting, I began to formulate the idea that our business could truly benefit from being more environmentally conscious. I presented the concept with much enthusiasm but with little evidence to support my convictions. Understandably my suggestions were met with a healthy skepticism but an openness to substantiation.

As the idea of "greening" our hotel gained momentum, I was given the liberty to question long-established policies and procedures. I was allowed to use my family's largest property, The Boston Park Plaza Hotel & Towers, an elegant, 977-room historic hotel, to test my ideas. Within three years, with the support and encouragement of my entire family and the energy of my colleague Liz Kay, we transformed every method of operation at the hotel and revolutionized the way we do business.

What began as a simple white-paper recycling project has blossomed into a comprehensive environmental campaign with more than ninety-five initiatives. We have sought to be creative while rethinking solid waste reduction, energy and water conservation, hazardous material elimination as well as education and communications.

Recently The Boston Park Plaza received the 1992 President's Environment and Conservation Challenge Gold Medal Award for Quality Environmental Management. In a discussion with one of the technical advisers at the ceremony, I discovered that what differentiated our effort from other innovative campaigns was that we "just did it." I am not advocating a careless approach to corporate environmentalism. I am simply suggesting that the time has come to take measured action rather than cautiously studying the problem or remaining paralyzed by the overwhelming prospect of changing business practices.

From the beginning of this entire process, a set of ideals has emerged that not only guides but continues to inspire me:

- Corporate environmentalism is good business.
- Efficiency is the common ally of business and the environment.
- Wastefulness is the common enemy of business and the environment.
- Environmental action need not mean lower quality or relaxation of standards.
- A comprehensive approach should balance economic viability with environmental responsibility.
- Daily choices have long-term effects.
- We all have a shared responsibility to reduce the depletion of our limited natural resources.
- We need to support a new consumerism that practices moderation.
- A long-term perspective is crucial.
- The key to success is commitment.
- Each of us can make a difference.

The environment is one of the few issues that touch all aspects of our lives and all segments of our society. It is both necessary and possible for all of us to think creatively about environmental initiatives. One of the primary goals of this book is to instill in others the same concern for the environment that I feel. Like a photographer who looks at everything through the lens of his camera, I now look at all my daily actions with an environmental perspective. Once you get caught up in this new focus, it changes how you view consumption. Oliver Wendell Holmes once said, "A mind that is stretched by a new experience can never go back to its old dimension."

I hope that the concepts and case studies presented in this book inspire other businesses and create a ripple effect that will benefit others. We can rectify our current situation only if we begin collectively to take environmental action—no matter how small. As Edmund Burke wrote, "No one made a greater mistake than he who did nothing because he could only do a little."

As a third-generation family businessman, I have found this personal and professional commitment to the environment to be one of the most powerful and rewarding decisions in my life. I hope that by these examples, other companies will recognize this opportunity. We must acknowledge the impact of our everyday actions and make changes to minimize their effects on the planet. "We did not inherit the earth from our ancestors, we merely borrow it from our children," aptly states a Native American saying. We cannot wait until our supply of resources has vanished before we give them the respect they deserve.

TEDD SAUNDERS

Introduction

"The time has come," the Walrus said, "to talk of many things: of shoes—and ships—and sealing wax—of cabbages—and kings—and why the sea is boiling hot—and whether pigs have wings."

Lewis Carroll

Environmental consequences are no longer simply a concern of a fringe element. Environmental issues are receiving broad recognition and growing popular support.

The time has come to speak of the single most effective safeguard against the encroaching global environmental crisis: To eliminate the root cause of environmental damage, we need to change the ways in which industries operate. A collective decision needs to be made to regard natural forces not as something to conquer but as forces with which we comply and cooperate.

Responding to the growing public demand, some farsighted companies are beginning to employ environmentally aware business practices. The aim of this book is to introduce the concept of business ecology as the best available way to meet society's environmental goals and to create more flexible and profitable businesses. The intent is to reveal strategies, management techniques, and emergent technologies various companies have selected to ensure continued or increased vitality while contributing to the resolution of pressing environmental problems.

It is easy to blame the business community for the ills the planet suffers, but the bottom line is that it is not in our best interest to see corporations destroyed or eliminated. Even diehard environmentalists use the products of some of the corporations we, as citizens, criticize. We rely on companies for employment, even when we would prefer them to provide us with more socially responsible workplaces. As often as not, businesses fail to comply with our expectations not deliberately or maliciously but because they lack knowledge or cannot foresee the far-reaching consequences of an action. Until social responsibility and ecology become a part of the business education curriculum, the leadership of a few companies, openly supported by the public, will dictate the actions of their peers.

Industrialization needs to be in the reclamation business, not the degradation business. As in all things, prevention is less expensive than remedial action. Companies that have resisted the change but have been forced to deal with pollution prevention find that their actions have increased profitability. When energy efficiency evolves into a revenue generator and reduces the impact on the environment, a message different from what we are used to hearing is sent. And when consumers begin to support a company's environmental activities, or organizations (including the media) applaud a company's efforts, the credibility and significance of the act is confirmed. All of these components combined create a new attitude toward corporate responsibility and performance.

Overview:
Business and the Environment

Before 1970 the corporate mission was simple—increase the bottom line. In the 1970s new management concepts began to appear: total quality management, high performance, self-managed work teams. As these concepts became better defined, they served to form a new corporate culture in which product was shaped by the demands of the customer.

The customer now demands that business take into account the environmental impact of a product or service. Businesses have had to rethink their mission to center their standards on the customer base and its environment. Many businesses are beginning to learn that customer satisfaction goes hand in glove with environmental responsibility.

Although it is unclear whether or not consumers are truly willing to make the sacrifices they profess to be willing to make, it is certain that they expect companies to demonstrate responsibility. Many companies have read the demands of the marketplace with uncanny foresight and have already incorporated environmental quality as part of their total quality management programs.

What is environmental management? It is a holistic, systematic approach to practicing environmental responsibility aimed at the thoughtful and ethical use of our natural resources. A comprehensive program incorporates concern for public health and respect for its environment and its community. A comprehensive initiative moves businesses beyond compliance and into the realm of environmental excellence. Striving for excellence is the ultimate total quality management effort.

It is generally recognized that grave environmental problems exist and that they may get worse if serious changes aren't made in the way we live and work. Although significant philosophical debate for or against environmentalism has taken place, very little information about practical approaches has been offered to businesses geared specifically for their use.

Business can no longer afford to react to consumers alone. The challenge is for business to balance the consumer desire for convenience, cost, and quality with environmentally sound practices. It is even better for the bottom line and for a company's credibility and competitiveness if the company takes a proactive approach and defines the emerging business ecology itself. Business ecology is a philosophy that contends that environmentalism and profitability are not mutually exclusive.

Understanding the Profit Inherent in Environmental Management

> *Clean and green engenders growth, profit and lasting competitive advantage.*
>
> **Tom Peters, *In Search of Excellence***

Commercial enterprise has always demanded the right to make a profit. Consumers have endorsed that privilege. Commerce and consumerism on a global scale have exacted an outrageous price: the potential collapse of human cultures and their environment. Economic self-interest can no longer be an acceptable excuse for international exploitation. Worsening water shortages presage famines. Deforestation is rife. The extinction of plant and animal species exceeds the rate of extinction of the dinosaurs. Irreplaceable topsoil is being washed away. Industrial pollutants poison the air. Ecological degradation, degeneration, and devastation are the debacle of the twentieth century.

We need to accept that we will continue to face burgeoning calamities and social upheavals around the globe unless we learn to attain a balance with our environment. Decisions made today by corporations, industry, and governments will do much to determine the quality of life we can enjoy in the future.

In this way, moneymaking has been perversely myopic. In tropical forests, efforts are concentrated on the harvesting of timber, even though this practice offers the lowest cost-benefit for the long term. The conservation of these forests and their natural resources in fact ranges from two to twenty times greater in monetary value than the short-term appreciation gained from clear-cutting timber.

It is unlikely that we will ever develop a universally quixotic economy wherein values and social responsibility move businesses to put the quality of life before money. Yet we may see a movement to balance values, society, and ecology with making money, so that companies and communities around the world can thrive together.

Businesses adopting an environmental approach to production are discovering solutions. The precepts are to rely on renewable resources, to ensure that they are renewed, and to avoid producing wastes that cannot become resources. It is difficult to make the transition from a high-consumption, high-effluent economy to a conservation-minded, renewable one; but many companies and consumers, here and abroad, are making a genuine effort to do so. By way of example, the San Francisco Hilton cut its garbage bill by nearly a third to $198,850 in 1991 from $289,613 in 1988 by recycling cardboard and paper. The nineteen-hundred-room hotel figures it also saved 3,281 trees. The Ritz-Carlton in San Francisco, after recycling less than a year, was able to reduce its garbage pickups to eight times a week from thirteen for a savings of $11,000 within the same time period.

The environmental action plan that we put into place at The Boston Park Plaza Hotel shook the foundation of the hospitality industry. We implemented over ninety environmental initiatives and, by doing so, created the most inclusive environmental plan existing in any service-related industry. The hotel's comprehensive "green" program not only reduced costs but attracted nearly a million dollars of new business in the first quarter of 1992 from meeting planners, event organizers, and transient guests choosing the hotel for its environmental initiatives.

Values are changing. Just as the civil rights movement changed the way we view minority issues and as the feminist movement altered concepts of gender equality, so the green movement has convinced the public of our shared responsibility for natural resources. Our values have evolved to embrace the sentiment that if we are to survive as a culture or a species, we shall do so only by contributing to the welfare of one another and to the world we share.

How to Use This Book

Corporations that think they can drag their heels indefinitely on genuine environmental problems should be advised: Society won't tolerate it . . . and other companies with real sensitivity and environmental commitment will be there to supply your customers after you are gone.

Edgar S. Woolard, chairman, DuPont
World Resource Institute, 12 December 1989

Inefficiency results in trying to reinvent the wheel each time a new environmental process is forwarded. The environment not only provides the opportunity for businesses to come together across competitive lines, it allows for a unified approach to solving a commonly shared problem. In most cases this requires technology to provide answers. Here the environment is poised to provide new methods for doing business, innovative approaches to traditional processes, and, above all, a fusing of new technology with existing methods. Just as companies have learned to incorporate an increasingly computer-driven means of communication, they will learn to incorporate recycling, reduction, and reuse in everyday business practices.

Each business profiled in this book will have varying priorities that drive their programs. Where government has not provided leadership, companies have established their own priorities—or hierarchy, if you will—that enable them both to comply with existing legislation and to fulfill their own vision of environmental sensibilities. While this book does not attempt to be an exhaustive study of every program throughout the United States, it is an endeavor to provide role models that others may find informative, enlightening, and compelling.

The businesses featured here have made great strides in awakening others to the fact that change is imminent. Their efforts are not token environmentalism, yet no company can hope to change 100 percent overnight and remain viable. The programs are not complete, and each possesses areas open to criticism. They should be viewed as works-in-progress. Each company has agreed that there is an educational process to implementation. As they learn more, they bring more of their operations on-line.

We applaud the initiative of these companies, regardless of whether they are motivated by consumer demand, government regulations, or philosophical beliefs. These companies are spearheading changes within their industries and setting precedents. Their environmental programs are benchmarks for other businesses. The practical advice collected in these case histories will provide readers with the framework necessary to create effective environmental action plans tailored to the needs of a business with two employees or to be incorporated by one that employs hundreds.

Background information on legislation, the implications of the laws, and voluntary recommendations from the EPA appear in the Addendum. The body of the text illustrates how businesses have adopted environmental concerns into their corporate cultures and quality assurance programs. We also provide guidelines and advice from others on how best to market and promote your environmental efforts. Evaluations and assessment checklists are included to help the reader establish an action plan. A comprehensive resource guide and bibliography offers information that will help guide the first steps on the journey.

CHAPTER ONE

Food Processing
Restaurants
Grocery Stores

It Began with an Apple

In a busy industrial district in Somerville, Massachusetts, flourishing with existing mills and works, Michael Durant founded his vinegar works company at 48 Washington Street. The year was 1865, when trainloads of apples from New England farms were hauled, daily, by horse-drawn carriages and delivered to this street, to be processed into cider and vinegar at the numerous mills lining the way.

M. Durant & Sons would eclipse its neighbors until, in 1907, it stood alone, the solitary surviving vinegar works in the city, the last of its era.

Durant & Sons evolved into larger companies under various names and owners. The company welcomed the twentieth century as the New England Vinegar Works under the sole proprietorship of Arthur Rowse, a former salesman for the company. The Rowse family has retained ownership since.

A Heritage of Doing Well and Staying Good

From the beginning the company was built on idealism. When Prohibition loomed, Rowse was offered half a million dollars for all the hard cider he had in stock, ten times its value. Rowse turned down the $1 a gallon (this when a dollar actually meant something), refusing to encourage men to drink and swagger home to abuse their families. To teetotaler Rowse drunkenness was a sin. During those years, gross sales figures for the Rowse company were $17,000.

Around 1920 the New England Vinegar Works was among the first to bottle vinegar in small containers rather than to sell it by the barrel to be dispensed at general stores. The plant purchased long-necked, secondhand grape juice bottles. They were washed, siphon-filled, and topped with crown caps. To transport the bottles, the company used egg crates with wood shavings deposited around the bottles to prevent breakage, a precursor to environmentally correct reuse and recycling to fulfill economic needs!

The company continued to prosper under the leadership of several generations of the Rowse family, despite some poorly calculated mergers and acquisitions and a few ambitious endeavors that failed due to technological mishaps. Growth precipitated a move in the 1930s to the heart of Nashoba Valley, Littleton, Massachusetts, . . . apple country.

Reusable novelty bottles were a consistent marketing strategy of the company throughout its long history. There were bottles that served as vinegar decanters and a cider bottle that could be reused as a pitcher when it was emptied of the product. Character bottles were kept for decorative reasons and are valuable collectibles today.

Over the years the company diversified. New technology allowed for the production of juices, among other product lines, and canned juices were much in demand during World War II. The name of the company, which denoted vinegar works, was no longer suitable. It was renamed New England Apple Products, which promoted its product line with the slogan "very fine." A few years ago, the descriptive "Veryfine" became a trade name for the company. But it was while trying to freeze-dry McIntosh apple slices, an experiment that failed to produce edible apple slices but succeeded in producing apple sauce, that Veryfine created a product that finally put its name on the map.

Environment, an Early Commitment

The company continued its personal commitment to improving the quality of its products and its facilities. The owners were always among the first to try to work with any advancements in industry technology, those that would benefit the company, its product line, its employees, its community, and its bottom line.

In 1965 the firm installed a wastewater treatment plant, the first privately owned facility of its kind in New England and in the juice industry. The installation occurred before the Clean Water Act was passed in 1970, at a cost of $75,000. The treatment plant dealt with the sulfide gases emitted when anaerobic bacteria from sugars and fruit acids were dumped into lagoons. Wastewater pumped into an eighty-thousand-gallon tank was agitated, like water in a washing machine, causing the aerobic bacteria to attack the sugars, giving off carbon dioxide instead of malodorous gas. Veryfine became a better neighbor in the process as well. Not only were the odors eliminated, but the sludge created by the process settled out, clean water was pumped into the lagoons, and the sludge, rich in phosphate and nitrogen, was composted, repackaged as soil amendments, and sold as compost to nurseries and consumers throughout New England. The residual from apples was supplied to farmers as a feed supplement for livestock.

In 1985 the Associated Industries of Massachusetts recognized Veryfine with its Ecologue Award for "commitment and success in solid waste management, water pollution control and plant beautification." Veryfine has a full recycling program for metals, plastics, paper, and wood that otherwise might be destined for landfills. The company also employs two full-time recyclers, who recycle all solid waste generated by employees.

With the money accrued from recycling cans and bottles, staff can purchase new equipment. Create an employee wish list for the use of the funds your office or department collects.

Veryfine Products has always moved quickly to address a wide range of environmental concerns. Veryfine's recycling efforts are a good illustration of the extent the company has gone to in order to prevent generations of solid waste in landfills. Its efforts predate the collective consciousness of the burgeoning solid waste disposal problem in this country. The company currently recycles 90 to 95 percent of the organic and solid waste it generates. It is the conviction of the company that all manufacturers have a responsibility to protect the environment. To that end, Veryfine has set up comprehensive programs that serve as models for many industries.

The philosophy at Veryfine, from the president on down, is that "we and our companies should have a deep and abiding concern for the earth and its environment." Company programs range from a review of the chemicals purchased to environmental education for all its employees. Five specific areas are the focus of their program:

1 Recycling
2 Source reduction/pollution prevention
3 Employee education
4 Habitat restoration/plant beautification
5 Product packaging

Like many of the companies reviewed in this book, Veryfine has taken the stance that a fragmentary approach to environmental implementation will not work. Its program is therefore based on a "holistic system" covering all areas of environment. The theory is that dealing with any one part without dealing with the concept of environment as a whole will lead only to a series of quick fixes resulting in less effective long-range impact. Short-term quick fixes end up costing more in the long run and are much less profitable than holistic, long-range plans. The business adage that "environment costs" is true only when companies fail to consider the wider impact of their practices.

"Understanding and protecting the ecological connectedness of all the environmentally complex interrelationships is important," says Sam Rowse, president of Veryfine. "At Veryfine, we believe that the multiple challenges of complex environmental decisions require the participation of our management and employees to reach its objective." Similar views are shared by all the successful environmental programs we have examined in other companies.

Waste Not, Want Not

Veryfine Products began a comprehensive recycling program in 1982. Currently it recycles 90 to 95 percent of all the solid/organic waste it generates.

Looking at certain numbers, one can quantify the enduring impact Veryfine is making on the environment. For example, the 350 tons of corrugated cardboard that was recycled in 1991 resulted in the following savings:

1 Approximately 7,650 trees

2 1,791,350 kws of energy (enough to power 349 average households for six months)

3 2,985,584 gallons of water

4 25,590 pounds of air pollution effluents

5 1,279.78 cubic yards of landfill material (such savings will work to reduce need for more landfills)

6 Taxpayer-funded waste disposal costs

Recycling efforts also work to turn trash into valuable resources, protecting natural resources from being wasted. Recycled paper is also produced in cleaner, less toxic processes than nonrecycled paper. Making new aluminum from used cans takes 95 percent less energy than producing aluminum from bauxite ore. The energy saved per can is the equivalent of that required to keep a hundred-watt bulb burning for three and a half hours.

Recycling efforts have also been economically beneficial to the company. "The environment is not an afterthought," claims Rowse. "It is essential to strong economic growth. Growth with a sustainable environment is feasible and necessary for our future."

In-Plant Practices

Source reduction and pollution prevention at Veryfine Products is defined as "In-Plant" practices that reduce or eliminate the water/product or other waste that is discharged to the waste treatment plant or put into the trash dumpster. Veryfine has done this in two ways.

1 Substitution: They review all chemicals they purchase, changing any environmentally damaging chemicals to more environmentally safe chemicals. They have changed lubricants, disinfectants, pH buffer chemicals, and ice melt, thus far. This effort intends to stop pollution before it starts, at the source.

2 Production process modernization: The company has upgraded or replaced existing production process equipment and methods with other procedures and processes that generate less waste, on the basis that pollution prevention through source reduction and sound recycling programs is highly desirable. This portion of the program is reflected in the company's adoption of new housekeeping practices, process line adjustments and process control equipment, and changes in methods of operation.

Veryfine has a vested interest in the water supply that runs under the ground where the plant is located. The plant was built over one of Littleton's major groundwater supplies. The company has installed eleven monitoring wells so that it and the town can monitor groundwater quality, flow, and elevations of the water table.

Water conservation has become an integral part of Veryfine's environmental program. The company believes conservation can temper or even curtail its demand for water. The era of cheap water is drawing to a close. Therefore not only does conservation protect natural habitats, it benefits the company's bottom line.

Veryfine has installed a cooling tower system that saves about 50 million gallons of water a year. To add to the efficiency of the system, C.I.P. (cleaning in place) systems have been added to clean the process lines. "We have changed the water hose to high pressure–low volume cleaning equipment," explains the company's environmental engineer, Bill Lindsey. "These changes have saved twenty-five thousand gallons of water a day, or about six million gallons a year. In the following years, we will be challenged to manage our water uses on a more reasonable basis. Our reward for conservation will be that all of us will come out ahead in terms of jobs, money, and water."

Employee Education and Public Outreach

It is the firm belief of all the companies with comprehensive environmental programs and of the authors that without an employee education component an environmental plan is doomed to failure. Veryfine Products is no exception to the rule. The company has paid for employees to attend the University of Lowell to become wastewater treatment operators. The company also produces a newsletter with an environmental column to keep employees informed on issues, technology, opportunities, and the internal program. An in-house training program provides information on hazardous waste handling and prevention, "right to know" information on chemical hazards, and spill control. Articles and pamphlets are regularly disseminated to employees, such as the EPA's *Recycle* or *Citizen's Guide to Pesticides* or the Earth Works Group's *Recycler's Handbook*. Employee education stresses the need to prevent pollution at all sources.

In 1992 Veryfine sponsored a water-quality educational program with the Massachusetts Audubon Society. The program involved field studies by teachers and children in the state. In addition Veryfine sponsors a recycling education program entitled "Garbage Is My Bag" in school systems in the Northeast. This forty-five-minute program educates children in kindergarten through eighth grade about solid waste problems and recycling issues. In 1993 this program was expanded to address parents and community officials.

Veryfine president Samuel Rowse participates in a speakers bureau program to address corporate environmental responsibility. Veryfine has developed an environmental trade advertising campaign that calls attention to the environmental issues facing manufacturing companies and their suppliers.

Veryfine has recently accepted the "CONEG Challenge" offered by the Coalition of Northeast Governors. As part of this challenge, Veryfine encourages other major companies to follow their lead by voluntarily implementing the Preferred Packaging Guidelines as endorsed by CONEG in 1989.

Currently Veryfine sponsors numerous environmental events. These include Save the Harbor, Save the Bay, Environmental Police Officers Association, Walden Woods Project, Waste Reduction Strategies Conference, Massachusetts Audubon Society Harvest Days, and Tufts New England Environmental Conferences, among others. In the future Veryfine will promote environmental messages through its vending machines and product packaging.

Natural Resources as Assets

The nation behaves well if it treats the natural resources as assets which it must turn over to the next generation; increased and not impaired in value.

Theodore Roosevelt

Veryfine has recognized the environment as a key economic asset. The company believes that achieving a satisfactory balance between environment and development in order to maintain a sustainable ecology is an urgent task. Veryfine has spent over a million dollars in landscaping and site beautification at its three industrial locations, Littleton, Ayer, and Westford, Massachusetts.

The Littleton facility is bordered on three sides by land zoned for residential use and is in full public view. To show concern for its residential neighbors, Veryfine built a 25-foot-high, 400-foot-long berm to obscure the view and dramatically reduce sound transmissions from the production facility. The top of the berm is planted with trees and shrubs.

A part of Veryfine's ongoing commitment to the environment was to build an $8.5 million state-of-the-art wastewater purification facility, opened in 1992, that has far surpassed the EPA standards. In fact EPA officials have visited Veryfine to learn about the facility's advanced technology.

They have designed and implemented a plan to restore a two-acre basin that has been part of the wastewater treatment system on the site since the 1960s. The new treatment plant provides a higher and more consistent level of treatment than was possible with the original water purification plant, making continued discharges to the lagoons unnecessary. Veryfine's facility saves nearly 20 million gallons of water a year and returns to nature water that is virtually as clean as—and sometimes even cleaner than—when it first came out of the tap.

Rather than simply abandon or fill the lagoon, Veryfine has renovated it to provide aquatic and wetland habitats for flood storage, water quality improvement, and wildlife. The initial steps in the renovation process entailed hydraulic dredging of the organic solids that had accumulated in the basin from the wastewater discharges. When removed, the organic solids were sent to a composting facility.

The hydraulic design criteria for the renovated pond address both the quantity and the quality of the site's surface water discharges. The basin functions to control the rate of storm water discharges from the Littleton facility to ensure no increases in flood peaks downstream; and the pond's morphometry and hydraulic characteristics are consistent with the EPA's National Urban Runoff Program (NURP) guidelines for effective treatment of runoff quality.

Wetland habitats are being promoted around the open water for both water quality improvements and wildlife use. Existing "floating mats" of emergent wetland plants such as cattails are being preserved and positioned to settle on the basin bottom as water levels are modified. The water level changes will also bring to the surface natural organic soils that will develop into shallow marshes. Planting around the periphery of the pond will further enhance its aesthetics and its appeal to wildlife.

At the Ayer distribution center, the company addressed the residential concern about views and sounds by again building a berm. At its corporate headquarters in Westford, Veryfine renovated a pond and left a 10-foot natural strip around the pond for wildlife. The insect and herptile populations have readily colonized the new pond, and new aquatic plant communities are established. Other vertebrate species, waterfowl, and aquatically linked mammals are using the pond. To provide food and cover plants for waterfowl, the sloping edges of the pond are planted with white water lily, pickerelweed, bur reed, and duck potato. The company has also created a nature trail for employees. Both the footpath and the wooden bridges crossing the pond are designed to ensure minimal intrusion.

Good Things Come in Packages

Packaging is a highly controversial issue and is a subject that often strikes fear in the hearts of manufacturers.

Veryfine is committed to producing an environmentally sound, superior-quality product and thoroughly researches all of its packaging decisions. Veryfine's packaging is made of 100 percent recyclable materials: glass, aluminum, and polystyrene foam.

Glass containers are 100 percent recyclable and can be made into new glass bottles and jars. Veryfine's glass packaging is made from the highest-percentage recycled glass currently available to glass manufacturers, which is at least 50 percent recycled glass. (The glass industry is dedicated to increasing this percentage through improved return systems and education.) Veryfine bottles are made from clear, or flint, glass. This is the type of glass that is most easily recycled. Recycled glass, or cullet, is used as primary raw material in the production of new glass. The cullet melts at a lower temperature than the materials used to make new glass, thereby decreasing energy consumption. Processing recycled glass also requires half the water used in making new glass and decreases the air pollution generated by 20 percent. It also cuts the necessary mining by 80 percent, conserving raw materials such as silica sand, limestone, and soda ash. Glass can be reused an infinite number of times.

Veryfine's aluminum cans are made of a minimum of 55 percent recycled aluminum and sometimes as much as 100 percent. Recycling aluminum saves 95 percent of the energy needed to make new aluminum while decreasing the amount of ore mining required to make new aluminum. It is ten times more expensive to turn ore into new aluminum than it is to reprocess used cans. There are strong economic incentives for recycling the material.

The labels on Veryfine bottles are made from 100 percent recyclable polystyrene foam. Chlorofluorocarbons are not used in the manufacturing of the labels, and the company is endeavoring to eliminate the use of hydrofluorocarbons in the future. Veryfine believes that the manufacturing of polystyrene foam labels is an energy-efficient process that is safe for the environment. Because of the protective action of these foam labels, the company can package juice in lighter glass. If a paper label were used, the bottle would have to be 15 to 20 percent thicker to avoid breakage during production and transportation. Manufacturing a thicker bottle would use additional unrenewable energy sources. When the bottles with the foam labels are recycled, the label does not need to be removed, because the polystyrene foam adds fuel value in the melting process. The label parts that burn off in the process do so safely and cleanly. Polystyrene foam has a very high energy quality, thereby accelerating and improving the combustion process in incinerators and glass furnaces as it burns, allowing more efficient operation.

When completely combusted, the foam, like paper, gives off only carbon dioxide, water, and trace levels of ash. When efficiently burned, 100 pounds of polystyrene foam yields one-hundredth of a pound of ash residue, while 100 pounds of mixed solid waste yields 25 pounds of residue.

The criticism most often voiced regarding Veryfine's use of foam labels is that when they end up in landfill they are not biodegradable. Veryfine contends that the labels cause no ecological harm. Although not biodegradable, they are chemically inert. They therefore do not emit any toxic gases, nor do they pollute the groundwater with chemical residue, as some of their biodegradable counterparts have been known to do.

Veryfine's controversial label can be recycled if it is removed from the bottle. Polystyrene foam is among the most recyclable of all plastics and can be used to make numerous molded or fabricated items that have long and multiple life cycles, including landscape timbers, household containers, and carpeting.

Additionally Veryfine products are capped with recyclable metal, packaged in corrugated cardboard trays, also recyclable, and wrapped with the thinnest polyethylene possible, also recyclable. Veryfine has eliminated the use of plastic six-pack rings around its aluminum cans. (However, we have recently learned that work has been done, and is continuing, to create plastic rings that biodegrade when exposed to sunlight.)

In November 1990 Veryfine became the only company to receive the Massachusetts Audubon Society's Audubon A Award in honor of its environmental leadership in the business community and for its outstanding achievement in environmental protection and the conservation of energy resources. The same year the company's sales rose to $200 million.

A curious footnote to the history of Veryfine was added in 1986 when success exacted an emotional price. Veryfine was compelled by a depressed vinegar market to leave the vinegar works trade of its birth. It was an easy financial decision, but a tough personal one for the Rowses. Yet the more things change, the more they stay the same. For more than 125 years, whether bottled as cider vinegar, apple sauce, or apple juice, the apples of New England orchards, first planted by the legendary Johnny Appleseed, have consistently borne fruit for Veryfine, and they promise to do so well into the future. At Veryfine, the apple, like all the earth's bounty, is legion.

Coca-Cola's Commitment
Is the Real Thing

In 1987 the Coca-Cola Company initiated an office recycling program at its Atlanta headquarters complex. On average, its employees divert 750,000 pounds of materials annually from the office waste stream.

Coca-Cola employees recycle office paper, computer paper, telephone books, laser printer cartridges, polystyrene cups, and food cartons, aluminum cans, plastic cutlery, plastic bottles, newspapers, glass, and corrugated cardboard. Proceeds from the sale of these items, more than $100,000 thus far, are donated to local charities. Coca-Cola encourages employees to bring in recyclables from home and to place them in bins at its drop-off center. This award-winning program serves as a model for all of Coca-Cola's international divisions as well as for other businesses.

Every day, Americans throw away thousands of perfectly usable pens, tape dispensers, paper clips, rubber bands, and other office supplies that end up in landfills. Think of how items can be reused or refilled.

The Coca-Cola Company was also one of the first major corporations to develop a comprehensive environmental education program for employees: an advanced laser disc Environmental Development Program. The program serves two purposes: to help employees understand environmental issues so they may conduct business in accordance with the company's principles and policies, and to encourage employees to take ownership of the issues so that they can do their part to enhance and protect the quality of the environment. The company offers similar information to its customers and its suppliers.

Coca-Cola has a lengthy environmental policy statement that is written from a global perspective. With a product recognized around the world, Coca-Cola has an impact on the lives of billions of people, and their written environmental commitment reflects the enormity of their responsibility to conduct business in an environmentally sound way.

Like most manufacturers of food products, Coca-Cola is governed by regulations and legislation. It is not surprising, therefore, that the first pledge it makes is to comply with applicable environmental laws. But, like most of the companies we have selected for inclusion in this book, they pledge to go beyond compliance in "the absence of governmental regulation to operate in an environmentally responsible manner." Coca-Cola has determined that it is financially beneficial, politically correct, and promotionally wise to incorporate environmental thinking into their corporate culture.

At the top of Coca-Cola's hierarchy of priorities is waste reduction. The company pledges to minimize the environmental impact of its operations, products, and packages through research and the application of new technology. Manufacturers are forced to address the issues of solid waste management, and Coca-Cola is committed to both reducing and recycling the solid waste generated in its facilities as well as to helping communities where it operates to implement recycling and sound solid waste management systems.

The company pledges also to minimize the discharge of waste materials by using responsible pollution-control practices and, recognizing the significance of the interrelationship between energy and the environment, the company promotes efficiency of energy use throughout its systems.

As a continuing component of its policy and its pledge to be environmentally accountable, the company periodically conducts audits of its performance and practices and shares that information with other businesses and the public.

The Challenge of Solid Waste Issues

According to Coca-Cola's research, which relies heavily on information gathered by the EPA, on average, every man, woman, and child in the United States generates 4.3 pounds of trash per day. Other developed countries, such as Germany, Great Britain, and Japan, face similar problems. In the United States, 67 percent is disposed of in landfills, 17 percent is recycled, and 16 percent is incinerated. Similar disposal trends can be seen in other parts of the world, although percentages vary.

Although landfills are the primary method of municipal solid waste control in many countries, the number of existing facilities decreases every year. It is increasingly difficult to establish new ones because of political and community opposition, or the "Not in My Backyard" syndrome.

Most world environmental agencies, including the EPA, recommend an integrated approach to solid waste management. The Coca-Cola Company supports this integrated approach, including the following solutions: source reduction, to minimize the amount and toxicity of materials being disposed of and to divert as much material as possible from becoming part of the waste stream; recycling, including collecting, sorting, and reprocessing items to make new materials and thereby, again, to reduce the amount of waste; and disposal, including waste-to-energy facilities and landfills.

Because its global reach presents Coca-Cola with widely varying contexts and conditions, the company has concluded that no single blanket solution will correct the solid waste crisis. Each community, worldwide, needs to employ the combination of approaches best suited to local circumstances and needs.

Life Cycle Assessment

It is Coca-Cola's policy to "use environmentally responsible, high-quality packages to effectively protect, transport, display and deliver soft drinks to consumers."

Coca-Cola employs "cradle-to-grave" analysis to evaluate packaging options for their total impact on the environment, including air, water, energy, and solid waste. The scientific practice of such an evaluation method is called life cycle assessment. Life cycle analysis is a scientific review of the resources and energy used, and the emissions and wastes released, as a result of the manufacture, use, and disposal of a product. This type of analysis can point to wiser ways of using natural resources and to ways to minimize the environmental impact of packaging.

The Coca-Cola system was designed to reduce significantly the amount of raw materials used to produce packaging. Glass bottles, aluminum cans, and plastic bottles have been reduced by 43 percent, 35 percent, and 21 percent respectively. This not only means that fewer raw materials are being used in packaging, it also enables trucks to burn less fuel transporting the product. Many bottlers have replaced corrugated shipping cartons, which are commonly recycled, with reusable plastic crates.

In 1991 in the United States, consumers recycled 62 percent of all aluminum cans, 31 percent of glass bottles, 33 percent of polyethylene terephthalate (PET) soft drink bottles, and 46 percent of steel cans. Coca-Cola is involved with a number of programs designed to increase the recycling rates by encouraging consumers to recycle soft drink packages through local programs.

The Coca-Cola Company distributes fountain syrup in refillable 5-gallon stainless steel containers called figals. These packages are returned to production facilities, where they are washed and refilled. They also distribute syrup in 5-gallon Bag-in-Box (BIB) containers, corrugated boxes that contain 20 percent recycled content on average nationally, and up to 60 percent in some areas. BIB containers also consist of a multilayer plastic bag that has been made lighter over time. To help customers recycle the box, Coca-Cola provides educational programs and technical support.

A recent innovation for Coca-Cola is the 2-liter PET bottle made with 25 percent recycled plastic. Considered a major breakthrough in plastics recycling, this was the first package using recycled plastic to be favorably reviewed by the Food and Drug Administration for use in direct contact with food. This technology was developed in a partnership between Hoechst Celanese and the Coca-Cola Company. This development will further expand end-use markets for plastic bottles, thereby contributing to the viability of recycling programs. This package earned Coca-Cola the 1992 *Discover* Award for technological innovation in the environmental category.

Coca-Cola launched a successful program with returnable PET bottles in Switzerland, Germany, the Netherlands, and Norway, in addition to its initiative to implement recycled content in PET bottles worldwide. The returnable and refillable bottles were tested for contamination using an innovative ultraviolet light technology developed by a Swiss company, Soudronic SA.

Individual Goals

Each production facility has its own environmental program to address solid waste management, water and wastewater management, underground fuel and storage tanks, fleet operations, and other related activities. On average, Coca-Cola's syrup branches divert from landfills at least 80 percent of all solid waste generated. In the United States, recovered soft drink syrups are sold to recyclers who convert the sugars into usable fuel additives. They also recycle motor oil, reuse coolant, retread tires, and return batteries to the manufacturers for recycling or proper disposal.

For sustainable recycling to work, Coca-Cola recognizes that collected materials must be used again. Its dedicated system uses recycled material in all primary packages. In the United States, recycled content exceeds 50 percent in aluminum cans and 30 percent in glass bottles. The company is working closely with suppliers of paperboard, can carriers, and corrugated cartons to increase the amount of recycled content in those items.

As part of its environmental stewardship, the company has also implemented a purchasing policy giving preference to products with recycled content that meet its quality and performance standards. They also work with suppliers to identify and develop products containing recycled content. In effect, companies like Coca-Cola are helping to build markets for recycled materials.

Building Partnerships for the Environment

Coca-Cola has learned that in the formation of partnerships with vendors, suppliers, communities, and environmental organizations there exist successful answers to some of the most complex environmental questions. The Coca-Cola system works in alliance with international, national, and local organizations to address those environmental issues that are pertinent to its business. One such organization is Keep America Beautiful, dedicated to improving waste-handling practices in local communities.

The Coca-Cola approach assumes that innovation and leadership will always be needed to achieve excellence in environmental responsibility. Like the authors, Coca-Cola believes that the process is never-ending. Perhaps nothing sets the standard better for other businesses to understand the "business and environment" mind-set than Coca-Cola's claim, "The Best Possible Environment for Our Success . . . Is the Best Possible Environment."

Ben & Jerry's, Naturally

The Ben & Jerry's time line lists the momentous occasion when Ben Cohen and Jerry Greenfield first met, in 1963 in seventh-grade gym class in Merrick, New York. The rest is ice cream history.

Ben & Jerry's, Vermont's Finest All Natural Ice Cream & Frozen Yogurt, was founded in 1978 in a renovated gas station in Burlington, Vermont, by childhood friends Ben Cohen and Jerry Greenfield with a $12,000 investment ($4,000 of which was borrowed). With the help of an old-fashioned rock-salt ice cream maker and a five-dollar correspondence course in ice cream making from Penn State, they soon became famous for their quirky, untraditional flavors, made from Vermont milk and cream. A year later their product was distributed in grocery stores and listed by brand name on restaurant menus.

By 1985 Ben & Jerry's had moved its corporate headquarters to Waterbury, Vermont, into a new 43,000-square-foot facility. In an ongoing effort to keep up with demand, Ben & Jerry's second manufacturing facility opened in 1988 in the community of Springfield, Vermont. The newest manufacturing site is located in the St. Albans, Vermont, Cooperative Creamery. Also in St. Albans, a separate manufacturing plant is scheduled to open for operation in 1994. The company owns and operates its own distribution center in Rockingham, Vermont.

The old gas station was demolished, and the company-owned "downtown" Ben & Jerry's Scoop Shop has been located at 169 Cherry Street in Burlington, Vermont, since 1981. Other Ben & Jerry's company-owned shops are located in Williston, Montpelier, and Waterbury, Vermont. There are nearly a hundred franchised/licensed shops in the United States.

Making all-natural ice cream creates a lot of natural waste. Ben & Jerry's has teamed up with two ecological-engineering firms to test a prototype solar aquatic treatment system on its ice cream waste. The system is a greenhouse, built near the company's waste and water pretreatment lagoons, that concentrates the natural purification process of a freshwater wetland. It combines solar energy with plants, algae, and microbes to break down the wastewater. The results: pure water, lush plant life, and nonhazardous by-products and odors. This system is the first of its kind ever used to process dairy waste.

Other Firsts Highlight an Exemplary Program

Ben & Jerry's has three "Green Teams" coordinated by the company's Environmental Program development manager. The Green

Teams are responsible for assessing the company's impact on the environment in all areas of operation and for developing and implementing new programs to compensate for that impact. The company's priorities are managing its solid waste stream, conserving energy and resources, exploring sustainable, renewable energy sources, and developing environmentally beneficial community outreach programs.

Like many companies, Ben & Jerry's was sending large amounts of waste material to the landfill. Once they analyzed what this was costing both the company and the environment, they made comprehensive changes in the way they were conducting business. Deducing that they generate about 18,000 pounds of cardboard per week, they equipped the manufacturing plants with cardboard balers and found a paper broker to pick up the bales. Every week they send out bales of cardboard to be recycled, saving the company $17,400 in annual hauling costs alone. Approximately every ten days, they sell five thousand boxes to a company in Canada called Rebox for reuse.

All Ben & Jerry's office employees have recycling containers at their desks for white, mixed, and glossy paper, and newspaper. The company motivates through memos, signs, fliers, and presentations that mix humor with information on how much recycling saves in energy, cost, and trees.

Simple addition illustrates that efficient purchasing, conservative use of office supplies and equipment, and modest measures to reduce waste add to a company's bottom line. This is just good common sense and sound business management.

The company was sending about a thousand 4.5-pound plastic egg pails to landfills every week. A partnership with Vermont Republic Industries was formed to have many of those pails cleaned, shredded, and sent to a plastic manufacturer for recycling. Remaining buckets are washed and reused. It costs Ben & Jerry's $235,000 a year less to reuse and recycle the pails than it used to cost to dump them in landfills. Production workers also recycle plastic bags and stretch wrap that come in from suppliers' packaging.

Ben & Jerry's switched to 100 percent recycled paperboard for its Brownie Bar and Peace Pop boxes and have phased out the use of trays in the Brownie Bar packaging.

To quote their collateral material, "We're learning all the time." Like the authors, and many of the companies we interviewed, Ben & Jerry's understands that environmental implementation is comprised of works-in-progress. By way of example, Ben & Jerry's assumed that their pint containers were nonrecyclable. Then, at a "green packaging" conference, they learned that there are five recycling plants in the U.S. specializing in polycoated paperboard. Now the only question that remains for the company is how to get empty containers to those recycling plants. They are open to suggestions.

The Solar-Powered Show Bus

Since spring 1991 Ben & Jerry's solar-powered show bus has been "barnstorming the country," transporting storytellers, jugglers, actors, musicians, magicians, and lots of ice cream. Solar energy powers the bus's freezers, appliances, and sound system, "keeping the ice cream cold and the entertainment hot."

In keeping with the funky names of their chunky ice cream flavors, Ben & Jerry's participates in environmental promotions with the same brand of idiosyncratic humor:

"Merry Mulching"—Vermont's Merry Mulch program sets up centers for chipping Christmas trees after the holidays are over. Vermonters who take a tree to a Merry Mulch center—thereby keeping it out of the landfill—get a free Ben & Jerry's cone coupon, along with as much mulch as they can take for landscaping their homes in the spring.

"Vermont Green-up Day"—In 1990 the company staged several truckload ice cream sales to benefit Vermont's annual Green-up Day. They printed free cone coupons on the peel-off backs of Green-up's "Don't Trash Vermont" bumper stickers.

"The Green Flea"—Employees donate truckloads of items to sell at a daylong flea market set up on the grounds of the Waterbury manufacturing plant. All proceeds go to the Environmental Federation of America/Earth Share, an umbrella group for several environmental organizations.

Well known for its donation of 7.5 percent of its pretax earnings to various nonprofit and charitable organizations (awarded through a grant application process) and for its Rainforest Crunch ice cream, which indirectly benefits rainforest preservation, Ben & Jerry's laundry list of environmentally and socially responsible actions is outstandingly impressive. They have really set the precedent for "Businesses doing well by doing good."

Yes, their printer ribbons are re-inked; yes, they print on recycled paper with water-based inks; yes, they use soy-based inks wherever possible and are researching ways to increase their application; yes, office pens are refillable; even holiday greeting cards are recycled. Currently they are investigating the viability of a companywide composting program. No environmental stone is left unturned.

Energy Conservation and Issues

Ongoing energy audits are being conducted at Ben & Jerry's Waterbury and Springfield manufacturing plants. A newly implemented energy conservation program at Waterbury could save as much as $250,000 a year.

Lighting has been improved, use of compact fluorescent lights has been initiated, and motion detectors are used in some areas, automatically turning off lights in unoccupied rooms.

Installation of numerous control devices on plant equipment, such as high-efficiency motors, has helped energy conservation. Research is being conducted on higher-efficiency refrigeration systems as well as the use of outdoor air in wintertime for refrigeration. Work is being done on a cogeneration project to increase energy efficiency.

With one vehicle already on the road, Ben & Jerry's is considering converting all its mobile ice cream sampling trucks to photovoltaic-powered refrigeration.

Ben & Jerry's on Energy and Hydro Quebec

The company has also taken a stand against the completion of the James Bay II project in Canada.

"We believe that our society should commit itself to conservation and to efficient use of our natural resources—including energy. At Ben & Jerry's our goal is to reduce our electrical consumption by 25 percent per unit of production over the next five years. We should not simply export the environmental costs of our wasteful energy use. We don't need more power badly enough to destroy a great wilderness."

That, they contend, is exactly what a group of Vermont utilities would do in purchasing power from Hydro Quebec, and they oppose a purchase of 340 megawatts that would be generated in part through an immense expansion of hydropower facilities in the pristine James Bay region of northern Quebec.

According to an informational flier published by Ben & Jerry's, "If completed, the James Bay Power Project will reshape the geography of Quebec's northern wilderness, destroy the homelands and hunting grounds of native people, and create serious threats of water salinity changes and mercury contamination."

Ben & Jerry's feels just as strongly about the many campaigns they promote through their shops. Postcards are distributed at outlets, encouraging customers to support efforts with the pread-dressed messages to those empowered to make the necessary changes. One example is "Have a Heart for Kids," a mail campaign to the U.S. House of Representatives asking them to provide guaranteed access to health care and preschool education programs to all children in America.

Investing in efficiency, conserving energy, managing waste, developing nondestructive, renewable energy sources and goods, and securing a sound future for others are synonymous with Ben & Jerry's. The company's mission statement is divided into three parts:

Assist environmental groups in their efforts with monetary contributions and other kinds of support. In other words, put your money and energies where your heart is. Such alignments increase the credibility of your message and oftentimes provide unexpected paybacks. This support can create dedicated consumers, increase your customer base, and bring in new business.

Product Mission: To make, distribute, and sell the finest quality all-natural ice cream and related products in a wide variety of innovative flavors made from Vermont dairy products.

Social Mission: To operate the company in a way that actively recognizes the central role that business plays in the structure of society by initiating innovative ways to improve the quality of life of a broad community—local, national, and international.

Economic Mission: To operate the company on a sound financial basis of profitable growth, increasing value for our shareholders, and creating career opportunities and financial rewards for our employees.

Total sales in 1991 were $97 million, up 26 percent over 1990 sales. Not bad for a business whose principle is to "live in harmony with its global neighbors and the natural world."

The Green Movement Around the World Has Captured Heinz's Imagination

H. J. Heinz was an industry pioneer. He actively demanded strict, uniform, and legislated standards to ensure consumer safety. "After more than 120 years, the H.J. Heinz Company continues to hold paramount the trust of its consumers," says Anthony J.F. O'Reilly, chairman, president, and CEO.

"As a company with consumers in more than two hundred countries, we find the environmental issue to be irresistibly global," he asserts. "The great chain of procurement, processing, packaging, and purveyance is, at each link, related to the state of our planet's ecology. This gives us a direct stake in the outcome of the environmental debate that presently occupies the international agenda."

Heinz and O'Reilly recognize that consumers are buying a company when they buy a brand name product. By virtue of brand loyalty, they become concerned about the company's reputation as well as its products. Assurance of product purity and safety and careful husbandry of the natural resources upon which we all depend, ultimately rebound, in the view of the Heinz Company, to the owners of the company. The mandate for Heinz is to anticipate and satisfy the "educated choices" that consumers make, knowing that when a match is made, a loyal and long-term relationship is formed.

A Pioneer in Pure Food

From the beginning, Henry J. Heinz, the company's founder, recognized that consumers wanted food that was wholesome, pure, and uncontaminated. This was a revolutionary concept in the days when fresh food was sold in the open, often from dirty bins, and when food processing was uninspected.

Heinz lobbied earnestly for America's first national legislation regulating food handling and processing. He and his fellow reformers achieved their goal with the passage of the Pure Food and Drug Act of 1906. In recent decades the company and its United States affiliates have not only concentrated on producing pure foods but have also centered technological efforts on ensuring the purity of America's air and waterways. They have pioneered treatment systems for wastewater and created energy-efficient and pollution-free power generating units. Additionally Heinz U.S.A., Ore-Ida, and other affiliates have joined various efforts to conserve wildlife and natural resources.

Green Revolution vs. Green Movement

It has been difficult for food product manufacturers to implement changes at the rate deemed desirable by most ardent green thinkers for the simple reason that consumers have not yet made an informed choice between the advances of the Green Revolution, an agriculture-based movement that ensures continuous food production, and the advancement of the Green Movement, intended to ensure sound environmental practices. Food manufacture is an industry that reflects the growing need for a thoughtful understanding of the balance between business and the environment. During the 1970s, the Green Revolution referred to a U.S.-inspired combination of science, technology, and agriculture. Although unable to eliminate hunger, disease, and war, the movement helped contain the spread of a seemingly inevitable scourge of these ills worldwide. It boosted agricultural productivity and preserved the American tradition of having the cheapest food basket in the world. "The achievements of the Green Revolution have a humanitarian as well as a financial dimension," claims O'Reilly. "They have kept alive a generation of the developing world. They have brought prosperity to a generation of the industrialized nations." The food manufacturing industry is quite concerned that the demand for pure food, air, and water not undo the benefits derived from the Green Revolution. The answer is in the proper mix of the two Greens.

No one questions that this should and can be done, but the answers require a prudent, intelligent, dispassionate investigation of all the possible consequences. And most of these decision-making factors are in the hands of consumers.

Charlie the Tuna Has a Reason to Smile

The message was delivered clearly when the issue of "dolphin-safe tuna" was catapulted to the headlines by the pleas of schoolchildren, parents, politicians, environmental advocacy groups, and the media. On 12 April 1990 the StarKist Seafood Company, a Heinz Company affiliate and the world's largest tuna canner, became the first major tuna company to adopt a dolphin-safe policy. Following StarKist's lead, at least two other canners announced similar programs.

StarKist's announcement included two major points:

- StarKist would not purchase any tuna caught in association with dolphins.

- It would continue its practice of refusing to buy any tuna caught with gill or drift nets, which are known to be dangerous to many forms of marine life.

Labels on cans of StarKist tuna sold in the United States carry "dolphin safe" symbols and the message "No harm to dolphins." In instituting this policy, StarKist went beyond government requirements to recognize consumer concern for the environment and, building upon StarKist's many years of work with boat owners and government, addressed the tuna-dolphin issue as a benchmark decision in the marketplace.

The policy applies to all StarKist products throughout the world and includes the tuna supplied for pet foods. "StarKist believes that dolphin deaths, injury, and harassment in association with tuna fishing must be stopped," says StarKist president and CEO Keith A. Hauge. The Marine Mammal Protection Act of 1972 established a maximum allowable quota of 20,500 dolphin deaths in the eastern tropical Pacific Ocean for U.S.-flagged boats. In 1992, according to Hauge, U.S. boats were far below quota.

Foreign boats are estimated to be killing substantially larger numbers of mammals. As the world's largest tuna canner, StarKist hopes to bring its influence to bear on the foreign-flagged ships that fish for tuna.

Praise for StarKist Seafood Company's "dolphin safe" policy came from scores of organizations. "This action sets an international precedent that will create a domino effect to end this needless killing of dolphins once and for all," declared Lesley Scheele of Greenpeace.

"StarKist's decision marks a milestone for both the consumer and the millions of gentle, intelligent dolphins that have been dying in tuna nets," said Patricia Forkan, senior vice-president of the Humane Society of the United States. "Now we can tell our more than one million constituents that they are free to purchase StarKist tuna for themselves and their pets." Similar endorsements came from around the globe, from environmental organizations, animal rights groups, politicians, the public, and the media. "The message to the rest of the tuna industry is clear," said David Phillips, director of the Earth Island Institute. "There is no reason why all tuna companies can't immediately follow Heinz's lead. Heinz has recognized that federal quotas and regulations are not enough. The public has spoken and Heinz has heeded the strong message that the killing of dolphins must be stopped."

"StarKist's new policy demonstrates the impact that environmentally conscious consumers can have on business," said Senator Joseph R. Biden (D-Delaware). "StarKist's decision shows that business, with consumer support, can change their products for the good of the environment."

"Now Charlie the Tuna has reason to smile," said Congresswoman Barbara Boxer (D-California). "I want to commend StarKist and its parent H. J. Heinz Company for the decision to voluntarily comply with the Boxer-Biden Bill (the Dolphin Protection Consumer Information Act). They are embarking on a course that will set a standard for the empowerment of the consumer and the exercise of corporate responsibility."

Environment in a Bottle

In 1983 Heinz pioneered and introduced the squeezable plastic ketchup bottle. The polypropylene-based GAMMA bottle represented a real breakthrough in plastic containers for highly acidic products.

The container involves four primary layers bound with two adhesive layers to provide the barrier that keeps oxygen out while retaining moisture, particularly important to maintaining product quality in food products made with perishables, like tomatoes, that are oxygen sensitive.

While the GAMMA bottle is technically recyclable, there are no economically viable polypropylene collection, cleaning, or end-use conversion systems now in place for this packaging. Consequently Heinz developed a new package, in partnership with Continental PET Technologies, a division of Continental Can Company, that would address environmental concerns while maintaining the consumer-preferred features of the GAMMA plastic ketchup package. The result: ENVIROPET™.

The joint effort has produced a bottle that is not only recyclable but also fits into existing curbside collection and recycling networks for plastic PET soft drink bottles. PET is the most widely recycled plastic in America. "Millions of bottles that would have ended up in landfills will now be recycled into other useful products," says CEO O'Reilly.

Until the development of ENVIROPET, PET's barrier properties, although vastly superior to most plastics, did not offer adequate resistance to oxygen permeation to protect some food products, including ketchup. The technical breakthrough that led to ENVIROPET was the discovery of a way to produce PET preforms containing thin layers of non-PET high barrier polymer without the use of adhesives to bond the layers. The preforms are converted into bottles in a process known as reheat stretch blow molding. The scrapless forming process actually improves the physical and chemical properties of the plastic, thus minimizing the amount of plastic needed.

Trials with major PET recyclers conclusively demonstrated that the ENVIROPET ketchup container can be processed through existing beverage bottle cleaning machinery without any modifications or negative impact. "The Heinz project was particularly well thought out, addressing the many concerns of processors and environmentalists," says David R. Hopkins, president of Conplex Inc., a technology and consulting firm. "Selection of material for which a recycling stream already exists was very wise. As curbside separation programs grow, we expect PET bottle regrind to be a major raw material in the extrusion industry and to contribute less and less to landfill solid waste problems."

In keeping with the famous Heinz 57 Varieties, Heinz has prepared a list of 57 products made from recycled PET:

1 carpet yarns

2 twine

3 filter material

4 shoulder pads

5 rope

6 paint brush bristles

7 necktie linings

8 tennis ball felt

9 automotive trunk liners

10 pillows

11 stuffing for ski jackets, cushions, and mattresses, sleeping bags, quilts

12 blankets

13 shampoo bottles

14 plastic egg cartons

15 detergent bottles

16 strapping

17 scouring pads

18 landfill liners

19 pond liners

20 furniture

21 automobile exterior panels

22 appliance handles, housing, and cases

23 automotive components

24 nonfood containers

25 belts

26 webbing

27 sails

28 woven bags

29 welcome mats

30 combs

31 oil funnel cans

32 recyling bins

33 plastic lumber for fence posts, boat docks, outside
    furniture, park benches, landscaping ties, decks,
    parking space bumpers, speed bumps

34 industrial paints

35 paint brush handles

36 pallets

37 housing insulation

38 refrigeration truck paneling

39 home and commercial freezer insulation

40 building and agricultural film

41 storage tank insulation

42 automobile bumpers

43 skis and surfboards

44 bathtubs, sinks, and shower stalls

45 boat hulls

46 swimming pools

47 corrugated awnings

48 marbleized materials

49 audio cassette cases

50 windshield wiper components

51 grills for cars

52 visors

53 highway barrier drums

54 engineered resins

55 home furnishings, bedspreads, draperies, furniture coverings

56 pile fabrics

57 industrial linings

ENVIROPET also compares favorably to glass in all areas of integrated waste management strategy supported by the EPA and most municipal and environmental groups. These categories are described, in the Addendum of this book, by Paul Sorensen, communications director for Camp Dresser & McKee Inc., enviro-engineering firm, as source reduction, recycling, incineration (waste-to-energy), and landfilling.

Green Meanz Heinz

Events in Europe have made its population more eco-conscious. The Chernobyl disaster spread contamination across the continent, and Europe's coastal regions and waterways have been polluted by chemical spills. Anticipating consumer concerns and following its own lead in the American market, Heinz has become environmentally active in Europe as well.

In the United Kingdom and in Italy, Heinz subsidiaries have launched independent initiatives to conserve resources and to ensure pure, wholesome products.

When Heinz-UK paid tribute to its founder in 1986, the centenary of his first sale of Heinz products in Britain, it did so environmentally. In association with the World Wide Fund for Nature, the company initiated a five-year, million-pound Guardians of the Countryside program. Successes so far include saving Cape Cornwall (England's only cape) by buying the land for the National Trust; sponsoring the fund's annual Walk for Wildlife; and publishing important educational materials.

The British affiliate has incorporated the environmental ethic into its daily operations. Both Heinz-UK factories run regular environmental audits, and all company cars are being converted to run on unleaded fuel. The subsidiary has invested heavily in packaging that is consumer safe and recyclable. The company's environmental record earned it recognition as the Best Company Manufacturer in the 1989 Green Awards, sponsored by *The Grocer*, a major trade magazine. The award prompted a few headlines of "Green Meanz Heinz," a play on Heinz-UK's popular advertising slogan "Beanz Meanz Heinz." According to *The Grocer*, "Going green is not only fashionable—it's commercially desirable."

Plada, Heinz's Italian subsidiary, is the leader in Italy's baby food market, which lends it a special bond with its customers. Plada anticipated consumer concerns with its "environmental shield" initiative. This program is a rigorous auditing and control procedure to ensure the purity of every ingredient Plada uses in its products.

Plada starts the process with a crop screening program. The company undertakes chemical research and inspection of its food supplies during the planting and harvesting, working with its farmers and contractors to provide a blend of organically grown product and food items that minimize the use of pesticides at levels lower than currently acceptable. Plada's *Oasi Ecologica*, "Environmental Oasis," marketing program brings the notion of product purity directly to the consumers. Strained meat and fruit varieties of Plasmon baby food, along with fruit juices, bear a "Plasmon Environmental Oasis Certificate of Guarantee," assuring consumers that the ingredients have been subjected to the company's scrutiny.

Plada's baby foods, under the Plasmon, Nipiol, and Dieterba brands, experienced a 20 percent growth in sales volume in their first year.

Heinz has shown that the environmental concerns of the marketplace are global in scope. Corporations with a global perspective need to deal with environmental issues throughout the many nations they serve. Pollution, contamination, and protecting resources are international problems. Companies like Heinz gain a greater foothold in each of their markets when they take a leadership role in solving the problems of their communities.

The Arches Are Green at McDonald's

Thirty-seven years ago, McDonald's reinvented the way Americans eat out. Now the company is hoping it can use its considerable influence to reinvent fast-food packaging.

As the largest quick-service restaurant business in the food processing industry, McDonald's has the enormous dual task of providing hot food quickly and efficiently while at the same time keeping packaging and its resulting waste to a minimum. But finding that balance has not always been easy. In fact, as McDonald's management discovered in the late 1980s, sometimes the only way to find innovative solutions is to create the demand for them first. Today the company is doing that by using the leverage of its more than eighty-five hundred franchises and thirty-seven regional offices in the United States to increase demand for recycled products and give suppliers of those products a much-needed boost.

This is not the first time McDonald's has been actively involved in environmental issues. Since the 1970s the company has taken steps to eliminate waste or unnecessary packaging. However, these steps were often unfocused as it struggled with the confusing complexity of environmental issues facing a company of its size. During the 1980s McDonald's watched as its once-loyal market became more environmentally aware and antagonistic against companies that contributed to a "throw-away society." Not only were consumers sending angry letters by the hundreds, but schoolchildren were protesting outside its restaurants—and much of the public perceived the company was guilty of negligence against the environment.

Facing increasingly negative publicity for its role in the waste that was piling up in overburdened landfills, and realizing that they could no longer provide an adequate long-term environmental strategy, McDonald's management took two major steps in 1990. The first was a program called "McRecycle USA," which represented an annual commitment of $100 million toward the purchase of recycled products for its franchises.

The second was the unprecedented act of forming a partnership with a leading environmental research and advocacy organization to develop a series of long-range initiatives. In this model collaborative effort, McDonald's was invited by the Environmental Defense Fund to discuss environmental solutions to the company's solid waste problems. Making such a move involved tremendous risk to both sides. For McDonald's there was the potential that the media would view this as a publicity stunt. And the EDF could lose credibility if the public thought it was selling out to the enemy. Despite possible criticism, both parties continued to believe the outcome would provide alternatives that neither could initiate alone.

An organization of two hundred thousand members, the EDF was typically able to effect environmental change in only small doses. And McDonald's knew that in order to meet the environmental demands of the 1990s, the company needed professional advice and expertise. Together they determined that the purpose of the collaboration would be to investigate a variety of cost-effective options the company could implement over a series of targeted years.

Several initial meetings led to the development of a task force comprised of four leaders from each organization. From the outset, representatives from each side were committed to remaining wholly independent, with each reserving the option to publish an independent report if they could not reach an agreement. In reality, the collaboration was enormously fruitful. EDF's executive director, Fred Krupp, said at the time, "We are hopeful that this process will illustrate ways in which business and environmental groups that have significantly different perspectives can nevertheless work together to achieve environmental improvements that are in the public interest."

McDonald's commitment to a long-term environmental strategy can be seen in its Waste Reduction Policy, a document that combines initiatives from both McRecycle USA and the EDF study. They read in part:

> We are committed to taking a "total lifecycle" approach to solid waste, examining ways of reducing materials used in production and packaging, as well as diverting as much waste as possible from the solid waste stream. In doing so, we will follow three courses of action: reduce, reuse, and recycle.
>
> ### Reduce
>
> We will take steps to reduce the weight and/or volume of packaging we use. . . .
>
> ### Reuse
>
> We will implement reusable materials whenever feasible, within our operations and distribution systems as long as they

do not compromise our safety and sanitation standards, customer service and expectations, or don't conflict with other environmental safety concerns.

Recycle

We are committed to the maximum use of recycled materials in the construction, equipping, and operations of our restaurants.

Conserve and Protect Resources

We will continue to take aggressive measures to minimize energy and other resource consumption through increased efficiency and conservation. We will not permit the destruction of rain forests for our beef supply.

To be an environmental pioneer in the quick-service industry, McDonald's knows only too well that some lessons will be learned the hard way. Take, for instance, its food packaging. In 1976 McDonald's came under environmental criticism for its paper food wraps. At the time, environmentalists were concerned that paper products led to the depletion of forests, as well as contributing to pollution. In response, McDonald's commissioned the Stanford Research Institute to compare polystyrene to existing food packaging. The institute determined polystyrene to be superior to paperboard because it was more easily recycled.

Once it became dedicated to polystyrene packaging, McDonald's found there were an insufficient number of recycling operations to handle the abundance of waste. But by 1989, the company had a program in place to take its polystyrene clamshell and coffee cup containers in bulk to a recycler, where they could be remanufactured into pellets. Ironically, within those thirteen years, environmental opinions had done an about-face, and McDonald's wound up on the wrong side of public sentiment.

Once hailed as a better alternative to paper, polystyrene was now considered an enormous disposal problem as well as a major contributor to ozone depletion, due to the release of CFCs during its manufacture. Unable to single-handedly support the slow-to-evolve polystyrene recycling industry, and given the opportunity to implement the Environmental Defense Fund's solid waste recommendations, McDonald's gave up on polystyrene in favor of the less-recyclable, but more practical, clay-coated paperboard.

While, technically speaking, polystyrene foam is more easily recycled, the company's recycling operation proved inadequate due to numerous problems in collection, separation, shipping, and cleaning the waste plastic. In the end, only *half* of the total plastic used was actually being recycled. From a strictly solid waste standpoint, then, paper wraps provided enormous *immediate* savings in waste volume, both in-store and after they were taken out of the store by the consumer.

Environmentalists hailed the decision as a major victory. To McDonald's, it was one small part of a very important learning curve. Perhaps this was one significant experience that gave the company an incentive to seek alliances and help build an infrastructure in future environmental strategies, realizing that it would be increasingly prohibitive for any one company to bear the burden of environmental solutions alone.

Reduce First, Then Recycle

During the research stage of the EDF study, the task force determined that the single biggest environmental challenge to McDonald's was solid waste. Findings from the EDF study indicated that almost 80 percent of on-premise waste in a typical McDonald's is generated behind the counter, or in the food preparation and serving areas. Since this represented a majority of the waste, as opposed to waste generated *after* products reached the consumer, the EDF strategy targeted many systems in the food preparation stages.

The highest priority was given to source reduction or "using less material that must be manufactured, shipped, stored, and eventually discarded and managed as waste." As packaging materials used by take-out and drive-through customers fall outside the company's recycling loop, source reduction currently offers the greatest environmental benefit. And with landfill fees continually increasing, all companies have to take into account the rising cost of waste disposal. Like many of the initiatives examined in this book, steps that produce environmental gains often translate into economic savings as well.

For example, the switch from polystyrene clamshells to paper-based wraps for its sandwich items has promoted conservation in many areas. Three years in development, the new wraps also offer substantial reductions in energy consumption, air emissions, and water pollution during manufacture, and four times less solid waste volume at the time of disposal, according to a report by the independent consulting firm Franklin Associates.

In researching the possibilities for *reusing* products, the EDF study found many opportunities to use bulk storage containers in-store and behind the counter. They included containers to replace individual packets for in-store condiments, including ketchup, salt, pepper, cream, syrup, and dressings. This one step in particular serves the dual purpose of recycling and reusing waste. Behind the counter, bulk storage can also be applied to cleaning supplies, food, and soda. Reusable lids for salads and breakfast servings and bulk dispensers for straws are also being tested or implemented in many franchises.

As a result of the EDF-McDonald's study, and with guidance from the environmental affairs officer, targets were set for implementation of forty-two specific *Action Items* and conversions. Those initiatives range from directing all suppliers to reduce waste within their own operations and in the manufacture of McDonald's packaging, to continually redesigning food wraps, to testing and implementing composting operations in a number of pilot franchises. Once incorporated on a broader scale, composting could also be developed for use in its own landscaping and thereby "close the loop" and allow McDonald's to achieve a commendable 80 percent reduction in total waste generation.

McRecycle, from Top to Bottom

Operating in tandem with the EDF initiatives, McRecycle USA has the potential to fuel an entirely separate industry. The most impressive element of the program is McDonald's commitment to spend a minimum of $100 million a year on recycled products that include paper, corrugated boxes, ceiling tiles, plastic construction lumber, patio tables and chairs, restaurant seats, roofing materials, insulation, interior tables and chairs, Playland surfaces, and decorative siding. After only three years, McDonald's announced in April 1993 that it had already spent $600 million on recycled products, exceeding its goal by $300 million—or twice its original estimate.

Each year in the United States approximately 375 new McDonald's restaurants are built, and more than 1,000 others are remodeled—representing an annual budget of $400 million. The diversity of the recycled product list means that the company can have a tremendous impact on many of its more than six hundred suppliers. In addition, McDonald's is a founding member of the Buy Recycled Business Alliance, initiated at the National Recycling Congress in September 1992. The alliance has a goal of encouraging five thousand more companies to make a similar commitment. These steps are providing enormous support to the growing recycling industry in ways many companies individually could not.

In one model franchise in Kent, Washington, principles of McRecycle USA can be seen in

- A copper roofing system made of recycled radiators and wires
- Seating and tabletops made from recycled steel, aluminum, and plastic
- Stainless steel equipment in the kitchen fabricated from recycled materials, as well as the menu board, condiment bins, and buckets
- Steel doors, frames, interior doors, windowsills, aluminum window frames, and insulation inside the walls and ceilings—all made from recycled materials
- Mops made from old McDonald's crew uniforms

Other McDonald's restaurants also use recycled tires for non-skid Playland surfaces, and used computer casings in roofing tiles.

But McDonald's commitment to furthering recycled products began even before many companies knew how to supply them. For example, in 1987 McDonald's pioneered the use of corrugated boxes created from 35 percent recycled content. At the time, that level was a significant challenge to an industry that had set 21 percent as the maximum allowable recycled content that would compromise neither strength nor durability. Undaunted, the company worked with an outside consultant to conduct extensive research into the industry's capacity to add more recycled material.

In a precursor to many of its methods today, McDonald's notified all of its suppliers in 1990—almost six hundred companies—that they must meet or exceed the 35 percent goal. To ensure this goal would be sustained, McDonald's established a monitoring and tracking system that annually reviews each supplier's box content. Yet another alternative under consideration includes replacing corrugated shipping boxes entirely with reusable containers.

McDonald's led the industry once again in the manufacture of recycled paper bags. The initial resistance to change seemed familiar. At the time, adding recycling paper to the manufacturing process was not considered technically practical, as it was expected to increase the bag's weight and expense. By late 1989, however, one supplier came forward with a design that contained 65 percent recycled newsprint. That innovation became the benchmark that led to other developments with suppliers. Soon one company created a brown paper bag containing 50 percent postconsumer waste and 50 percent postindustrial waste—the design McDonald's finally chose. In other words, due to its challenge to improve quality beyond existing standards, McDonald's was the first in the quick-food industry to implement a bag manufactured completely from 100 percent recycled material.

Where existing suppliers are unable to meet the new demands and maintain McDonald's strict quality standards, new suppliers will be sought. And each supplier's performance toward meeting the program's goals will be reviewed on an annual basis. Ed Rensi, president of McDonald's USA, admits that the limited market of recycled products and manufacturers has been a barrier to its success. "There is an urgent need to expand the market for recycled materials so that individuals, communities and businesses can sustain and even increase their recycling efforts," he said in *Recycling Today*.

In response, the company began a McRecycle USA Registry Service with a toll-free 800 number that manufacturers of recycled products could call to learn about McDonald's materials needs and to register their companies. As an unexpected side benefit, the registry now serves as a public data base listing hundreds of manufacturers and suppliers of recycled products. The company provides this list to any interested parties.

In addition, the company opened the McRecycle USA Information Center at the corporate headquarters in Oak Brook, Illinois. Located with McDonald's test kitchens and training centers, the Information Center is the focal point of all recycling efforts. It also serves as a resource for suppliers and others who would like to learn about recycling opportunities and specifications.

An important point to note here is that while the overall strategy is applied across the board in all franchises, some municipalities are further ahead than others in establishing an infrastructure to support recycling. As stated in the study, "While the corporate office can mandate a packaging change to all of its restaurants, it cannot mandate use of a particular recycling program on a national basis. This increases the need for strong regional leadership on waste reduction issues." In other words, McDonald's has its work cut out for it.

The company determined that to ensure an adequate long-term approach, any new program would need a strong structure for research, analysis, design, implementation, and monitoring consistency. In effect, it would cross many departmental lines. The program now in place involves five departments: Purchasing, Quality Assurance, Product Development, Operations Development, and Environmental Affairs.

Only one, however, has the responsibility for overseeing the program's success in all areas and by all departments. This position is described in a brochure titled *McDonald's Commitment to the Environment.* In it the company states, "A commitment to a strong environmental policy begins with leadership at the top of an organization. Therefore, our Environmental Affairs officer will be given broad-based responsibility to ensure adherence to these environmental principles throughout our system. This officer will report to the Board of Directors regarding progress made toward specific environmental initiatives."

To facilitate a realistic appraisal of environmental initiatives in all areas of the country, each of McDonald's thirty-seven regional offices maintains an environmental coordinator who directs the local recycling efforts. Results are then consolidated into an annual report submitted to the environmental affairs officer.

The Consumer Is King

As McDonald's found out during its clamshell upheaval, consumers represent the greatest link to the company's overall identity as an environmental champion. To further its public message, McDonald's has established many outreach efforts, including an All-Star Green Teens program in conjunction with the Student Conservation Association. This program recognizes high school students for their local environmental achievements and will send a group of them to Yellowstone National Park for two-week internships during the summer months.

Other promotional vehicles include placing monthly advertisements about McRecycle USA in trade periodicals and recycling magazines, and the use of specially designed carryout bags and tray liners describing McDonald's environmental policies and initiatives.

Beyond 1993, McDonald's will investigate still more environmentally sound operating practices. If technology does not exist to develop an alternative to plastic cutlery and wax-coated paper wrap (which is currently difficult to recycle), it is hoped that research along those lines will continue until all options are exhausted.

In addition, the authors hope that the company's next stage of its evolving environmental strategy will give energy alternatives the highest priority. As a member of the EPA Green Lights program, McDonald's has shown its commitment to improving lighting efficiency in each franchise and the home office. With the potential to introduce new heating and lighting measures to eighty-five hundred stores, renewable energy markets can be given the same much-needed boost that recycled products will receive with McRecycle USA.

Possibilities exist at each franchise for incorporating systems such as solar panels to supplement energy use, and waste-to-energy conversion of the type developed by Herman Miller Inc. As proven in its EDF partnership and McRecycle USA, a company the size of McDonald's can provide the leadership and financial support necessary to make environmentally sensitive principles a way of life— much as it has made the fast-food hamburger one of America's staple foods.

Hannaford Brothers Builds a Better Market

Intent on finding a new and better way to sell his family's produce, Cape Elisabeth farmer Arthur Hannaford opened a tiny wholesale fruit and vegetable shop in nearby Portland, Maine, in 1883.

His brother, Howard, soon joined him in the business, incorporated in 1902. Both brothers were dedicated to providing their customers with the finest fruits and vegetables at the fairest prices. The company flourished and by 1918 was the leading produce wholesaler in northern New England. In 1927 Hannaford Brothers became a wholesale grocery business. In 1944 the Hannafords created their first retail outlet by financing a supermarket for William T. Cottle, a manager with retail experience. This type of equity partnership, in which Hannaford Brothers owned a controlling interest in the supermarket and the partner owned 49 percent, would come to play an important role in the strength and expansion of the company.

The next quarter century saw a number of acquisitions and mergers. The purchase of Progressive Food Distributors with equity partner Ralph Perry created Progressive Distributors, Inc., now a supplier of pharmaceuticals, health and beauty aids, specialty foods, and general merchandise to all Hannaford stores.

In 1971 the company sold common stock to the public for the first time. In 1977 Hannaford introduced its first Universal Product Code scanning systems, along with unit-pricing shelf tags that helped customers compare prices. In 1982 the company established Hannaford Trucking Company as a wholly owned subsidiary.

While staying at the technological forefront with computerized programs for costs and pricing, shelf management systems, and data bases on customers' family and medical histories, Hannaford also broke new ground in store formats. In 1983 it became the first company in Maine to open a combination supermarket and drugstore. The following year Hannaford opened its first three Super Shop'n Save stores as well as its first Sun Foods super warehouse store.

Growth has been constant for Hannaford and a key factor in its strong performance. Hannaford expanded its market territory and built and acquired stores in Massachusetts and upstate New York. The company constructed a distribution center in Shodack, New York, and opened its largest store—an 84,000-square-foot food and drug superstore—in Utica, New York. This store provides a dry-cleaning service, a walk-in beverage cooler, and one-hour photo processing.

It combines the low grocery price and limited service philosophy of the Sun Foods warehouse store operations with the full service and everyday low price philosophy of Shop'n Save.

With sixty-five supermarkets and thirty-five Wellby drug stores by 1987, Hannaford reached sales of $1 billion dollars. Living up to its projections, Hannaford now owns over ninety-four supermarkets and maintains annual sales of over $2 billion.

Always a Trend Ahead

It takes a tremendous amount of foresight to become a billion-dollar company, and Hannaford Brothers has always been prescient about the marketplace.

It is not surprising, therefore, that the company opened the first United States store with midtemperature refrigeration and air-conditioning systems free of CFCs and HCFCs and that it is currently testing a new low-temperature refrigerant with zero ozone-depletion potential (AZ-50), a major step toward creating the first supermarket completely free of ozone-depleting refrigerants. Nor is it surprising that Hannaford Brothers began recycling efforts as early as 1975, sending corrugated cardboard for recycling. Today it recycles stretch wrap, scrap wood, unsalable products, high-density polyethylene (HDPE) pill bottles, office paper, and shopping bags. Its new composting programs recycle 75 tons of waste weekly.

Hannaford's Earth Matters™ programs combine waste management and consumer education. Changing its waste handling practices has reduced by 40 percent the amount of solid waste sent to landfills and incinerators. The company hopes to further utilize composting to increase that number to 50 percent. The annual budget for the Earth Matters program totals approximately $20,000.

In 1990 Hannaford introduced the first plastic bag recycling program in the United States. This supermarket-based program continues to collect used bags and to process them into new bags containing up to 50 percent recycled material. Refunds are given to customers who reuse bags. Since April 1990 customers have reused over 10 million bags, receiving over $389,000 in refunds. The bag programs help promote recycling, reuse, and help keep bags from becoming litter or trash. Hannaford has assisted other supermarket chains to implement similar bag programs.

The shopping bag also becomes a medium for environmental messages. Without using extraneous paper, Hannaford provides information on recycling, composting, energy conservation, and related topics by putting messages on the bags themselves. Hannaford educates its sixteen thousand employees and more than a million customers a week on improving the environment.

Hundreds of its employees volunteered to clean up their individual communities for Earth Day 1992. These "Clean It Up!" projects ranged from picking up trash to cleaning a feeder canal. Each spring and fall, volunteer associates continue to work on clean-up projects cooperatively with local organizations.

The Hannaford Environmental Program is most comprehensive, combining all the significant elements of source reduction, solid waste management, energy conservation, employee education, and outreach programs.

Hannaford's extensive environmental policy statement can be summarized in its commitment to its Earth Matters efforts.

> With these and many other creative efforts, we strive to lead, offer factual information, and to constantly remind ourselves of our environmental stewardship. Ongoing environmental assessments are an integral part of our business. Each new supermarket and distribution facility must be designed to optimize recycling and composting efforts and to minimize the environmental impact during development and construction. Existing facilities are being retrofitted to permit maximized recycling of all recyclable and compostable materials, the elimination of CFC's, and optimizing energy conservation.
>
> We should continually search for, and share, new information and technology. We have learned that we must all work together in partnership by listening carefully to the changing needs of our communities and by responding in the most effective manner.

Awards in recognition of Hannafords's efforts are numerous, but one of the most significant honors was bestowed on Hannaford in 1992, the President's Environment and Conservation Challenge Award, the nation's highest environmental accolade.

Step-by-Step

Efforts to conserve energy and reduce ozone damage include installing high-pressure sodium lighting systems, automatic light dimmers, door replacements with better insulation and tighter seals on dairy cases and freezers that save 60 percent on energy, systems to heat water and air by waste heat from refrigerators, and efficient, computer-controlled programs for heating, ventilation, and air-conditioning.

Hannaford's introduction of the nation's first CFC-free super-market refrigeration and air-conditioning system was a benchmark in the industry. The company uses R-134a, a new hydrogen-based refrigerant alternative to conventional CFC refrigerants, and state-of-the-art technology in its air-conditioning and midtemperature refrigeration. Refrigeration systems require a working fluid, traditionally a CFC, that boils at a relatively low temperature. This fluid is alternately compressed and expanded, changing from a liquid to a vapor state. The compressor system consumes a lot of energy as it cycles the liquid to vapor, removes the heat, and changes the vapor back to liquid to repeat the process. The direct effects of the ozone-depleting CFCs are coupled with the indirect effects of using fossil fuels as an energy source. The less efficient the refrigerant and systems, the more carbon dioxide is emitted by power plants in producing additional electricity, thus increasing the global warming impact. R-134a has no ozone-depleting potential, and its global warming factor is about 90 percent lower than that of the CFC refrigerants often used in supermarkets. Supermarkets account for almost 20 percent of CFC consumption for cooling in the United States.

When replacing appliances, contact your local utility for information on purchasing the most energy-efficient ones and carefully read all labels to determine which satisfy your energy needs.

The New York State Energy Research and Development Authority and Hannaford, plus a consortium of utilities, refrigeration equipment manufacturers, and consulting engineers, worked together to develop and demonstrate the use of R-134a. Engineered from the ground up, the individual components were designed and manufactured as a fully integrated system. The use of R-134a has required extensive modification to compressors, piping, lubricant oil, expansion valves, control systems, and installation practices, including a unique leak-detection system. Refrigerant loss occurs through leakage in system piping and components and often during servicing of equipment. Leaks can account for about 30 percent of a system's CFC emissions. Because the low-temperature refrigeration loads still contain HCFCs, the new system's ability to locate and eliminate leaks is expected to cut emissions up to 50 percent. This important development will go a long way toward making all refrigeration systems more environmentally safe. In addition to being the first to use the new CFC-free refrigerant, Hannaford's new compressor technology makes it one of the most energy-efficient supermarket chains in the country.

Because of recent efforts to press for an end to CFC production by 1995, coupled with international pressure ultimately to ban transitional hydrochlorofluorocarbons as well, Hannaford's system has monitoring instrumentation to measure the refrigeration system's reliability and efficiency.

Indicative of its continuing conservation efforts, Hannaford trucks are equipped with map-routing computers to ensure that trucks travel a minimum number of miles. Trucks automatically shut down after five-minute idling. They use electronic fuel injection, limit speed electronically and use cruise control, reduce wind resistance with air shields, and reduce friction with radial tires.

Solid waste management programs include waste-flow analysis at corporate, retail, and distribution center locations. The company works with local, state, and national organizations to develop solid waste reduction and recycling plans. It also conducts environmental seminars, workshops, and conferences. Another precedent-setting program of Hannaford's is its composting of organic wastes.

Unlike programs used by other retailers and manufacturers, where mixed inorganic and organic wastes are shipped to a composter in a commingled state, Hannaford's program emphasizes the separation of organic materials to ensure that the composter receives contaminant-free material. This results in a higher-quality composted product.

The program involves the collection of unsalable materials such as produce trim and outdated or unsalable produce, bakery, or deli items. Each Shop'n Save supermarket generates 2 to 3 tons of organic wastes weekly. This represents an average of 75 tons of solid waste that is being diverted from the waste stream and recycled into a usable product rather than being placed in a landfill.

Hannaford recognizes the critical importance of recycling as many materials as possible at the source and properly preparing each material for the market, thereby ensuring the highest recovery value. Composting can significantly reduce waste. Ted Brown, Hannaford's environmental affairs manager, has chaired a nationwide food industry task force that has been looking at this issue and has concluded that composting is an effective tool in the food industry's effort to reduce solid waste. "We are all very excited about our composting program and encourage others to learn more about the benefits of composting as an effective waste management solution," says Brown.

Educational programs for employees, customers, and the communities Hannaford serves are key components of its environmental program. The company sets up environmental store tours for interested parties and concentrates on programs that educate and influence grade school children. Environmental shelf messages are placed throughout the stores, informational brochures are available, recycling information boards post updated information, a bulletin is issued quarterly, and consumer environmental discussion groups are sponsored by the stores.

All Hannaford associates are involved with internal efforts to reduce, reuse, and recycle, and, as one might imagine, these interoffice efforts are monumental. The checklists in chapter 6 of this book give guidelines for incorporating comprehensive internal programs implemented by companies like Hannaford, Smith & Hawken, Ben & Jerry's, and The Boston Park Plaza Hotel.

Choices Are the Key to Future Successes

Hannaford Brothers is working with manufacturers to reduce unnecessary packaging and is taking steps to reduce its own brand's packaging, while preserving the integrity and safety of the products. Every effort is made to pass on suggestions Hannaford's customers volunteer in their discussion groups.

Offering customers a choice plays a key role in Hannaford's marketing. For instance, most paperboard beverage cartons, like milk cartons, are nonrecyclable because they are plastic coated instead of wax coated as they were years ago. These cartons add to the solid waste stream. Plastic milk jugs, on the other hand, are made of recyclable high-density polyethylene (HDPE2). Hannaford advises customers to purchase milk in plastic jugs, if HDPE is recycled in their area, and to recycle them to reduce solid waste. Hannaford provides information in its stores for customers to help them determine which plastic and glass containers are reusable or recyclable. The stores also provide Earth Matters plastic bag recycling bins for their customers.

Hannaford is working to offer a greater range of environmentally friendly products. The difficulty is determining what constitutes environmentally friendly products or packaging. To date there are no nationally or regionally recognized standards covering this area, although work is being done to create such standards. In the meantime Hannaford is proceeding cautiously to ensure that the environmental products it sells are favorable to the earth and its resources and meet strict health and safety requirements.

The company has introduced the Green Meadow line of paper products produced from 100 percent recycled fibers, and Hannaford continually works with its vendors to eliminate excess packaging, to encourage the use of recycled materials, and to use nontoxic inks on labels.

Hannaford will continue to take a proactive role in working with businesses and municipalities to develop environmental programs, and with legislators to meet state and federal waste management goals. Hannaford has discovered that its efforts have strengthened its partnership with its customers. The company's efforts have propelled Hannaford to the forefront in both the marketplace and in helping worthy environmental programs succeed, providing credibility to the adage that "success is turning knowledge into positive action."

CHAPTER TWO

Service Industries

AT&T Calls for Environmental Excellence

With 2.4 million registered shareowners, AT&T's is the most widely held stock in America. Likewise AT&T takes great stock in America with environmental efforts dating back almost fifty-five years, beginning in 1940 with recycling copper and telephones. Thirty years passed, however, before a proactive environmental policy was formalized in 1971 with the creation of AT&T's Environment and Safety Organization, forming the basis of its ongoing environmental programs.

As parent company of the Bell System, AT&T's primary mission for more than a century was to provide universal telephone service to practically everyone in the United States. With the divestiture of the Bell Companies in 1984, AT&T turned its focus to worldwide high technology markets with only its long distance operation remaining under government regulation.

AT&T now provides communications services and products as well as network equipment and computer systems to businesses, consumers, telecommunications service providers, and government agencies. Other business interests include a general-purpose credit card and financial and leasing services. All in all, there are some twenty business units within AT&T, over forty major manufacturing sites, and some twenty-five hundred administrative locations.

The Midas Touch

Tying all levels of AT&T together in its efforts to achieve both economic and environmental goals is what the company calls its "golden thread." Commitment, grants AT&T, must begin stitch-by-stitch from the top, then cascade down through the company to each process owner or end user. Contending that its thread is even stronger than government regulations, AT&T says that its goals "go further and faster than laws, regulations, or international guidelines require."

Overall, most of big business has not adopted environmental policies on the basis of altruism alone. Government is the needle that has sewn the new patterns. In the throes of adhering to government regulations, companies often begin to recognize that there's gold in them thar environmental hills. Initiating environmental reforms rather than waiting for them to be imposed can save a corporation millions of dollars annually by avoiding or minimizing direct and indirect costs. Direct costs typically include labeling, transporting, and landfilling or incinerating waste; taxes on toxic, hazardous, or virgin materials; penalties and fines for noncompliance; legal fees; and Superfund liabilities, among many others.

In the climate of the 1990s, few companies are willing to gamble with indirect costs resulting from a failure to show a commitment to the environment. Negative publicity influences stock prices and shareowner relations; it makes consumers think twice about doing business with a company that appears to have no regard for the well-being of the planet. Persistent assaults by environmental groups diminish employee morale and confidence, affecting productivity. One could hardly envision AT&T tumbling in the wake of one or all of the above, but stranger things have happened. Who would have thought a decade ago that a corporate giant such as Wang Laboratories would be reduced to a pint-sized company that is fading fast because of greater competition, mismanagement, and a poor economy.

Success Stories

Designed to put AT&T on track toward preventing pollution at the source rather than depending on abatement-type compliance (the so-called end-of-the-smokestack approach), the company's current environmental goals were unveiled in 1990:

- Eliminate CFC emissions from manufacturing by the end of 1994.

- Eliminate reportable toxic air emissions 95 percent by the end of 1995.

- Decrease total manufacturing process waste disposal 25 percent by the end of 1994.

- Increase paper recycling to 60 percent by the end of 1994.
- Reduce paper use by 15 percent by the end of 1994.

The first facility to leap into action was AT&T's factory in Singapore, engineering out CFC emissions in mid-1990. The company's Little Rock, Arkansas, plant was second, becoming CFC-free in late 1990. Typical of the company's local initiatives is AT&T's Atlanta location, a 2-million-square-foot complex that manufactures communications cable. A team of AT&T managers from different areas was convened, and a champion for each of the goals was designated. Assistance was also provided by outside consultants. Atlanta's successful methods and processes are being repeated in the company's plants worldwide. By the end of 1991 AT&T reported

- a 76 percent reduction in CFC emissions
- a 75 percent reduction in reportable toxic air emissions
- a 39 percent reduction in manufacturing process waste disposal
- recycling of 45 percent of its waste paper (45 million pounds, saving $2 million in waste disposal fees)
- a 66 percent reduction of 33/50 Industrial Toxics Project (ITP) emissions

AT&T now boasts a whole wall of citations in recognition of its accomplishments, including the 1990 Council on Economic Priorities Corporate Conscience Award, a presidential citation from the 1991 President's Environment and Conservation Challenge Award, the 1991 EPA Region II Administrator's and Stratospheric Ozone Protection Awards, the 1991 and 1992 National Environmental Development Association Honor Roll Awards, and the 1991 New Jersey Governor's Award for Outstanding Achievement in Pollution Prevention. And they keep on rolling in.

The 1991 Renew America Environmental Achievement Award is also prominently displayed, received by AT&T, along with the state of Arizona, for a program in Arizona that allows "telecommuters" to work at home one or two days a week, communicating with their offices through fax machines, modems, and telephones. This accounted for nearly a hundred thousand fewer employee miles driven to and from work, preventing an estimated 1.9 tons of vehicle-related air pollutants.

Design for Living

While recovery and cleanup is crucial to coping with decades of corporate and consumer debris, preventing pollution rather than correcting it has become the major focus for many companies. AT&T's Design for Environment (DFE) policy dictates "Think environment" in the development of new products and manufacturing processes. Before research and development conceives a new design, before an idea moves to the manufacturing stage, before managers implement a product or plan, all are encouraged to ask, "How can we create and deploy an environmentally preferable product, designing waste out of the process from the beginning?" The answer, says AT&T, is "to anticipate the negative environmental impacts of your products and processes; then engineer them out."

The next step in getting its engineers to think environment is getting all its engineers to think the same, notes AT&T. In pursuit of this, AT&T (among others) is adding DFE software to its computer-aided-design systems, containing guidelines and options for making products easily recyclable, choosing the least harmful materials, and minimizing hazardous waste and energy use in manufacturing. AT&T's Bell Laboratories is developing a rating system for DFE products. In 1993 AT&T expects to introduce a "green" business phone that uses minimal lead solder and is easier to disassemble for recycling.

The Paper Trail

Continuous communication to employees through annual reports, posters, video, print and electronic media, and exhibits encourages employee participation in AT&T's environmental goals. In most of its locations, teams, known by such names as Planet Protectors, help to collect used paper, magazines, newspapers, corrugated boxes, and computer printouts for recycling. One employee in Dallas took it upon herself to learn everything she could about recycling and for that effort was chosen leader of her quality improvement team. Her team recycles 11,000 to 13,000 pounds of cardboard every two weeks. Eight employees at the Warrenville/Westwood, Illinois, facility formed the Westwood Ecology Quality Circle in 1990. Beginning its recycling drive in April 1991, the group collected over 29 tons of paper by year's end. The NSEC West Headquarters in Ballwin, Missouri, recovered 147 tons of paper in 1991.

All in all, as of 1991 AT&T employees recovered about 45 million pounds of paper annually, saving 374,000 trees and 55 barrels of oil. Given that paper takes up the most space in landfills and never biodegrades, the best news may be that 72,600 cubic yards of waste annually is rescued from that fate. Its dollar savings from paper recycling—revenues from sales of recycled materials plus costs avoided in waste disposal fees—totaled $3.4 million in 1992 alone. AT&T teams have extended their recycling efforts to plastic spools and tubes, wood, aluminum cans, cardboard, and polystyrene foam.

Enlist the aid of employees from all levels of the company in your program and recognize their efforts. Involvement in a program of this kind empowers employees and raises staff morale.

In the face of such employee enthusiasm, the AT&T executive branch could do no less. Recycled paper is used for many company publications, the most significant of which was AT&T's 1991 annual report, the largest ever printed on recycled stock—660 tons. The accompanying proxy statement used another 260 tons of recycled stock. A "compressed" bill has replaced AT&T's sixteen-page format for its PRO WATS service, in response to thousands of complaints from customers who criticized the waste of paper. Estimated savings in paper and postage is $3 million annually. In just two years, AT&T increased its use of recycled paper by a whopping 700 percent—from five tons in 1990 to 3,500 tons in 1992. The amount is still rising. As of 1 January 1993, AT&T was using recycled paper for virtually all of its direct-mail literature to its customers.

Safeguards

Overall corporate responsibility for AT&T's environmental and safety management lies with the 170-person staff of the Environment and Safety Engineering Organization (E&S). The group's mission is to establish the direction, standards, and engineering support for all of AT&T's operations necessary to protect employees, customers, shareowners, the public, and the environment. Impressing the importance, especially to business-unit leaders, of supporting its people "in the trenches" with necessary finances and staffing is another essential E&S responsibility.

All facilities, from customer Phone Centers to massive, complex factories, have safety issues, notes AT&T, which is "working hard to improve its protection across the company." Its 1991 E&S report recorded a drop in the lost-workday rate from 0.87 in 1990 to 0.83. While its Oklahoma City plant was awarded STAR status by OSHA in 1989, this didn't help AT&T's overall job-related injury rate for 1991—2.65 cases per 100 employees, a 1 percent increase from the 1990 rate of 2.62. Two job-related fatalities occurred in 1991, one in Network Cable Systems and one in Business Communications Systems.

A joint Bell Laboratories/E&S benchmarking team has been established to assess a "Best in Class" accident/injury prevention program for AT&T companies. Additionally, a new employee training program on environment and safety has been rolled out to manufacturing and nonmanufacturing locations. The program outlines each manager's responsibilities in these areas.

Customer Driven

Quality is the driving factor in its whole operation, avers AT&T, which defines quality as "consistently meeting our customers' expectations." AT&T is well aware that a company's environmental integrity is a potent, visible consumer issue and is seriously considered when the quality of the products that company has to offer is evaluated. In a marketplace where some 70 percent of Americans identify themselves as "environmentalists" and worldwide consciousness is ever-increasing, AT&T is reaching out to touch everyone with "an environmental record that works for us, not against us."

Reader's Digest Digesting Waste

Addressing the Gravure Association of America's 1992 Environmental Conference held in Durham, South Carolina, Robert G. Whitton, Jr., associate director of the Reader's Digest Association's production department, summarized the company's environmental policy as having two major goals: "To work with suppliers and industry groups to reduce, minimize, or eliminate the generation of waste or the release of potentially hazardous waste to the environment, and to conform to environmental laws and regulations in each country where we conduct business."

Publishing enterprises, too, are affected by changes in environmental awareness, regulation, and technology. Reader's Digest is a global publisher of magazines, books, and home entertainment products, and it is one of the world's largest direct-mail marketers. It conducts business from more than fifty locations in thirty-one countries and is known in virtually every nation on earth. From a business perspective, there are three things that characterize Reader's Digest's environmental interests: the "givens," those aspects of business that are governed; the "gray areas," where it's less clear what level of participation by the publishing community is required; and "personal," those determined by the publisher as clear environmental concerns of its own.

The Digest as Watchdog

The givens are such things as EPA compliance and recycling of plant waste. To meet these goals, the magazine works closely with its printing and converting suppliers to meet current and emerging requirements. In this way, Reader's Digest can rely on its printers and suppliers to control the segregation and disposal of preconsumer waste from the manufacturing system and to comply with the local, state, and federal guidelines and laws for the proper handling of by-products from the work done for Reader's Digest.

The gray areas refer to the nature of inks, coatings, or adhesives needed to manufacture or fabricate its products, promotion pieces, and other customer communication items. Certainly some of these materials present obstacles to worker safety or recycling technology. Inks and adhesives are specified by the creative director or production manager to achieve a predictable result, and Reader's Digest is cognizant of the responsibility it holds for the consequences of these directives. The company therefore measures or moderates its quality expectations in order to give greater emphasis to environmental responsibility.

Reader's Digest differs from many of our selected case studies in that it is not directly responsible for the manufacture of a product, but produces indirectly by fulfillment. Yet it is not passive on the subject of environmental issues, recognizing that the cost of capital, materials, utilities, and labor incurred by its printers and suppliers in controlling or recovering waste and pollution will be reflected in invoices. The company is equally aware that sweeping changes in regulation or an unfavorable site inspection at one of its printers' plants could pose a threat to its reputation and business as well.

The clear concern of Reader's Digest is reducing municipal solid waste. It foresees the possibility of having to pay disposal fees for paper destined for landfills or even of outright prohibitions against paper disposal. The newspaper industry has been largely transformed by mandated recycling of old newspapers and requirements for recycled content. Proposed legislation could promote similar change in the printing and writing grades. A related issue is product and packaging recyclability. In the Digest's estimation, every publisher must work to improve the recyclability of its products. This means working with suppliers to create quality inks more compatible with de-inking plants (where postconsumer paper is washed, repulped, and processed), and includes the disposal of the resulting sludge. Similar actions are taken with varnishes, coatings, and adhesives. The company is also working with its suppliers to evaluate the potential for recyclable or soluble pressure-sensitive labels. The Digest has elected to support paper companies who will increase the fiber yield from de-inking, thus reducing waste that must be incinerated or dumped in landfills. Reader's Digest is using its buying power to induce change.

Business can buy recycled goods to create a perpetual demand. By insisting on recycled products as well as other environmental changes from vendors, companies send a clear message. A company can use its buying power as a positive inducement, especially if the company is a major user of certain products. Smaller companies can form cooperatives to increase the impact of their buying power.

"Another issue is recycled paper," says Robert Whitton. Currently there are many tradeoffs in the use of recycled magazine paper in areas of performance, availability, and price, he explains. Although grades have proliferated, quantities of recycled paper are limited.

Some recycled offerings don't print as well as virgin fiber, and only test quantities of coated number 5 are available in basis weights below 38 pounds. "Bear in mind," adds Whitton, "that the motive to use recycled paper is not saving trees; it's reducing municipal solid waste. Recycled paper will become more available, of higher quality, and more cost efficient as printers gain more experience and as customers, compelled by legislation or not, become more willing to use it. Some years from now, we'll wonder what all the fuss was about." In Whitton's view, publishers must work to reduce the number of unsold copies, while printers must continue to wage war on waste. There is room for improvement with better copy counts and lower press and finishing spoilage. The effort at process improvement, he asserts, provides a good link between environment and quality management.

Papermakers have long used chlorine bleach to whiten their products. Yet chlorine is harmful to the atmosphere and is a known precursor of toxic substances like dioxin. The U.S. paper industry has made significant investments in the elimination of all but barely measurable trace amounts of dioxin in their effluent streams. In Europe, where there are older mills, the paper industry has been targeted by Greenpeace to eliminate chlorine altogether. While many European mills have rather painlessly converted their pulping capacity to so-called chlorine-free, the price tag for U.S. industry is considerably higher, with estimates as high as $10 billion being cited within just a few years. Reader's Digest is actively aligning with papermakers and regulators in search of a cost-effective solution to the issue.

These partnerships have become a major component in Reader's Digest's environmental efforts. It will continue to work with its suppliers to understand the level of its commitment to licensing, permitting, regulatory compliance, and removal and disposition of drums, boxes, bales, and compacted materials of the trade. In exchange, it looks to its suppliers to help to qualify substitute or alternative consumables, including paper, ink, and adhesives, for trouble-free operation on the equipment employed to do the Digest's work. The raw material suppliers, especially paper mills, must offer improved substrates for testing. For its part as publisher, Reader's Digest must be ready, willing, and able to evaluate these new paper grades or inks out of a genuine desire to make the partnership work.

Reader's Digest's objective is to use more recycled materials in the workplace, in promotions, bills, products, and packaging. In time, the company believes, recycled materials will become the norm. "The supply chain will figure out the logistics, manufacturing, and quality problems," says Whitton. The company's suppliers will then have "ample capacity to match demand, and price will be less of an issue."

The Publisher as Educator

Perceptions and emotions drive much of the environmental effort today. When an activity is perceived to be harmful to the environment, people are against it. Whitton capsulizes this attitude with the old saw "My mind is made up; don't confuse me with the facts." Reader's Digest has taken the position that a critical issue is to educate legislators and regulators about the genuine ambiguities it sees in expectations versus feasible actions. It encourages spontaneous dialogue with regulators and consumer groups who oppose present industry standards. In the company's view, "We have a positive story to tell about our environmental actions, and we should become more proactive among those who would criticize."

Reader's Digest magazine annually publishes about half a dozen articles that touch on the use and abuse of the environment. Reader response to this category has invariably been praise. The company receives roughly three hundred pieces of masthead mail a year that include negative comments about the environment, and the majority of that group, according to Whitton, is critical of the magazine's promotional mail.

Although the amount of direct mail *Reader's Digest* generates may be open to criticism, a lot of thought and discrimination goes into the *Reader's Digest* selections of paper stock and inks for direct mail, and additional efforts to prevent multiple mailings to the same address are controlled by diligent monitoring of its mailing lists.

As an advertising vehicle, *Reader's Digest* found that at first advertisers were enthusiastic to tell about their goods and services and company behavior "friendly" to the environment. However, this climate changed. Negative publicity garnered by some advertisers who had made unsubstantiated and excessive claims for their products, such as the green marketing of Hefty trash bags, scared other advertisers into extreme caution. As a result, ads that do mention environmental issues do so with modest claims or heavily substantiated ones.

From the perspective of *Reader's Digest*, environmental advertising has diminished, and marketers are choosing very narrow, manageable messages, like Procter & Gamble's concentrated detergent packages, or "soft" messages, if they use print or broadcast media at all.

Employees Pitch In

The Reader's Digest Corporate Environmental Statement addresses the need for an internal workplace initiative as well. Its general policy is to "encourage all employees worldwide to practice concern for the environment in their daily activities as they create, produce and market our products."

In its Pleasantville, New York, headquarters, employees separate paper products for recycling from garbage. Offices are equipped with separate bins to collect almost 250,000 pounds of newspapers, computer printouts, and other paper products that used to be thrown away every month. "In addition to helping our environment, recycling makes good business sense," says Al Chaleski, facilities manager at the Reader's Digest Association. "It's helping us to save thousands of dollars a year in the United States, and similar recycling activities are underway in the company's other locations worldwide."

In addition to recycling efforts, individual departments have converted to the use of environment-friendly products and exercise energy conservation efforts similar to programs found and detailed in other case studies in this book. Using newsletters and educational programs, the company's employees have readily committed themselves to the environmental policy.

Reader's Digest's greatest contribution to the environment and business story is its willingness and ability to use its buying power and prestige to influence an entire industry. "Industry groups, such as Gravure Association of America, need our support as we go about the business of educating one another and the general public," concludes Whitton. "In addition, all the literature available points to the need for concerted action among a wide array of industry groups, many of whom may have conflicting, narrow agendas. Publishers and others alike can act to shape consensus around the main issues affecting the vision of where we want to go, and the legislation, guidelines, or voluntarism necessary to get there."

Eco-tourism in the Urban Jungle

The term *eco-tourism* has often been narrowly defined as the practice of merely encouraging travelers to recognize the value of an exotic location and act responsibly to maintain its uniqueness and authenticity. Responsible travel should extend beyond safaris in Tanzania or treks through Nepal. Whether a hotel is located in a bustling urban center like Boston or on the idyllic islands of Hawaii, every property has a shared responsibility to lessen its impact on the earth's limited resources. Many companies in the travel industry are recognizing their obligation to protect the assets that make their daily and long-term economic survival possible.

With 977 rooms encompassing 750,000 square feet, The Boston Park Plaza Hotel & Towers is the largest independent, family-owned and -operated hotel in the United States. Since 1927, when it was built as the flagship of Ellsworth M. Statler's company and later owned and operated by Conrad and Barron Hilton, it has been renowned for its grandeur, elegant design, and ultimately for its innovative service to guests. In fact Statler was responsible for first introducing radios, sewing kits, and chilled drinking water to hotel rooms, and he also created the ingenious valet guestroom doors for laundry and dry cleaning, still in use today.

My family, the Saunders, wishing to expand their real estate business, went into hotel ownership during the Depression. My grandfather, Irving M. Saunders, and his brother, Sidney, purchased the Broadway Hotel, the Copley Square Hotel, and the Lenox Hotel, all located in Boston, Massachusetts. My father, Roger, at age fifteen worked his way up the ranks of our first property, the Broadway, gaining invaluable hands-on experience as an elevator operator, bellman, and housekeeping employee. The day after graduating college, he began working at the Copley Square Hotel, and twelve years later he became the manager of the Lenox Hotel across the street. My brothers, Gary and Jeffrey, began managing the Lenox and Copley Square hotels respectively after years of learning the ropes at other distinguished hotels, such as the Waldorf Astoria. Fifteen years ago, my father and his brother Donald purchased The Boston Park Plaza Hotel, then still known as the Statler Hilton, as well as the connecting Statler Office Building. Saving the complex from the wrecker's ball, they chose to restore and renovate. My family's philosophy is that the preservation of historic buildings is an invaluable asset to the overall quality and charm of a city, and it is undeniably an efficient use of resources. This purchase was therefore consistent with the family's tradition of taking older, underused facilities, recognizing them for their ultimate value, and transforming them into landmark properties. In the 1990s our company's focus on preservation expanded to include the practice of conservation.

It is within this context that the concept for our environmental program was able to gain momentum and to take hold. Because of the top management's ongoing commitment to a comprehensive environmental campaign, I had the mandate and financial support necessary to create and implement a long-term strategy. The Saunders Hotel Group Executive Committee, composed of my father, my older brothers, and my twin, Todd, supported me in my goal to make our company more environmentally sound.

The stability of private ownership enabled us to recognize that many of the suggested investments were not only good for the environment but, from a long-term perspective, made solid business sense as well. This approach allowed us to find a workable balance between short-term cost-saving measures and long-term investment.

In the spring of 1990, I joined forces with an environmental communications consultant, Liz Kay, to create a framework to help guide the overall process and strengthen our contacts. Gary, as president of the hotel, gave us the freedom to question all standard operating procedures as we addressed the key issues of source reduction, material reuse and recycling, hazardous material elimination, energy and water conservation, and education and communication.

What began in the fall of 1989 as a simple white-paper recycling project has grown into a comprehensive environmental campaign of more than ninety-five hotelwide initiatives. The need for an environmental policy to help guide our decisions and focus our efforts became evident. This signed policy, framed and posted throughout the hotel, serves as a clear statement of the family's commitment:

> "If one individual convinced two people to do something for the environment, and the next day each convinced two more people, and so on, and so on . . . it would take less than a month to get everyone in the United States to take some kind of action."—anonymous
>
> We at The Boston Park Plaza Hotel & Towers are taking dramatic action to help secure our future and to make our world a cleaner, safer place for ourselves and our children.

With the implementation of this sweeping environmental program—unprecedented in scope—we are setting an example not only for the hotel industry but also for diverse businesses and for individuals themselves. We have scrutinized our hotel operation and have identified every area where we can reduce waste, recycle materials, and conserve energy and water. We also pledge to maintain the superb standard of quality which we have provided our guests throughout three generations of hotel ownership.

Through this ambitious environmental program we hope to educate both our guests and ourselves, to foster an environmental conscience, and to effect positive change that will extend far beyond The Boston Park Plaza Hotel & Towers.

We established a hierarchy of action steps based on the most critical environmental issues facing our region. Available landfill space in the state was quickly disappearing, as it is nationwide. We therefore focused on reducing certain sources of trash, like excess packaging. We involved the purchasing director in reviewing all procurement decisions, encouraging bulk purchases and reusable and recyclable products whenever possible.

Our initial implementation step was to establish a list of priority issues:

1 Reducing waste at the source
2 Purchasing reusable goods
3 Conserving water and energy
4 Recycling and buying recycled products
5 Eliminating household hazardous materials
6 Examining environmental health and air and water quality standards
7 Fostering education and communications

What distinguished this program from many other green efforts was not only the desire to incorporate an environmental policy into every facet of the company but also to create an aggressive communications and education campaign for our employees, guests, and the general public. Training seminars for staff were conducted in a multitude of languages. Newsletters were employed to disseminate information. Printed collateral information, on recycled materials, was created especially for various guests, ranging from a meeting planners guide tailored to help planners create "green meetings" to room service menus on recycled paper. Ultimately, we are asking our many constituencies to rethink and change their daily actions.

Hotel employees volunteer to be on our Green Team. They monitor existing programs, encourage continuing participation among their peers, suggest new ideas, and help to keep the flow of information circulating around the hotel. One Thursday a month is Green Day at the company's employee cafeteria. A theme is selected and the cafeteria is decorated accordingly and environmental gifts are raffled off. This is a creative reminder of our combined efforts.

Employees are now creating new ideas as well as successfully maintaining the program. It is the commitment to positive, ongoing education and environmental awareness that has helped the program catch on among the diverse employee groups at the hotel. The campaign has taken on a life of its own, with creative solutions appearing regularly. One good example of this is packaging materials. As part of our ban on polystyrene and as an alternative to foam shipping pellets, the hotel uses shredded paper from offices to pack all boxes. We also created a small card to educate and encourage the receivers to do the same. Likewise we reuse wooden shipping pallets, rather than junk them, and ask our vendors to do the same.

The program has also been integrated through all levels of operation. In fact, the division heads as well as the hotel's volunteer Green Team gather monthly for the sole purpose of discussing their departments' recent environmental accomplishments and goals. And we are now implementing similar programs at the Saunders Hotel Group's other historic Boston properties, the Copley Square and Lenox hotels. This ripple effect is critical to the long-term viability and success of the campaign.

The following are some of our accomplishments.

Solid Waste Reduction

- As part of the hotel's solid waste reduction program, we recycle all paper, aluminum, glass, cardboard, steel, #1 and #2 plastic (most readily recyclable plastics), and telephone books. On an annualized basis the hotel's efforts have prevented over 120,000 pounds of trash from reaching our landfills, saving $6,000 in the process.
- We negotiated the return of all fifty-five-gallon steel and plastic drums as well as shipping pallets, printer

toner cartridges, and clothes hangers to their supplier for reuse. Initially, many of the drums were fitted with covers and utilized in the building as back-of-the-house recycling receptacles. The remaining containers are rinsed, re-labeled, and sent back to the vendor for reuse.

- As part of the effort to close the recycling loop, we have purchased all new paper products, including dioxin-free stationery and office forms on recycled stock. Over a three-year period, nearly 100 percent of the hotel's printed materials were switched to recycled paper, ordered only as supplies were depleted.

- Partially stained white linens are resewn into chef's aprons and neckerchiefs by our seamstresses, reducing waste and an entire budget item, and providing a use for an otherwise unusable product.

- All disposable tableware in the employee cafeteria, serving over 170,000 meals annually, has been replaced with reusable china, glass, and silverware. Employees use ceramic mugs instead of 5,000 throwaway paper cups weekly, saving more than a quarter million cups per year.

- Perhaps the most visible initiative in the program, and the first of its kind in the country, was the creation of an elegant pump dispenser system for all bathroom amenities. By cutting out the cost of throwaway repetitious packaging, we are able to spend our money where it counts, on higher-quality, all-natural amenities for our guests. In addition, this dramatic change eliminates almost 2,000,000 one-ounce plastic containers from the landfill annually. Just think of the waste that could be eliminated if all 400,000 hotels in the United States followed suit. This new amenity plan has been overwhelmingly well received by our guests and is a perfect example of a win-win situation. We save on the cost of amenities, our guests receive a higher grade of product, and our landfills are saved from needless waste.

Water Conservation

As a result of the multi-billion-dollar, decade-long Boston Harbor cleanup, in 1992 alone Boston water rates rose by an incredible 15 percent and are expected to experience dramatic increases within five years. In the case of The Boston Park Plaza, the annual increase would have been over $150,000. Fortunately the hotel had already undertaken numerous water conservation steps, cutting water costs by over a third. To reduce annual water consumption by more than 16.5 million gallons and 29,000 gallons of fuel to heat that water, we have

Flushing a toilet typically uses five to seven gallons of water. Using a toilet dam can save up to 40 percent of the water wasted.

- installed the highest-quality low-flow shower heads and aerators in each of the hotel's eleven hundred bathrooms;

- replaced the outdated, water-cooled machinery, such as banquet ice machines, with more efficient air-cooled models, saving 1.5 million gallons of water annually;

- renovated eighty-seven bathrooms and retrofitted them with new 1.6 gallons-per-flush water-saving toilets at a cost of $26,000 and a two-and-a-half-year payback;

- investigated a laundry water conservation system for The Boston Park Plaza Hotel that will save 2 million of the 2.6 million gallons presently used. The Lenox Hotel has already installed a $6,000 system and estimates a sixteen-month payback.

Energy

With the constant emergence of new building technologies, we have numerous opportunities to upgrade the property's energy efficiency. Although energy use was not a major factor when the hotel was built in the 1920s, it is now taken into consideration in all new building renovations. We can also test and pilot new products and technologies as they come to the marketplace.

- Thermopane windows have been installed in all 1,686 guestroom windows at a cost of nearly $1.2 million. These windows not only save approximately

$50 per window annually but also open easier and cut back on both noise and indoor air pollution.

- We have installed energy-efficient fluorescent lighting in selected locations, including all renovated areas, signs, and nondecorative fixtures. We are still seeking energy-efficient lighting for guestrooms and chandeliers that fulfills the many requirements for aesthetics, safety, and performance.

- We have consolidated hotel transformers during off-season and "shoulder" months.

- Closed-loop, energy-efficient chillers for renovated basement and lobby-level areas use water as a cooling agent and reclaim the heated water for the hot water system.

We use our nighttime security staff to conduct energy audits as they inspect the premises and to turn everything off as they make their rounds.

- Numerous ongoing energy-efficient programs are also in place throughout the facility, including lighting timers, motion detectors, and a rigorous cleaning and maintenance schedule for all equipment.

Household Hazardous Materials and Environmental Health

- We are continually on the lookout for new biodegradable products that perform to the satisfaction of our guests and our employees.

- The housekeeping department has installed mixing stations with refillable spray bottles for new biodegradable, zinc-free cleaner concentrates. This has eliminated the use of thousands of throwaway aerosol cans and has dramatically reduced pollutants. In fact members of our housekeeping staff confirm that the new solutions not only work well but are easy on their hands and smell better.

Switch to nontoxic cleaning supplies. Some commonly used disinfectants are classified as pesticides by the EPA and are considered hazardous waste. When we switched to environmentally sound products, allergic reactions like skin rashes ceased to be a problem for staff. Using refillable containers creates less waste and saves money.

- We have installed Holofill carpet (made entirely from recycled plastic soda bottles) in the service area corridors. We are testing whether or not this carpet can withstand wear and tear. Holofill is not yet available in the carpet quality and design we require for our guests, but when it is, we will examine the possibilities of its use in our front-of-the-house facilities.

Education

Education is key to implementing innovative ecological programs and effecting long-lasting change.

Early on we found that employees in a service industry must understand the goals of the program and be encouraged to participate. In the four years the program has been in existence, we have gathered and used hundreds of different tactics to educate our employees, guests, and public about this effort. We therefore implemented the following programs:

- We harnessed the employees' enthusiasm and concern by forming a Green Team of volunteers from all departments. With growing interest in the program, and more employees directly involved, new ideas arise constantly.

- We translate information into numerous languages. *The Insider,* the hotel's monthly employee newsletter, is also written in French and Spanish and includes recent accomplishments and simple things employees can try at home.

- Ongoing training and information sessions for every department keep them abreast of new initiatives and involved in the process. This year the training program will be run by members of the Green Team.

- We have created monthly and annual Environmental Action Awards to publicly recognize individual employee contributions.

- An incentive program for employees to collect soda cans was created and the housekeeping department purchased eleven new vacuum cleaners with monies from these redeemables and a matching gift from the hotel.

- Brass eco-educating plaques in each of the 977 guest rooms and every office remind guests and staff of the impact they have on energy and water usage, and how they can help support the hotel's environmental commitment.
- A pamphlet explains our efforts and results, with eco-tips on the back for guests to bring home and take action.

Sales and Marketing

This effort is paying off—not only environmentally, but financially. The hotel has received new business totalling almost one million dollars in additional group bookings from companies who wish to align with a business that has taken a strong environmental stance. Aggressive marketing and sales tactics are now in place, resting solidly on the integrity and visibility of the program.

Aware that skeptics might question the sincerity of our green marketing stance, we purposely waited more than a year into the program to announce our efforts publicly. This strategy has proven successful for the hotel. We have relied totally upon media editorial coverage in lieu of advertising and can clearly show not only image-building but tangible results. As an individual property, otherwise overshadowed by corporate chains, we have gained unprecedented name recognition due to this campaign.

Coverage has included CNN, "NBC Nightly News," "CBS This Morning," Monitor TV's "The Good Green Earth," the *New York Times, USA Today, Business Week, Good Housekeeping, Metropolitan Home,* and numerous hospitality, environmental, business, and consumer trades. We have authored articles for hotel and meeting trade journals and have been featured in others.

In tandem with this media exposure has come national recognition. In December 1992 The Boston Park Plaza Hotel received the President's Environment and Conservation Challenge Gold Medal for Environmental Quality Management in a ceremony at the White House. The program has also received accolades from numerous environmental and industry organizations. We received the Edward Bernays Best of Show Award from the Hospitality Sales and Marketing Association International for our overall public affairs, education, and communication efforts.

What We Have Learned

In assessing the success of the program, we have found that some elements are vital to its integrity. The individual responsible for the program, for instance, must be in a position of power or have direct access to decision makers to carry out the campaign's goals. Personal passion for the issues empowers employees at all levels. Constant visibility and a hands-on approach encourage others to become involved and create a synergy that will ultimately ensure a program with long-lasting effects.

As we integrated this new thinking into all hotel operations, the staff began to recognize that these policies and procedures were part of the new corporate culture at the hotel. The financial investments were a tangible sign to employees that the hotel had a long-term commitment to the program.

Although some efforts do require investment, others need only common sense to be integrated into workable procedures. There are costs associated with taking on a comprehensive program like this. However, the long-term benefits of increased marketing opportunities and streamlined operations justify the investment. One of our greatest goals is to cause a ripple effect—to encourage a new way of thinking. We want our employees and guests to leave the property at night, or after their stay, inspired to make changes in their homes, schools, and workplaces. We speak around the country and abroad in order to affect our peers and our industry. If we can play a role in encouraging collective responsibility for the environment, and if we can foster positive changes through our actions, we will have helped to make the world a better place for ourselves, our children, and generations to come. This is the most significant bottom line of all.

If the Shoe Fits, Buy It

He was sixteen when he left the family farm in Sweden and arrived in America with five dollars in his pocket, unable to speak a word of English. The year was 1887, and the man was John W. Nordstrom.

He worked his way across the United States in the mining and logging camps that dotted the frontier. One Sunday morning in 1897, John Nordstrom read a newspaper headline announcing that gold had been discovered in Alaska; he headed north for the Klondike that very afternoon. The enterprising Nordstrom struck it rich. With his stake, he settled in Seattle, Washington, and opened a small shoe store in 1901. The business grew to become the largest shoe chain in the country.

Three generations later, Nordstrom is a fashion specialty retailer offering a wide selection of apparel, shoes, and accessories for women, men, and children. The company operates fifty-two large specialty stores and four small specialty stores in Washington, Oregon, California, Utah, Alaska, Virginia, New Jersey, Illinois, Minnesota, and Maryland, plus five smaller specialty stores, fifteen clearance stores, and leased shoe departments in eleven department stores in Hawaii. Almost a century later, Nordstrom remains committed to its founding principles of quality, value, selection, and service. In addressing the needs of it customers, it has a commitment also to the environment. This responsiveness pays off. In 1991, sales totaled $3.18 billion, compared with $2.89 billion in 1990, a 9.9 percent increase. Clearly, putting the customer first is a profitable attitude.

Earth Focus

Early into its program, Nordstrom prepared an environmental statement, as follows:

> At Nordstrom, we realize the earth is our common home. We also realize it is our responsibility to respect and preserve the earth's precious resources.
>
> Nordstrom believes that success in today's world is achieved by joining economic vitality with environmental stewardship. It is our goal to make choices that demonstrate a spirit of partnership and reflect our interdependent relationship with the earth.
>
> Nordstrom has taken an active role in managing the solid waste generated by our facilities. We are implementing extensive recycling programs and working with our vendors

to develop markets for the materials we recycle. We have also initiated comprehensive energy and water conservation programs.

In the area of packaging reduction, we are working diligently with our suppliers to eliminate excess materials and provide earth-friendly packaging that uses recyclable and post-consumer fibers. When selecting required packaging, Nordstrom incorporates a "full life cycle" view ranging from design to disposal.

Nordstrom will continue to encourage practices which promote environmental excellence. Together with our customers, employees and suppliers, we will work toward innovative solutions to sustain and improve our world.

The Nordstrom Environmental Program began in 1990 as a grass-roots effort by several employees in various regions. One regional group formed the Nordstrom Environmental Awareness Board (NEAB). This Seattle-based coalition supports the environmental activities of the company, its community, and concerned individuals. NEAB efforts range from employee education to community tree-planting projects.

If your company is big enough, appoint an environmental coordinator to keep current on regulations, alternatives, and technology and to address the environmental concerns of your constituency.

Nordstrom has always encouraged its salespeople to provide outstanding service. The staff's aptitude and success at satisfying their customers enabled the company to grow from a few dozen employees in the 1920s to over thirty thousand today. Employees have shown their confidence in management, and management is committed to responding to its employees' needs. Support of NEAB's efforts to improve the environment demonstrates management's willingness to adopt the concerns of the people it employs.

On the heels of NEAB came the appointment of individual Nordstrom environmental coordinators, including a full-time corporate environmental coordinator, responsible for company environmental goals and programs, including monitoring and implementing new processes, products, and activities. Additionally, each region has an organized team of employees to establish environmental efforts.

"Nordstrom, as a corporate citizen, has an opportunity to make a difference," states corporate environmental coordinator Alice

Johnson. "Source reduction and recycling are not our bottom-line business, but we do believe we have a vital role to play."

Nordstrom recognizes its employees for outstanding ideas that contribute both to the environment's well-being and the company's bottom line. Prizes are awarded each quarter for the ten best ideas presented during that time period. The company also acknowledges the efforts of its vendors toward environmental improvements. "Nordstrom believes it can make the greatest impact working together with vendors to reduce unnecessary packaging, to conserve natural resources, and to utilize recycled products," adds Johnson.

Companywide Efforts

Nordstrom has made impressive progress in the conservation of energy and water. Utility companies across the country have identified Nordstrom as a leader in helping to create innovative programs for commercial users. One program developed in the Pacific Northwest not only saves energy but is structured to provide financial assistance to low-income utility customers.

Companywide energy conservation resulted in savings of 8.1 million kilowatt hours in 1991 and 1992. Each twelve-month energy savings is the equivalent of the amount of energy used to light eighty-nine thousand average households for one year.

Nordstrom has installed electronic ballasts and energy-efficient fluorescent lamps throughout many of its older stores in the Northwest. Aluminum reflectors have been replaced with new energy-saving devices and are being recycled whenever possible. Water-saving technologies have been incorporated in new and existing stores.

Most Nordstrom stores are equipped with cardboard baling devices, allowing an average store to recycle over 80 tons of cardboard each year, thereby reducing an enormous amount of garbage that would otherwise be sent to landfills. Paper recycling bins have been placed at each cash register to enable employees to recycle. Several regions are also adding plastic recycling programs as well.

All Nordstrom signature gift boxes are made of 100 percent boxboard, containing a minimum of 35 percent postconsumer fibers. Furthermore Nordstrom uses merchandise bags containing 15 percent postconsumer recycled material, printed with environmentally safe ink, and recyclable in most regions of the United States. Each of these bags is imprinted with the following message: "We ask that you benefit the Earth even more by reusing this bag." To enable customers to recycle the paper shopping bag, plastic handles have been replaced with paper twist handles. These bags also contain 15 percent postconsumer recycled material and carry a message of environmental encouragement.

The Brass Plum department at Nordstrom provides customers with a plastic drawstring bag composed of 10 percent postconsumer plastic. These signature bags have been printed with earth-sensitive inks and are durable enough for reuse. Rack bags contain 6 percent postindustrial plastic. As supplies of these bags are depleted, new rack bags will also be printed with the safer inks.

Each year Nordstrom employees correspond with customers to inform them of new merchandise and upcoming events. Over 50 percent of these small direct-mail pieces are printed on recycled paper using postconsumer material. All business cards, note cards, and notepads are printed on recycled paper and can be recycled. Over 75 percent of business forms are printed on recycled paper, most with safer inks. As supplies are depleted, more forms will incorporate these environmentally friendly features. Credit card receipts are printed on recycled paper and produced without carbon paper. During a single year, Nordstrom uses over 55 million of these forms, keeping tons of carbon from landfills. Credit card applications were redesigned so that two types were combined to make one new application. The result uses less material and eliminates the return envelope, saving more than a million envelopes annually.

In May 1992 Nordstrom began a companywide conversion of billing envelopes mailed to credit card holders. Previously, envelopes had a window that prevented the piece from being recycled. The new envelopes have recyclable glassine windows and can be recycled along with other paper products. To eliminate waste, supplies of the old envelopes were depleted before the new envelopes were used.

Vendors who ship merchandise to Nordstrom are encouraged to use packaging made of recycled content. All corrugated cardboard boxes used by Nordstrom for shipping goods are made of recycled material, some up to 100 percent.

For years packing peanuts used to ship merchandise to Nordstrom have been reused to send merchandise to customers. The program, which uses only clean, undamaged peanuts, has been so successful that Nordstrom distribution centers have needed to purchase only small amounts of new Styrofoam packing material. Some are using instead a crimped paper product called Quadra-pak, which is so environmentally sound that it may be added to a gardener's compost pile. When bubble wrap is needed, Nordstrom uses plastic wrap that includes 15 to 50 percent postconsumer plastic and may be reused and recycled where facilities exist.

By using its computerized information service for employees, the company reduced the amount of report paper needed in 1991 by 20 percent. Over the span of three years this computer network will save Nordstrom approximately 167.9 million pages of paper. Laid end to end, that many sheets of paper would encircle the world.

In February 1992 the company unveiled a new logo. A complete changeover of the logo will be slowly implemented due to the company's commitment to the environment. Current supplies of materials will be depleted before new supplies incorporating the new logo are ordered. Many of the environmental programs we examined follow this procedure. A few companies, enthusiastic about their new environmental programs, mistakenly dump all of their old supplies to make room for the new. But this dumping defeats the beneficial effects the new products are intended to have.

Nordstrom's food outlets have converted to using many ecologically correct materials and food items. All napkins used at Café Nordstrom and the espresso bars are made from 100 percent preconsumer recycled fibers. To further conservation efforts, Nordstrom specifically designed a smaller (5-by-5-inch), single-ply napkin to reduce the amount of paper used in each napkin. The boxboard chosen to package Nordstrom's own Shoe Box Lunches are made of 100 percent recycled paper. Up to 70 percent of the paper used in these boxes are postconsumer materials. Whenever possible, durable plastic Sparklelite drinking cups and porcelain coffee mugs are used in the Cafés to eliminate the waste of their disposable counterparts. For hot drinks, such as coffee, Nordstrom espresso bars and Cafés use paper cups that include a statement encouraging users to "help preserve the environment" by using a single cup for multiple servings. Dolphin-free tuna is being used in the majority of Cafés at Nordstrom. This tuna, also called tongol tuna, has received Greenpeace's "dolphin-free" verification.

Other areas in which Café Nordstrom and the espresso bars are practicing sound environmental practices include the use of reusable menus, recycled paper trays, and recycled paper bags for carryout orders. Some locations have started recycling plastic milk jugs and metal cans.

Nordstrom's housekeeping department is using refillable, concentrated, citrus-based cleaners. Aerosols containing harmful CFCs have been eliminated in almost all cases in the housekeeping departments.

Earth Supportive Merchandise and Services

In keeping with its pledge to care for the environment, Nordstrom has made several unusual products available to its customers, and the list is always growing. Here is a sampling of such products:

- The Incredible Paper Making Kit turns ordinary junk mail into hand-crafted stationery in just half an hour.

- Nordstrom Essentials is an exclusive line of body products made from natural colors and essential oil fragrances. Whenever possible, natural ingredients are used instead of synthetic ingredients.

- MAC Cosmetics skin treatments are allergy-tested and contain no animal by-products. The products are not tested on animals. MAC creator Frank Toskan designed a series of T-shirts to promote cruelty-free beauty and donates proceeds from the sale of these shirts to the search for alternative testing methods.

- The Bodyography line of beauty treatments for men and women offers products that are sensitive to the earth's needs. These products are free of mineral oil and alcohol, are completely biodegradable, and have not been tested on animals. The company encourages customers to recycle by returning empty containers to Nordstrom for 50 percent credit toward their next Bodyography purchase. Its Save the Rain Forest shampoo uses tropical extracts to provide economic incentives to preserve the rainforest, and 5 percent of the profits are donated to the Rain Forest Action Network.

- Select Pantry, Nordstrom's food products, are made from all-natural products. Select Pantry labels are printed on recycled paper with water-soluble inks. Select Pantry gift boxes are beautifully designed so further gift wrap is not necessary. They are created from 100 percent recycled cardboard and finished with water-soluble varnish. Inside the boxes, glass bottles are protected by Sizzle Pack, which is an environmentally sound paper packing product.

"Although Nordstrom still has many opportunities to enhance our current environmental programs, we are please with our progress so far," says Alice Johnson. "Both Nordstrom customers and employees have expressed their enthusiasm for the changes we have made to benefit the earth. We will build on these successes and continue to aggressively implement environmentally positive programs."

Dydee Changes Diaper Habits

Dydee Diaper Service, based in Dorchester, Massachusetts, is the nation's second oldest diaper laundry and the largest in New England. Founded in 1933, Dydee employs eighty-five people and still handles its own washing rather than farming it out to a commercial laundry. In fact in 1990 the company installed a $500,000 continuous batch tunnel washer that uses only one-fourth to one-fifth of the water used by conventional washing machines.

Closely regulated by the Massachusetts Water Resources Authority (MWRA), Dydee easily met all wastewater standards for processing through MWRA treatment plants until the installation of the tunnel washer. Strangely enough, the equipment that Dydee elected to purchase to save water was the reason for its failure to pass the routine testing of its wastewater discharge in 1991. Traces of zinc, a heavy metal, were found that exceeded MWRA allowances. Dydee was deemed in violation of its permit.

Getting to the Bottom

"How could this happen?" asked a perplexed Steven Landry, Dydee president. Zinc is a heavy metal typically found as a by-product in such industries as metal plating. How then did zinc turn up in Dydee's wastewater? The answer was astonishing but elementary—diaper rash. For generations parents have treated their babies' sore bottoms with zinc-oxide-based ointments.

Among the 200,000 pounds of cotton Dydee laundered each week were enough zinc-laden diapers to cause the problem, and the tunnel washer was the culprit. Since it uses less water, the concentration of wastewater contaminants increased. To rectify the problem Dydee was faced with two solutions: the installation of

1 a wastewater pretreatment system at a $200,000 initial investment plus a $30,000 annual maintenance cost (it must be tended by a licensed operator); or

2 a closed-loop ozone-activated laundering mechanism that eliminates water discharge altogether.

Number 1 began to look more acceptable to Landry since his research indicated that the new technology of number 2 was not yet ready for application to diaper services.

Going to the Source

Facing the prospect of such an enormous expenditure, Landry continued to search for a more economical alternative. He had to come up with something fast, however, since the company's violation had been reported on Boston's nightly news, and some customers were abandoning ship "due to adverse publicity." Addressing the zinc problem at its source became Landry's third, and ultimately implemented, alternative.

Since occasional diaper rash is a fact of life for babies, another method of treating the rash could rectify Dydee's problem. Through letters and the company's monthly newsletter, Dydee asked its customers to trade in their zinc-oxide products for zinc-free, "equally effective" ointments, creams, and powders. The response was so overwhelming that zinc levels dropped by more than 50 percent after the first five months of outreach efforts, well within compliance.

Saving More Than Face

This brainstorm was not without cost, but when compared with the prices for the first two alternatives, it was a drop in the diaper pail. Some $1,000 worth of free samples were passed out and a $1 bounty was paid to customers for each offending product passed in, totaling another $7,000. The difference between the actual cost and the below-market price for zinc-free options offered to customers was also absorbed by the company. In all, some $10,000 was spent to clean up a mess that could have cost Dydee hundreds of thousands, perhaps putting the company in financial peril.

Dydee enlisted the assistance of the Office of Technical Assistance (OTA) of the Massachusetts Executive Office of Environmental Affairs. OTA's mission is to help industry reduce the use of toxic chemicals and/or the generation of toxic manufacturing by-products. Its nonregulatory services are available at no charge.

For its "exceptional action on behalf of the living environment," Dydee and its customers were presented with the 1992 Audubon Award by the Massachusetts Audubon Society. The society recognized Dydee "as a business leader on environmental issues, most notably for its innovative customer education program and the positive response by customers, resulting in the reduction of zinc contamination in wastewater discharges at its plant."

Disposable vs. Cloth

Customer participation in the solution of Dydee's dilemma was not surprising given that this segment is predisposed (pun intended) to cloth over plastic disposable diapers. Dydee's customers are, for the most part, a self-selecting group that uses cloth diapers for environmental reasons. Immediate response to a call to arms to combat yet another ecological hazard was a natural for them.

Although no one has yet proven conclusively that cloth is better for the environment than the throwaways, or even that one is more damaging than the other, the positive weight of evidence appears to be teetering on the side of reusables. In 1988 Carl Lehrburger, a recycling and waste reduction specialist, completed a study of quantitative and qualitative impacts of diaper use on solid waste management. Funding was provided in part by the National Association of Diaper Services (NADS), but the report begins with the assurance that the NADS had no editorial control over the study's research design or contents. A recognized authority in his field, Lehrburger develops recycling programs and markets secondary materials for Energy Answers Corporation, a waste management company based in Albany, New York.

According to the study, the impact of single-use diapers on the nation's solid waste disposal system is staggering. Single-use diapers create over seven times more postconsumer solid waste and over three times more manufacturing or process solid waste than reusable diapers. Nearly $300 million, continues the study, is spent annually to discard disposables, which now account for approximately 90 percent of all diapers sold in this country. Of this 90 percent, 82 percent ends up in landfills and 8 percent is incinerated. Cotton diapers constitute the other 10 percent and are reused fifty to two hundred times, then recycled as rags.

Of course, the disposable diaper industry has conducted its own studies, which reveal that cloth and disposables have about the same overall impact on the environment, just in different ways—cloth uses more water and energy while disposables create more solid waste. Kimberly-Clark, makers of Huggies, points out that besides using more water, the laundering of cloth diapers releases detergents, bleaches, and disinfectants into the environment. Kimberly-Clark cites an environmental study by Arthur D. Little, Inc., that concludes that disposables are "a response to significant societal needs."

Disposable diapers account for less than 2 percent of all waste that goes into landfills, asserts Kimberly-Clark. In a July 1992 article in *Smithsonian* magazine, garbage gurus William Rathje and Cullen Murphy gave an even lower estimate. They said that disposable diapers constitute no more than 1.4 percent by weight and no more than 4 percent by volume, dispelling the "myth," as they called it, that diapers are major constituents of American garbage. Both archaeologists connected with the University of Arizona, Rathje and Murphy are coauthors of *Rubbish! The Archeology of Garbage*, published by Harper Collins (1992).

Kimberly-Clark does not argue with the EPA's suggestion that the best way to reduce waste is to produce less of it in the first place. The company avows that it supports source reduction by using the fewest materials possible to make Huggies, and it reduced volume by 13 percent in 1991. It pledges "to continue to enhance the performance [of its diapers] and their environmental compatibility." Other companies such as Procter & Gamble, makers of Pampers, are making similar promises. A card in each package of Pampers expounds on P&G's benefits and policies for protecting the environment.

Claims of "biodegradable, recyclable, and compostable" by single-use diaper manufacturers are also red flags to their critics, who point out that attorneys general in ten states prohibit the use of the words *recyclable* and *compostable* in regard to disposables. Also disdained is the hype on the use of biodegradable plastics in single-use diapers, which Lehrburger's study says does nothing for the scope and cost of landfilling or for the elimination of the spread of infection caused by feces. Moreover, "biodegradable" plastic probably does not decompose as rapidly as manufacturers claim, notes the study, and even if broken down, it is of little benefit to the environment.

While the controversy centers on the diapers, packaging is also an issue. This, too, adds to waste. In defense the disposable diaper industry has for the most part replaced bulky boxes with lower-volume packaging. As an example of other innovations, Kimberly-Clark uses plastic handles made partly from recycled plastic milk and water containers in over 90 percent of Huggies packages.

A Healthy Argument

The threat to public health posed by fecal material contained in the diapers should be examined more closely by local, state, and national governments, the Lehrburger study urges. Although manufacturers' instructions on each package counsel that fecal material be flushed before disposal, one-third of these diapers are nevertheless thrown out, contents and all, and this human waste ends up as solid waste, to be incinerated or dumped in landfills. Babies are usually immunized with live polio virus and other vaccines, so they are effective carriers of enteroviruses. These virus-embedded diapers are considered a threat to the health of those who handle solid waste and to society at large.

Manufacturers of disposable diapers tell another story. They claim that there is no scientific evidence to suggest that waste from disposable diapers migrates from landfills into groundwater or poses any health risk to sanitation workers, landfill operators, or the public. They also maintain that disposable diapers are more sanitary since cloth is often stored in soaking pails, an ideal place for bacteria to grow, and that bacteria and viruses remain even after cloth diapers are laundered.

Caring and Sharing

Bottoms Up, a monthly newsletter published and distributed by Dydee leaves little doubt as to the company's commitment to the environment and to the well-being of its babies. Each newsletter contains a lead article on issues that most affect the readers—sources of lead poisoning; guarding against Lyme disease; replacing household products that could be harmful to babies and/or the environment with "old-fashioned" concoctions that are as effective, safer, and less costly; and even "green" gift ideas for the holidays.

In another recycling effort, Dydee's drivers annually collect around 5 tons of clothing for the Clothes for Kids campaign, a nationwide annual cooperative effort between the National Coalition for the Homeless and participating members of the National Association of Diaper Services. Since 1986 Dydee has also worked with the Marine Corps Reserve in the Toys for Tots campaign to deliver toys to needy children for the holidays.

Convenience or Conservation

The cloth diaper industry experienced a boom in the late 1980s, growing almost 70 percent between 1988 and 1991, when many parents were alarmed by news stories of plastic disposable diapers clogging overburdened landfills. But other concerns, such as the recession, soon pushed this issue out of the headlines. Furthermore,

convinced by manufacturers' persistent claims that disposable diapers offer health, comfort, and convenience benefits unmatched by
cloth diapers, nine out of ten parents now choose disposable diapers.

Though nothing has yet taken the place of a cloth diaper as an
over-the-shoulder protection for baby burping, disposables have been
embraced as the most convenient by a fast-paced society to protect
baby's bottom. Is this nearly unanimous election for convenience at
the expense of the environment? Only time will tell.

CHAPTER THREE

Manufacturing

General Electric Brings
Green Things to Life

"Every single person in GE has to be an environmentalist. Our products have to be thought of in those terms. Our processes, too. Everybody has a role to play. And the companies that don't understand this and don't do it, won't recruit the best, won't sell their products, won't be viable, positive enterprises in the 1990s." General Electric's CEO, Jack Walsh, made this statement in 1990 as the new year, GE's 112th year, began.

Given GE's size and diversity, it's not surprising that environment, health, and safety issues confront the company in a variety of ways. "Today we're in transition from a reactive mode—fixing old problems, cleaning up old sites, responding to government regulations—to a preventative mode, where 100 percent compliance is the floor, and we have systems in place to ensure that level of performance," declares Steve Ramsey, vice-president of GE Corporate Environment Programs. "These are coupled with programs to eliminate waste and to reduce workplace injuries; training to make our employees aware of their responsibilities; and outreach efforts to ensure we are being a good environmental neighbor in the communities where our plants operate."

GE's environmental goals include

- 100 percent compliance with laws
- Continued progress toward minimization and elimination of workplace injuries and illness
- Continued progress toward minimization and elimination of waste emissions
- Cost effective cleanup of remedial sites
- Good environmental citizenship

GE, like other industrial companies, faces the task of meeting regulations and finding solutions to environmental problems that were created in the past but that affect the present and the future. In the 1960s GE and other companies stepped up efforts to control waste and to prevent its escape to the environment. The first oil-water separators were among GE's contributions to a growing effort to control and contain pollution from industrial plants. In the 1970s pollution control became an integral part of GE's manufacturing operations across the country. At the same time, state and federal regulations governing industrial pollution changed the way industry as a whole needed to conduct business in the United States. In the 1980s it became apparent that controlling and containing pollution was not enough. GE began to shift its approach to environmental programs and practices that recognized the entire life cycle of products and processes, from design and production through use and disposal. Striving for environmental excellence had become a serious component of GE's corporate culture.

> Each member of a Green Team should be given a task or area to coordinate. In this way, each person becomes a resident expert and is a part of the solution.

Environmental Programs at GE

During the 1980s GE launched a series of programs aimed at ensuring compliance, managing remediation efforts, and preventing pollution in the first place. These programs, which have received even greater commitment since 1990, have inspired this motto at GE: "The mess you never make is the mess you never have to clean up."

GE employs an EHS (Environmental Health and Safety) self-assessment tool of its own innovation called PULSE. It uses a checklist to help GE's diverse businesses evaluate their environmental performance. Another program, called POWER (Pollution, Waste, and Emissions Reduction), was established to provide a company framework and guidance for pollution prevention. Looking for solvent substitutes and cleaner processes, POWER aims to reduce the creation of waste rather than waiting until it gets to the end of the pipe. It gives the site a starting point and a way to measure progress on key environmental and health and safety issues. A best practice program called PEP (Plant Emergency Preparedness) assists plant managers in determining potential hazards and outlining emergency plans. PEP also involves local plant communities.

Education and Networking Work for GE

To ensure the transfer of best practices and to identify state regulations and trends, a program called Environets, which is unique to GE, links environmental professionals and GE state government representatives on a state-by-state basis, with regularly scheduled forums. Through dialogue, GE can transfer knowledge, address common issues, leverage resources, and meet directly with state legislators. By using this mechanism, GE managers understand the best way to deal with state environmental and health and safety regulations. In turn, they have been extremely effective in getting GE's views across to state lawmakers and in getting the company's best thinking focused on the issues.

Training courses in environmental skills and awareness are now required for every GE plant manager as well as employees in engineering, transportation, and marketing. The company offers a series of regional plant management training courses. Every plant manager in the company has been through a two-day course developed to bring together forty to fifty managers and some CEP (Corporate Environmental Program) staff to talk about the environmental issues GE faces, how these can be addressed at the local level, and how EHS values can be integrated into the total business culture, not just pegged as an EHS manager's responsibility. Each manager has an opportunity to understand how to manage these issues. GE's goal is to make EHS awareness, training, and integration routine. In this way it will possess educated staff prepared to take advantage of opportunities to improve productivity, quality, and public image. Furthermore GE is able to rely on its individual plant managers to lead and champion this effort. Given GE's size and number and variety of outlets, an intensive training program at the plant level, where most regulation infractions and most worker injuries occur, ensures a successful transition from reactive to proactive implementation of its environmental and health and safety goals. The leadership of plant managers combined with the leadership of the heads of GE's individual businesses is critical to achieve the quantum cultural change it seeks throughout the company.

Its concern for prevention has prompted GE to make some great advances in reducing waste and improving products and processes. GE's Plastics Division reduced its toxic releases by 75 percent by the end of 1992. GE Appliances reduced all wastes by 40 percent between 1988 and 1991 and is working toward eliminating the use of chlorofluorocarbons in refrigeration products. Several GE businesses have reduced use of CFC-based solvents by substituting water-soluble citrus-based cleaners. GE's Lynn, Massachusetts, plant achieved a 75 percent reduction in CFC use in four years and is committed to a total phaseout. GE's Research and Development Center has conducted a series of seminars and demonstrations to acquaint GE's varied businesses with viable alternatives to CFC-based cleaners.

In 1990 GE created an Environmental Research Center and Environmental Technology Laboratory in Schenectady, New York, to help find innovative, cleaner technologies. GE's Corporate Research and Development Center in Schenectady has pioneered in bioremediation research aimed at breaking down PCBs in the Hudson River. This technology shows great promise for other applications, including oil spills.

Remediation

"It's no secret that GE has a large number of sites that are targeted for cleanup under federal and state programs," admits Ramsey. "The point is, you can't clean up a hundred years of problems in one year, and you can't just throw money into these things willy-nilly." Last year GE spent $100 million on environmental cleanup efforts companywide. To make sure its money is being spent on the right problems as economically as possible, GE formed a Remedial Council. The Environmental Research Center (ERC) serves as a resource for the Remedial Council and GE's other groups that need solutions to environmental problems. The ERC investigates new technologies that can help clean up at lower cost and with less adverse environmental impact. The company has invested in a $50 million biomediation project as an example of how this system works.

Environmentally Friendly Products

GE's products have also become more environmentally friendly. No product has gone untouched by the trend, from the low-noise, fuel-efficient GE90 aircraft engine to energy-efficient light bulbs. Here are some of the more significant product developments:

- GE Plastics has tested a variety of ways to use recycled plastics and has demonstrated them in its widely publicized Living Environment Concept House in Pittsfield, Massachusetts.

- Recycled GE plastic computer housings have been installed as roof panels on several McDonald's restaurants around the country.

- Another company business, GE Environmental Systems, is a turnkey supplier of air-pollution control systems for power plants all over the world. GE flue gas desulfurization technology is the worldwide market leader in power plant applications.

- GE gas turbines are leaders in emission reductions. The MS7001F (7F) gas turbine, in a combined cycle application, has an efficiency rating 15 percent greater than the efficiency of a typical coal-fired plant. The 7F will meet the power needs of 114,000 people at any given time, and, since it can be fired by natural gas, it produces fewer emissions per megawatt of power.

The basic scientific approach adopted by GE is one seen more and more throughout industry, namely, "product life cycle analysis." In this case, GE pulls together its engineers, designers, EHS people, and others to incorporate the EHS vision into a product right from its inception.

GE as Good Neighbor

"Every public opinion poll says the public really cares about anything affecting the environment. Lawmakers listen and continue to enact tougher laws and come down hard on violators," explains Ramsey. "We need to reach out to our communities and let them know we're being responsible and that if any problems develop, we'll be there to take care of them."

A good example of this occurred in West Lynn, Massachusetts. Groundwater contamination was discovered at GE's Aircraft Engines plant, which the company is remedying. The state wanted GE to take samples in people's homes to check for possible contamination. GE argued that this would be intrusive; it also wanted to avoid negative public reaction. A team of Aircraft Engines employees went door-to-door, and spoke at a PTA meeting, to describe what the company was doing and why. The outreach effort was appreciated by the residents and went a long way toward keeping things calm.

Many of GE's businesses have sponsored local projects focused on particular community issues, and these have fostered good relations between the company and the public. Employees of its Medical Systems created a habitat for swans. Other businesses' employees have worked with local chapters of the Elfun Society on mostly sweat equity projects that have had a positive impact on the public's perception of GE. These projects range from restoring housing projects in the inner city to establishing and maintaining hiking trails. Local chapters have restored acres of prairie grass, planted native wildflowers, and adopted highways for cleanup.

"The point is, being a good neighbor is also good business and good policy," declares Ramsey. "It pays off and it benefits the community as well as GE."

GE continues to work ahead to upgrade EHS resources, awareness, and training at all levels. "It is imperative that we manage our manufacturing processes with the utmost concern for environmental and safety issues," says Ramsey. "Our employees demand it, our communities demand it, and our customers demand it." For Steve Ramsey, "prevention" is the operative word and the environmental theme of the 1990s and the next century for all businesses.

Paper from Paper: Marcal

In September 1992 Marcal Paper Mills was authorized by the New York State Department of Environmental Conservation to use the "recycled" emblem on all Marcal roll towels, paper napkins, and facial and bath tissues. This officially recognizes that Marcal tissue products meet the state's guidelines, which require manufacturers to use a specified level of recycled secondary and postconsumer fiber when they make recycled product claims.

Under New York State Environmental Conservation Law, titled 6 NYCRR Part 368 Recycling Emblems, tissue manufacturers must prove to the state they use minimum levels of recycled paper in order to promote the recycled claim on their packages or in advertising. Across all categories, Marcal exceeds state guidelines by producing its products from 100 percent recycled fiber. Marcal then meets the minimum postconsumer content levels of 40 percent on towels, 30 percent on paper napkins, and 30 percent on Marcal bath and facial tissues.

New York's labeling law is one of the toughest in the country and surpasses the EPA procurement guidelines for postconsumer fiber content in tissue products. New York requires manufacturers to outline the types of secondary and postconsumer feed stocks used, their sources, and what levels are used in the manufacturing process for various tissue products applying for labeling authorization.

For Fifty Years, Every Day at Marcal Has Been Earth Day

Born in Sicily in 1893, nine-year-old Nicholas Marcalus and his sister arrived in America at the turn of the century through Ellis Island. The two wore tags addressed with their destination in Passaic, New Jersey, where relatives lived. Soon afterward Nicholas chose to return to Italy with his sister, who had fallen seriously ill. Fate was unkind, for the girl died upon their return to Italy.

Nicholas set out again for America when he turned fifteen. He lived with relatives for a year before going out on his own. "I remember him saying he left with nothing but the tools in his pocket," says his grandson, Nicholas, president and CEO of Marcal.

Nicholas became a self-taught engineer, apprenticing with skilled engineers to learn his trade. He started his first business at nineteen. His son, Robert, attributes his father's success to his "innate ability to invent mechanical processes and an intuitive sense for business, for knowing the most effective way to manufacture at the least cost and the lowest manpower." During his lifetime, Nicholas was granted over fifty patents for a variety of inventions, the last when he was in his eighties, just before his death in 1979.

It was his first patented product that launched Marcal. At the urging of his wife, Mildred, he began working on a way to improve waxed paper. Waxed paper was then the primary means of wrapping food for storage. However, it was only available in waxed sheets, which stuck together in hot weather and warm kitchens. The solution became the now-familiar wax paper on a roll, packaged in a box with a serrated edge.

Nicholas and a partner began manufacturing Cut-Rite wax paper through the Automated Paper Machinery Company in Elizabeth, New Jersey. Later the company was sold to R. E. Davis Baking Powder Company, then Scott Paper Company, and finally to Reynolds Aluminum, which now owns the Cut-Rite brand name.

This brainstorm led to the founding of Marcalus Manufacturing Company in 1932, in the thick of the Great Depression. The company rented the basement of the Charms Candy Building in Bloomfield. Nicholas began manufacturing an improved wax paper, only to be sued by the new owners of his original patented invention. When the case was argued before the U.S. Supreme Court, Nicholas won.

With that victory, Nicholas began to expand his line. He began buying tissue and napkin paper from paper manufacturers and converting it into finished products. In 1939 the company moved operations to Elizabeth, where Nicholas bought fifteen acres of land in Elmwood Park, then known as East Patterson. He built his first paper machine, which freed him from the pricing whims of outside suppliers. In 1947 he came up with an innovative way to turn wastepaper into pulp. Although Nicholas was truly a visionary, the decision to use recycled products was an economic one, not an environmental one. He couldn't afford to continue buying pulp, and recycling required less capital than moving to an area and starting a pulp mill that would use virgin fiber.

The future brought many changes. Along the way the company changed its name to Marcal to be more closely aligned with the brand name used on its products. When son Robert entered the company, he brought with him strong management, finance, and administrative skills. The company acquired a number of small paper mills, expanded its capacity, and improved its technology. Gradually a third generation of Marcalus family members has joined the mill.

Curiously it is Nicholas's namesake grandson who has inherited his grandfather's inventive ability. He has implemented two packaging innovations the company takes great pride in: the Poly-case™ bundling system, which wraps multiroll packages in a plastic casing, allowing the finished product to take up 20 percent less storage space in trucks and warehouses, a design adaptation of a system widely used in Europe; and the reusable Draw and Store bag, a drawstring bag that Nicholas also adapted to package retail multiroll products. "I think we all inherited the hand-me-down mentality of the Depression Era in which my grandfather lived and did business. Products that have a second life go along with the thinking of not wasting anything," says another grandson, Peter, vice-president of corporate communications.

A Growing Advantage

Recycling is not only a part of Marcal's corporate culture, it is a family tradition in business. Water used in wastepaper cleaning and pulp-making processes is recycled for reuse. A cogeneration plant on the company's now sixty-acre site converts enough natural gas to electricity for the plant's use, with excess to sell to the local utility. Paper packaging, cores of rolled products, and some boxes are all made from recycled materials.

Consumers need to support the environmental efforts of business. It is a shared responsibility. They have to learn to distinguish between efforts that are sincere and those that are merely "greenwashing." Once they are satisfied, consumers should let companies know they recognize and appreciate the effort.

With annual sales of upward of $200 million, Marcal launched a $20 million expansion of its facilities three years ago, funded in part by a $3 million low-interest loan from the New Jersey's Department of Environmental Protection, the sale of more than $13 million in tax-exempt bonds, and the business's own private capital. With this money the company is increasing its de-inking and papermaking equipment and technology to permit it to recycle even more paper. Marcal processes 150,000 tons of wastepaper annually and hopes to boost that figure over 30 percent.

Much of the augmentation is expected to come from its municipal collection program. For many years the company relied on printing plant overruns and errors as the main source of recyclable material. In 1990 it began accepting high-quality postconsumer waste from municipalities to create the "Marcal Mix"—a blend of magazines, junk mail, and office paper that undergoes a plethora of cleaning processes to become pulp for paper manufacturing.

Currently Marcal accepts recyclables from over six hundred municipalities, representing a thousand-plus communities in the Northeast. Two hundred are in New Jersey; the remainder are in Pennsylvania, New York, and New England. By recycling its high-quality wastepaper, a municipality can reduce its solid waste stream by 8 to 10 percent as well as decrease its landfill budget by a considerable amount. While Marcal does not pay for this material, sending it to the mill instead of the landfill has its own payback for participants. For example, one thirty-five-mile trip to Marcal with 12 tons of waste material costs Morris County, New Jersey, anywhere from $150 to $250 in hauling fees, while a trip to the nearest landfill using the same mode of transportation, calculating the $131 per ton tipping fees, would cost $1,500 to dump.

Marcal is expanding collection efforts to include undeliverable third-class mail from the postal system. It accepts mail from about thirty metropolitan-area post offices and hopes to increase that number. Under the supervision of Peter Marcalus, the company conducts educational outreach seminars, one-day recycling events, school programs, and other public presentations in an effort to convince communities to participate in its recycling program.

The company believes plans for expansion could be expedited with more assistance from the state. The time required to obtain permits for recent expansion was "not as short as it might have been," says Nicholas. "When we seek to expand or improve our processes, we are frequently confronted with bureaucratic delays and inaction."

He would like to see the state increase its support of efforts of companies like Marcal, which recycle and use materials generated in the state. He believes that the state needs to revise it permit-granting process for new facilities.

Marcal is working on increasing its use of proprietary processes that allow it to manufacture tissue products without using chlorine bleach. Marcal's lines of bath tissue, paper towels, and napkins are made without chlorine bleach.

The Bottom Line Is Environmental

Although the choices Marcal has made have been determined more by economics than environmental impact, their conclusive evidence that tightwad techniques are both good for business and for the environment clearly illustrates our contention that "the bottom line of green is black."

The results of Marcal's innovative business style have not gone unrecognized by environmental groups. The Environmental Action Coalition, a Manhattan-based organization founded after Earth Day 1970, awarded Marcal a Green Star Award (the company was one of four companies so honored) for demonstrating that "you can make a profit without selling out." In 1992 Marcal received the Environmental Protection Agency's Region II Environmental Quality Award, and in 1991 it was distinguished by the New Jersey Department of Environmental Protection and Energy by receiving its Outstanding Achievement in Recycling Award.

To create a demand for more recycling programs, buy supplies with recycled, postconsumer content to "close the loop."

Marcal has elected to temper the sentiment that is usually associated with recycling endeavors, and it is critical of companies that advertise how many trees they saved in producing recycled items. Even though their slogan is "Paper from paper, not trees," the company feels the basis for its program is commonsense business practice. "We should never be waving the flag that recycling saves trees," acknowledges Nicholas. "The paper industry regenerates trees more quickly than it uses them. The benefit of recycling is not in saving trees but in reducing solid waste. We've created a market for materials that before could only be sent to landfills or incinerators. When you buy Marcal, you close the recycling loop."

A Computer Company Where an Apple Is Always Green

As we've seen, manufacturing confronts some of the greatest challenges in environmentally safe production, but it also has some of the best opportunities for innovative solutions.

Take the personal computer industry, for example. Heavily involved in manufacture, in many ways it is setting the example for production processes that consider the environment at all stages of development. This is partly due to its being one of the youngest industries in the world. Most computer companies are barely a decade and a half old, and they have usually been led by business mavericks. This is the industry that made the "two guys in a garage" style of entrepreneurship famous.

Preferring to operate outside established business methods, computer manufacturers inherently concern themselves with social and "alternative" issues. It's only natural that the environment is often a primary concern.

In fact at Apple Computer, concern for the environment is at the center of standard operating procedures. And it has been almost since day one. Since 1982, when the company was still relatively young, Apple has given cash and equipment donations to nonprofit environmental organizations. To date that includes more than 130 recipients. Currently the company has a partnership with the World Environment Center, a nonprofit, nonadvocacy organization that provides developing countries with assistance programs, training, and information services related to urban and industrial pollution control. In addition the company recently established an EarthGrants program that donates personal computer systems worth $613,000 to nineteen institutions in various countries working on environmental issues.

But the management at Apple realizes that the company must do more than assist environmental organizations. In addition to manufacturing high-quality products, Apple must produce them "in a manner that conserves the environment and protects the safety and health of our employees, our customers, and the community," as its Policy on Environmental Health and Safety states.

To that end, a wide variety of programs have been introduced since 1989. The most impressive is the company's commitment to eliminating chlorofluorocarbons, or CFCs, from the manufacture of printed circuit boards.

From Toxic to Green with No-clean

Electronic companies use CFCs to clean electronic parts and printed circuit boards. Standard soldering materials leave behind a residue that in time tends to corrode and lead to equipment failure. In 1989, cleaning was considered absolutely vital by most assembly engineers. And at Apple that process accounted for 90 percent of CFC use. But when it was determined that the chemicals contributed to ozone depletion when released into the air, Apple engineers began researching alternative approaches to CFC cleaning agents.

They were given additional impetus when, in the 1989 Helsinki Declaration, eighty-one nations agreed to phase out CFC use by the year 2000. Accordingly, Apple began intensive research with a self-imposed deadline to eliminate CFCs from manufacturing by 1993. In the process, the company promised to treat all research, development, and implementation as nonproprietary.

Setting goals was the easy part. Harder was establishing alternative methods that would ensure the highest quality circuit boards without substituting other environmentally compromising results.

At the same time, most electronics manufacturers were developing replacements to their CFC cleaners with water-cleaning systems. But Apple took the position that water cleaning and the resulting hazardous waste effluence would create its own set of environmental problems, the least of which would require significant machine retooling to overcome.

Instead Apple's engineers decided to develop a no-clean method, although prevailing opinion in the industry held that skipping the cleaning step would seriously compromise the quality and reliability of the unit. By working with its vendors to develop a new solder paste and liquid flux material, Apple engineers were able to design a process that would decrease the corrosive nature of the soldering materials and leave behind only benign residues. By June 1992, through collaboration with suppliers, the company's engineers achieved their goal of employing a no-clean method—a full year ahead of their own schedule. Using this no-clean technology has reduced Apple's worldwide CFC emissions from a peak of 270,000 pounds in 1990 to less than 2,500 in 1992.

The steps they followed in this conversion provide an example of the type of guidelines necessary for making such a large-scale change possible.

First, strategic relationships were developed with other progressive electronics and manufacturing companies—including competitors—to promote sharing of data and research efforts. The company became involved in technology exchange agreements and discussions at industry consortia, such as the CFC Reduction Task Force of the American Electronics Association. This often led to joint development work with other companies. It's worth noting that collaboration of this type is a consistent pattern among environmentally sensitive companies. They frequently forge partnerships across competitive lines to foster mutually beneficial solutions.

Second, direct material vendors were consulted and encouraged to provide new fluxes and solder pastes that could be left on the boards without affecting quality or performance.

Third, equipment vendors were consulted regarding the designs of new spray fluxers that would be necessary to handle the new approach.

Fourth, each manufacturing site notified its suppliers of the new policy and encouraged them to eliminate CFCs from their own operations.

Finally, training was used both to instruct the production assemblers in the new method and to assure product managers and customers that the process was in fact reliable and met their high quality standards.

As the process was tested and developed, new design configurations were adopted when residues left behind were found to interfere with circuit board performance. Crucial to the evolution of a completely new manufacturing process was the ability to continually adapt to new sets of circumstances and to explore untested methods until a viable, environmentally sound alternative was realized.

The company says that its primary costs during this time of conversion were in the research stage. Implementation of the process added no new costs to production and actually provided savings when CFC solvents and the expensive disposal and monitoring equipment involved were eliminated. In addition, since one step was removed from the manufacturing process, throughput increased. As in any production line, that translates into savings.

Recycling and Packaging Reduction

Apple uses the same type of collaborative involvement in other environmental initiatives as well. When the company decided to switch from white cardboard shipping boxes—which Apple had pioneered the use of—to unbleached brown cardboard, Scientific Certification Systems was contracted to compare the environmental effects of three cardboard designs: bleached white with all virgin materials; unbleached brown with all virgin materials; and unbleached brown with high recycled fiber content. The study found that by using the third choice, the company could eliminate toxins such as dioxin and chloroform used for bleaching and could give a boost to the market for recycled pulp.

In October 1991 all Apple shipping boxes were converted to the unbleached, recycled material. Interestingly, the move did not result from external pressures but was made in response to an internal environmental review of the company's packaging and procedures that indicated opportunities for improvement. To date, the switch to brown recycled boxes has enabled Apple to realize a $3.2 million savings and 50 percent cut in materials costs.

Packaging and waste reduction are also a focus throughout all facilities. The company continually examines ways to significantly reduce the amount of paper and plastic wrapping used in shipping and to eliminate polystyrene foam when possible. Making user manuals smaller is another means of cutting down waste.

The company also collects electronic scrap generated by the R&D and service departments to reclaim precious and heavy metals for reuse.

Apple promotes recycling even beyond the company. Through the Apple Clean Earth Campaign, U.S. customers can return Laser-Writer Toner Cartridges free of charge. For every cartridge returned, the company donates $1 to either the National Wildlife Federation or the Nature Conservancy. Customers can also return used rechargeable batteries from their personal and lap-top computers. Realizing that the disposal of these batteries constitutes significant hazard, Apple facilitates their recycling by turning them over to recyclers where possible or ensuring proper disposal where no recycling operations exist.

In the areas of energy and resource use, Apple has recently created a new department within the facilities management organization to implement conservation efforts.

Employee Involvement

Central to a successful corporate environmental program is the support and active participation of a company's employees. Apple employees are encouraged to engage in a two-way dialogue with management for suggestions and tips on environmental initiatives.

Paper recycling is an employee effort in Apple facilities around the world. In Canada a Green Team has been recycling since 1989. In Paris "Apple Goes Green" boxes collect paper throughout the building. In the Cupertino, California, headquarters, the Apple Recycling Department collects high-grade paper, glass, aluminum cans, paper, and cardboard. The company calculates employees now recycle about 10,000 pounds of aluminum and glass each month and about 85,000 pounds of paper.

The Commute Alternatives Program seeks to reduce the use of single-occupancy vehicles by rewarding employees with a dollar, redeemable at the company store, each time alternative methods for commuting are used. And each month employees are invited to an Environmental Brown Bag Lunch to hear a featured speaker from the environmental community.

To facilitate an active exchange of ideas and suggestions, the international employee newsletter includes a "Green Report" with tips, suggestions, and information of the company's environmental efforts and those of its employees. One newsletter featured a report about an employee who recycled so much at home that she threw out only a single bag of trash every three months. Even the company's international electronic bulletin board maintains a folder with tips and advice for employees on improving their environmental practices at home and at work.

Promoting much of this effort has been the responsibility of an environmental issues manager, who spends most of his day in meetings, on the phone, or sending computer mail encouraging employees to keep environmental issues in mind when they design, manufacture, and distribute Apple products.

Machines That Sleep

Apple has unveiled computers that automatically "sleep" or go into a low-power state when not in use. As a participant in the U.S. Environmental Protection Agency's new Energy Star Program, Apple is one of a dozen charter companies involved in this business and government partnership. Since mid-1993 the Energy Star logo has been used by manufacturers to identify products that use low-energy technology in their systems.

Studies project that this technology will provide energy savings as high as 60 percent or more, since tremendous energy is currently wasted when computer systems are left on overnight and during weekends. It is estimated, in fact, that computers and peripherals are used only 20 percent of the time they are turned on. An automatic sleep feature will significantly reduce energy consumed during a machine's idle time.

But the company realizes there is still much work to be done. Initiatives under consideration include using recycled paper in all user manuals, improving product design whenever possible to be more environmentally sensitive, and encouraging suppliers to eliminate unacceptable risks to the environment—all the while understanding that protecting the environment is not just one company's problem.

3M Aims for Letter Perfect with 3 P's

The Minnesota Mining and Manufacturing Company, better known as 3M, is one of the nation's leading blue chip companies and one of the world's premier new-product companies, developing and manufacturing more than sixty thousand products for business, industry, government, and consumers around the globe. Two of its best-known products are Scotch brand tape and Post-it brand notes. It employs over eighty-seven thousand men and women in fifty-seven nations.

Since 1975 3M has operated an environmental program called Pollution Prevention Pays. For nearly twenty years it has been cleaning up its operation before state and federal government enforced their mandates. Although among the first to initiate a structured environmental plan, 3M continued to earn the baneful distinction of being one of the country's major air polluters. This reputation no doubt stemmed from the very nature of its business—the manufacture of products that produced hazardous chemical wastes.

> Stay in contact with local and national environmental groups for updated information. Their concerns and knowledge of the issues will help to redefine the program as it grows.

Then in 1989 3M added another *P* to its Pollution Prevention Pays, to create 3P Plus. The enhanced plan has helped to create an environmentally sensitive corporate culture and has spawned an entire generation of new environmental programs. Now both environmentalists and financial analysts credit 3M for its dedication to cleaning up all of its operations.

In 1990 NBC, CBS, and PBS highlighted 3M for its environmental efforts, and the *New York Times* did a positive profile of the company's environmental achievements. Although it continues to emit large quantities of toxic chemicals, it nevertheless has a good record of achievement in prevention and ambitious goals to make that record even better. In the process 3M has saved hundreds of millions of dollars by avoiding the generation of wastes that would have had to be treated, and it has reduced pollution by more than half of what it would have been considering 3M's growth.

Insurance Policy

Going beyond regulatory requirements is uppermost on 3M's priority list, which also includes

- preventing pollution at the source
- conducting detailed environmental audits

- removing ozone-depleting chemicals, PCBs, and loose asbestos
- removing or upgrading underground tanks
- reviewing environmental marketing claims, labels, and symbols for accuracy
- conserving natural resources
- developing products with minimum environmental impact

Most of these policies have specific deadlines.

Senior managers from each operating division are required to incorporate 3M environmental policies, objectives, and standards into their operations, including research and development long-range planning, capital, and operating budgets. Several management programs facilitate achievement. Management's 3P and Environmental Leadership programs provide additional incentives for employee involvement. Quarterly progress reports on and audits of the implemented initiatives are among several control mechanisms that give senior management objective data to measure performance improvement.

Educate employees. Include as many as possible in the design and implementation of your program. If you have not informed everyone, from management to the cleaning crew, of your intentions, the program will appear exclusive and may create problems.

A graphic illustration that 3M has more than good intentions is the investment made to rid Hutchinson, Minnesota, of the chemical odor emitted from the company's two plants there, a long-standing problem for area residents. Some $26 million was spent for equipment to recycle and burn off solvents even though the two plants were already meeting EPA standards. By 1995 3M expects to achieve a 95 percent reduction in the approximately 25 million pounds of volatile organic solvents that were emitted into Hutchinson's air in 1989.

The company invested another $175 million in 1993 to install the most sophisticated pollution control equipment in its other plants throughout the world, cutting air emissions 90 percent from 1987 levels.

Success Begets Success

The company's 3P program has proved that preventing waste and pollution at the source saves both the environment and money.

The company believes that its success has had a great impact on the way business and government look at environmental strategies, and it cites, as documentation, comments by many members of Congress describing 3M as "exemplary" and a statement by former President George Bush, who said 3M has "clearly demonstrated the benefits of doing it right."

Sharing its success stories with others has also influenced the thinking of industry and government, asserts 3M, pointing out that 3M's environmental professionals have met with more than two hundred other companies since 1975 to provide them with detailed descriptions of 3M's initiatives. Its representatives also appear regularly at seminars and conferences, make presentations to business, state, government, academic, and technical groups, meet with the news media, and frequently confer with congressional and EPA staffs. The company assisted the EPA in the planning of a series of four pollution prevention conferences in 1977, the first ever held.

Few can argue with 3M's successes. Results already achieved from the 3,007 initiatives implemented from 1975 to mid-1992 are reductions by 134,000 tons in air emissions, by 16,900 tons in water pollutants, and by 126,000 tons in sludge and solid waste. Some $540 million was saved. Its Energy Management Program has cut energy use by one-half per unit of production and associated air emissions of criteria pollutants by more than 25 million pounds a year. New pollution control equipment that burns solvents will still emit CO_2 but will result in a reduction well below the 3.9 billion pounds per year anticipated by 3M.

The Commute-a-Van program has conserved more than 3 million gallons of gasoline and eliminated more than 60 million pounds of air emissions since 1973. Since 1985, 3M has saved more than $120 million from its resource recovery operations, which cover metals, plastics, solvents, papers, and other materials.

Not willing to rest on its laurels, 3M has set standards to

- reduce air emissions 70 percent from 1987 levels by 1993

- reduce energy consumption 20 percent from 1990 levels by 1995

- reduce list of seventeen compounds (EPA's 33/50 Project) 70 percent by 1995

- reduce generation of waste 35 percent by 1995

- reduce generation of waste 50 percent from 1990 levels by 2000
- reduce all discharges to air, land, and water 90 percent from 1987 levels by 2000
- approach zero pollution and achieve sustainable development after the year 2000

Creditable Actions

Companies earn Emission Reduction Credits from the federal government for achieving the required reduction of air pollution in advance of time allotted. The credits can be sold or traded within the same geographic area. A company that hasn't adhered to the government's mandate to clean up its act in a certain period of time looks to buy credits from a company that has. The purchase of these credits gives the delinquent company more time to meet requirements. The theory is that companies that clean up their act quickly should be rewarded, while those that drag their feet should be penalized by having to pay for extra time.

The 3M Company adopted a policy of not profiting from the sale of these credits. It returns the credits to the local environmental agency rather than selling a license to another company and allowing it to pollute the atmosphere. Exceptions to this policy are considered, however, according to the wishes of the local community. In the case of its Camarillo, California, facility, 3M sold credits to a company that would create jobs and turned the profits over to a trust fund to benefit a local environmental agency. So far, 3M has returned credits that would have added thousands of tons of pollutants to the air, sacrificing several million dollars for the sake of a cleaner atmosphere.

Environmental Consideration

Noblesse oblige also extends to two other significant areas of 3M's policies. First, no business interests will be bought or sold unless they are consistent with 3M's commitment to environmental responsibility. This policy applies to any acquisition or divestiture that involves occupancy and/or ownership of land and buildings. (Of course, points out 3M, liability issues also dictate this policy.) Large and diversified, 3M is constantly pursuing the purchase and sale of business interests, and this puts an interesting twist on negotiations.

Moreover, all environmental claims, symbols, and slogans for new or existing products must be submitted to the Environmental

Marketing Claims Review Committee for approval. Approval will be based on technical accuracy and substantiation as well as on clarity. To pass the litmus test, a claim cannot be construed as likely to mislead customers or the general public. The company wants to guard against slogans or symbols that make broad environmental claims such as "safe for the environment" or "environmentally friendly"—nice catchphrases on the surface but ambiguous and impossible to document.

Advertising claims have gotten more than one company in hot water. Plastic garbage bag manufacturers touted their products as "biodegradable," yet the truth is that biodegradation doesn't begin for decades, maybe not for eons. Even food is discovered almost intact when dug up in landfills twenty and thirty years after it was placed there.

The Big Picture

Nearly 7 percent of 3M's sales (more than $900 million) is devoted to research. Of that amount, 17 percent ($150 million) is directed to environmentally oriented projects such as removing hazardous chemicals from products and processes. These investments in the future are helping 3M attain the status it seeks as a "sustainable growth" corporation, defined as one whose products, facilities, and operations have minimal environmental impact. Therefore its business can continue to grow without adversely affecting the earth. A sustainable growth corporation is also one that has maximized the business opportunities the environmental issue has presented.

With its holistic pollution prevention process in operation, 3M intends to continue to minimize its environmental impact, but some of its initiatives need reinforcement. Waiting in the wings are pollution prevention opportunities with suppliers and customers, education, water conservation, wildlife habitat enhancement on its properties, and the elimination of household hazardous waste. With this agenda, one can safely assume that 3M will not retreat on environmental issues.

Fujifilm Attempts to "Capture the Earth's Beauty"

Fuji Photo Film U.S.A is the U.S marketing subsidiary of Fuji Photo Film Co., Ltd., of Tokyo, a leading manufacturer of imaging and information products, including film and cameras, color copiers, photographic paper, and photofinishing supplies, videotape, audio cassettes, floppy disks, and many other related products. Fujifilm professes to have lived for almost thirty years by the concept "What nature gives to humanity, we must return to nature." The company pledges "to continue to act as a responsible corporate citizen, considering always how its actions will affect the environment and people's lives."

Initial environmental efforts began with the founding of the company in 1934. In 1965 an antipollution committee was created at the Ashigara factory, followed in 1970 with the appointment of an environmental group at each of the company's production facilities and, a year later, at the Tokyo head office. In June 1989 an environmental committee directly answerable to the president was created. Based on its avowal "to preserve nature and the precious environment in all procedures, action programs and technological research," Fujifilm introduced (in the early 1990s) its new environmental slogan, "We Capture All the Earth's Beauty."

Faintly reminiscent of a scout oath, the charter driving Fujifilm's present and future environmental programs states:

1   We shall do our best to safeguard the environment and uphold water and air qualities.

2   We shall exercise constant vigilance to ensure that our products are not injurious to health and safety.

3   We shall strive in every sphere of corporate activity to conserve energy and resources.

4   We shall make concentrated efforts to study, propose, plan and implement programs that will advance environmental causes.

Water, Water Everywhere

As a major water user in the manufacture of emulsion products, Fujifilm's policy is "No discharge till effluent is clean enough to keep fish alive." Factory effluents at the Ashigara plant are routed through a fully equipped wastewater treatment plant. Cleaning processes take a full day and night. First passing through several checking reservoirs, the treated water is discharged into the surrounding river system only when that water is clean enough to support aquatic life. Despite a fourfold increase in production over the past fifteen years, Fujifilm has reduced water consumption by 20 percent. This was accomplished by experimenting with various methods of cleaning and rejuvenating industrial water over the past twenty years.

Appreciating that it takes clean water to keep wetlands wet and safe for habitats, Fujifilm is cosponsoring, with the Nature Conservancy of South Carolina, the publication of five thousand copies of a book to help raise funds for a river basin forty-five miles from its Greenwood plant. The book features photographs of the basin by Thomas Blagden, Jr., of Charleston.

One of the Atlantic Coast's most pristine and ecologically diverse areas, the ACE Basin (so named for the merge of the Ashepoo, Combahee, and Edisto rivers) provides an important winter home for ducks and is host to several other animal and bird species. Fujifilm hopes that the book, published in 1992, will increase public awareness of the ACE Basin project. A segment on this project was aired in December 1992, on CBS's "Sunday Morning with Charles Kuralt."

Aboveboard

Acutely sensitive to the danger an undetected leak can have on the environment, Fujifilm constructs its storage tanks and pipelines above ground to keep them under constant visual surveillance. A containing wall and multiple layers of protection ensure that in the event of leakage, the liquid will be contained before hitting the ground. As repeatedly exemplified by other companies in this book, Fujifilm recognizes that prevention is less costly than remedial action and less damaging to the environment.

In the fight against air pollution, Fujifilm converted to cleaner fuels to decrease emissions. Other cleanup measures include the use of water sprays in the solvent incinerator, recycling of exhaust gases, and two-stage combustion. Nitrogen oxide emissions have been reduced by 60 percent. Hydrocarbons are tackled on many fronts, including catalytic incineration of weak solvent gases. Warnings of high oxidant emissions are strictly heeded and remedied, to the point of halting production lines temporarily until levels are reduced.

Adhering to the Three *R*'s

Recovery, recycling, and revolutionary new energy-saving products are all part of Fujifilm's policies. Unique among the various detoxification and recovery measures for fumes and noxious gases produced by organic solvents is Fujifilm's water spray absorption of the solvent gas that is generated during polymerization.

Silver is retrieved from film trimmings and from 5.2 mm2 bits of motion picture film perforations. Other wastes such as iron, tin cans, cardboard boxes, and plastics are regularly collected for paper base manufacture. Also recovered and recycled are methylene chloride and methyl alcohol as well as whatever is reusable from cellulose triacetate and polyester.

A revolutionary X-ray system developed by Fujifilm is saving resources as well. The world's first computer-based radiographic imaging system, the Computed Radiography (CR) provides increased diagnostic accuracy with reduced X-ray dosage. The X-ray image is first recorded on a reusable, high-sensitivity imaging plate and can be reproduced either on a high-resolution TV monitor for direct diagnostic viewing or on a dedicated CR film, which uses less silver than conventional X-ray film. This reduces the amount of metal elements released in the waste stream and minimizes the use of a precious resource.

In 1991 a new minilab film processor was debuted that utilizes low-replenishment chemistry and reduces chemical waste disposal. A revolutionary rinsing device that can be replenished with ordinary tap water produces significant savings in wastewater disposal. Fujifilm also addressed one of the largest concerns of the photofinishing industry by developing for minilabs a new reduced-formaldehyde stabilizer that drastically reduces concentrations of this carcinogen but retains the same high level of image stabilization.

A long-standing tradition in Japan, recycled paper packaging for film products began in the United States in 1991. Also underway is a nationwide collection system to retrieve used components of Fujicolor Quicksnap, a roll of film fitted with its own lens and shutter functions. Fujifilm is working with industry associations and members to standardize materials used in the manufacture of the film canisters and other components to facilitate the recycling of these items. Fujifilm also asks its suppliers to use recycled products whenever possible in packaging as well as in shipping materials and display and merchandising cards.

A new high-speed auto-reversal type COM microfilm features an auto-reversal emulsion. Eliminating the full reversal process, commonly used by service bureaus, makes this film substantially safer for the environment. Chemical consumption and waste are dramatically reduced by converting to a two-bath process allowed by this film, and silver can be easily reclaimed and recycled, unlike full reversal processing systems.

Solid Solutions

A nationwide environmental program dedicated to finding "Solid Solutions for Solid Waste" (SSSW) was begun in 1990 by the National Audubon Society thanks to a grant by Fuji Photo Film U.S.A. Conducted over a three-year period, the two-stage grass-roots project was aimed at helping communities formulate realistic and environmentally sound solid waste management policies.

The first step was the publication of a guidebook entitled *Audubon's Community Solid Waste Management Program,* which suggested practical, cost-efficient, and environmentally sound waste management procedures. The second phase was the implementation of pilot programs in various communities to test and refine the guidebook. Fujifilm and Audubon also joined forces to publish a free booklet, available for the asking, entitled *Solid Solutions for Solid Waste,* giving advice on how Americans can reduce solid waste at home, in the workplace, and in their communities.

The program and the free booklet were publicized extensively through press releases and a video news release. Celebrity appeal was also used to get the word out. John Ratzenberger of "Cheers" fame was featured in a satellite media tour, and Florence Henderson starred in a series giving environmental tips, which was syndicated to radio stations around the country.

Education is an important component of any program. Keep customers, vendors, and employees informed with the use of collateral material printed, of course, on recycled paper with nontoxic inks.

Elementary, My Dear

Some 750,000 elementary school students are expected to participate in a program labeled Saving Our Part of the Planet as part of a Fujifilm-funded project known as Fujifilm PhotoPals. Designed to match up third-, fourth-, and fifth-grade classrooms around the country, PhotoPals encourages the exchange of pictures representing the different cultures, customs, lifestyles, and backgrounds of each participating class.

For the Planet section of the program, students are forming investigative teams to find out what their schools and their communities are doing about environmental issues. After researching their topic, conducting interviews, and taking pictures to document their findings, students send the material to their designated PhotoPals. Nature appreciation is another segment of the PhotoPals project.

On Every Front

Fujifilm realizes that a comprehensive environmental program needs many ingredients to be fruitful and successful. Reaching out to the community at large and involving employees as well as management are two of those elements. To get its word out to the public, Fujifilm conducts active public relations and ad campaigns. A *We Care* booklet gives a summary of its environmental program and is available upon request.

All of the company staff are exhorted to become involved and are urged to develop "environment consciousness." Staff are also asked "to act, within both personal and corporate spheres, as a caring inhabitant of the planet"—wise advice for anyone.

"Extra, Extra" Is More Than a Scoop at the *Los Angeles Times*

Newspapers alone take up as much as 13 percent of the space in America's landfills, and the *Times* has an impressive record for trying to stem the tide.

Each day the *Los Angeles Times* produces and distributes 1.24 million papers, yet it is not a cavalier drain on our natural resources. Just the contrary! The *Times* initiated environmentally conscious practices way back in the 1970s, long before they became fashionable. A general concern for the environment was a leading motivator in the newspaper's pledge to implement environmental initiatives. Later, when meeting state regulations became a driving force in the industry, the *Los Angeles Times* was way ahead of the pack, having gotten an early start. From raw materials through the manufacturing process, the *Times* continues to demonstrate and execute its concerns for the environment far beyond statutory requirements.

Comfortable in its role as a practitioner of what it preaches, preach it does in its own pages through promotional advertisements and consistent coverage of the environmental beat. In fact the *Times* was ranked first in a listing of America's Ten Most Influential News Organizations in environmental coverage by the *Business News Reporter* newsletter.

The *Los Angeles Times*'s long, rich tradition of concern for the environment is woven into the workplace, the work force, and the news pages. Indeed its commitment extends beyond its business practices. The company recently established a twenty-four-hour recycling center in downtown Los Angeles, where its employees can drop off newspapers, plastic, glass, and metals brought from home. Proceeds are donated to the Times Fund, the *Times*'s charitable arm, which benefits underprivileged youth in Southern California.

All the Print That's Fit to Save

Eighty percent of the paper used annually to publish the *Times* is recycled newsprint, approximately 320,000 tons containing at least 50 percent recycled fibers. It is the largest consumer of recycled newsprint, with a far higher recycled fiber content than California law requires for the year 2000.

Waste newsprint or newspapers generated at the *Times* plus all unsold newspapers from street rack sales are sold to a recycler, the Independent Paper Stock Company (IPS), a division of Jefferson

Smurfit Corporation. This company converts the wastepaper into usable newsprint and resells it to the *Times.* The total recovered annually is approximately 45,000 tons.

Conserve paper by making two-sided copies. Use the back of letters received for memos and internal communications. Before you put a piece of paper into the recycling bin, ask yourself if it has any other use. Use envelopes several times over for interoffice mail, and order labels to place over the labels of mail you receive so that envelopes can be reused. Imaginative use and purchasing can be a money and environment saver.

Even the waste ink sees new life. All that is generated by the *Times*'s downtown and Orange County facilities is accumulated and sold to be used as bunker fuel, a residual fuel used in large boilers, in paper manufacture, and in asphalt. The systems in use at the Olympic plant and the Times Valley edition plant in Chatsworth, California, are able to reclaim most of the waste newspaper ink for reuse in the production cycle. A similar system is being developed for the company's other two major production facilities. Anything that cannot be reclaimed for reuse in the production cycle is also reused as bunker fuel.

In late 1992 the Olympic plant converted to soy ink, replacing the more toxic petroleum-based inks. By the end of 1993, the *Times*'s other two plants will complete their conversion to soy ink. The cost is almost twice that of petroleum-based ink but is expected to decrease.

All of the aluminum printing plates used on the presses, approximately 340 tons annually, are sold to El Monte Steel and Iron for recycling. Additionally, an average of 236 tons of scrap steel, iron wire, and miscellaneous metals is sold each year to El Monte, which in turn sells the metals to appropriate recyclers.

One Picture Is Worth Gallons of Clean Water

All of the *Times*'s plants are equipped with a silver recovery system designed to extract silver from photo solutions to render the remaining liquid harmless for drainage. The silver is sold to Canadian Silver. About 33,900 gallons per year of photo solution is processed in this manner. All film, too, approximately 100,000 pounds annually, is recovered and resold to Canadian Silver, which extracts the silver.

Back at the Office

The *Times* has set up its Times Recycling Task Team to conduct an office paper recycling project in thirteen company departments. Separate recycling boxes are placed at each employee's desk.

About 7,000 tons of other paper products are recycled each year, as are more than 7 tons of plastics, consisting mainly of film and soda bottles. Outside bins are in place for employees to bring in aluminum cans, glass, and plastic goods. Seventy-eight percent of compactor trash, some 5,200 tons each year, is recycled at the Los Angeles, Olympic, and Orange County facilities. The Valley plant will soon implement a similar program.

> Used toner cartridges can be returned to the copier manufacturer, where they are disassembled for parts. Some copier manufacturers will pay for the returned cartridges.

On the Road—Again

At home and away, the *Times* extends its conservation efforts in every possible way. Although Mr. Goodyear may not be too happy to hear this, *Times* delivery trucks are equipped with retread tires. More than 250 retreads are used each year.

Virtually nothing is wasted, including used engine oil. This is picked up by Rosemead Oil Company to sell to Petroleum Recycling Incorporated, where it is processed and sold as bunker fuel. About 4,800 gallons of oil are recovered annually. Recycled oil is used by all *Times* vehicles, which have been fueled since the 1970s by clean-burning propane.

Solutions for the Solutions

Little, if anything, has escaped the scrutiny of the *Times*. Dirty cleaning solvents are pumped out of the twenty-one parts washers throughout the four facilities. The washers are serviced by Safety Kleen, which replaces the dirty cleaning solvents with a new recycled product on a regular basis, accounting for nearly 3,300 gallons recycled annually. The *Times* is investigating new, more environmentally safe solvents.

> Determine what kind of receptacles are appropriate for your company. Perhaps an extra bin on each floor will suffice. The Boston Park Plaza Hotel now has at least four clearly labeled recycling containers per department for aluminum cans and various qualities of paper.

Above and Beyond

Conceding that state regulations were a force behind the initiation of more stringent environmental policies, the *Times* points to "general concern" as the "leading motivator." More important than the motivation are the results. As the 1991 winner of the most prestigious President's Environment and Conservation Challenge Award, the *Times* can eloquently document its commitment and its claims as a leader and innovator.

The *Times*'s programs are outlined in an attractive brochure featuring the form of a thriving tree, but even that doesn't tell the whole story. Correspondence we received from the company was printed on both sides of the paper—one side relating in capsule the *Times*'s conservation efforts, and on the other side, an explanation of the mission of the American Farmland Trust, an organization of farmers and conservationists dedicated to preventing the loss of productive farmland to development and to promoting farming practices that lead to a healthy environment. This is a clear indicator that the commitment by the *Los Angeles Times* extends well beyond its own boundaries.

BMW: Providing a Green Lap of Luxury

"As provocative as it may sound, the greatest risk to the automobile is its own success. An increasing number of people use this most individual means of transport to an ever-increasing extent. . . . This, in turn, requires a policy maintaining the role of the automobile in future . . . from an ecological and economic perspective." So says the BMW brochure, *A Consistent Initiative to Protect the Environment: BMW Car Recycling.*

Car companies by nature have tended to be antagonists of the environment; and the public has considered them to be the combination of two extremes: necessary assets yet contributors to air pollution, ozone depletion, landfill waste, and overdependence on fossil fuels. But BMW may be changing the image of an industry that has been inclined to favor sales over environmental awareness.

Government legislation has usually provided the impetus for car manufacturers to improve fuel efficiency standards and lessen carbon monoxide pollution. "Cars and the environment were once a question of what came out of the tailpipe, but today the challenge is much more complex," says Karl Gerlinger, president and CEO of BMW North America.

Preempting an Almost Certain Future

BMW knows what the future will hold: a greater number of cars being discarded than landfills can absorb. Europeans alone will junk nearly 20 million cars annually by the year 2000. To stem the tide, BMW has invested a significant amount of money in efforts to make cars as recyclable as possible by the turn of the century. Waste, the company contends, "is entirely man-made."

Actually the metal in most automobiles—which amounts to 75 percent of total weight—has been recycled for decades. Today automotive dismantlers drain fluids, extract chlorofluorocarbons from air conditioning units, and remove batteries. In addition, engines, brakes, windshields, axles, struts, heaters, starters, alternators, seats, tires, hoods, trunks, doors, and other removable parts are recovered or reconditioned for resale. But the remaining 25 percent of each car—the plastic, rubber, upholstery, and glass, collectively called fluff—piles up in landfills. To further each car's total life cycle, BMW has been cooperating with other German carmakers and with raw materials suppliers since 1990 to make this remaining fluff reusable.

Cars with New Parts That Are Old

To that end the company has invested more than $18.8 million to expand the recyclability of its cars, including a $2 million pilot vehicle-recycling plant built in Landshut, Germany, to test materials and develop new ones that would make recycling easier. Results of this test facility have enabled the new 3-series models to include two luggage compartment linings that are made entirely from bumpers recycled from the former 3- and current 5- and 7-series models. In addition, any waste material generated in the manufacture of the new 3-series bumpers is used again for production of front bumper panels. Another model, the Z1 roadster was recognized by *Business Week* for being "the first car ever designed properly from the outset for optimum recycling." The model includes body parts made from thermoplastic, which can be ground up and remanufactured.

During the research process, the Landshut technicians also discovered a number of barriers to the efficient recycling of car parts. The primary inhibitor is the use of more than twenty different types of plastics per car. Because future trends indicate an increase in the percentage of plastic used, BMW has established a number of steps that the company believes need be taken by all car manufacturers to increase recyclability of plastic parts:

- Reduce the number of types of plastics used.
- Mark all plastic parts clearly so dismantlers can sort them for efficient recovery.
- Make all parts of "pure plastic," that is, plastic parts that are not riveted, glued, painted, or dissimilar.
- Contract with plastics suppliers to take back their plastic parts for use in remanufacture.

In addition, BMW established the following guidelines for all other parts prior to manufacture:

- Parts and components should be easy to disassemble.
- They should not contain any pollutants.
- Use of different materials should be kept to a minimum.
- Parts and components should not be made of inseparable combinations of materials, such as a mixture of plastic and metal.
- Rules and directives must be provided to suppliers.

Currently nearly 81.5 percent of the new 3-series sedans and coupes can be recycled. This has been achieved, in large part, by identifying the recyclability of parts during their production. In a company brochure, for instance, an illustration of a transparent car shows a green color code for all parts that can be sorted, ground up, and used again.

BMW has already established authorized recycling centers in Europe and the United States, where cars can be taken for dismantling. The U.S. pilot program, launched in cooperation with the Automotive Dismantlers and Recyclers Association, has recycling centers in the Bronx, New York, Sante Fe Springs, California, and Orlando, Florida.

Beyond Recycling

But BMW's environmental efforts go even further than recycling. In September 1992 the company was the first carmaker to announce that it had eliminated all chlorofluorocarbons from its complete line of cars. This includes CFCs that are used in the manufacture of dashboards and interior components as well as those used in air conditioners. Instead the environmentally friendly hydrofluorocarbon-134a (HFC134a) refrigerant is being used for air conditioning.

The company has also set standards in efficient use of water in its manufacturing process. Currently, advanced recycling procedures allow a little more than 2 cubic yards of water per car to be reused up to six times.

Like many car manufacturers, BMW is also developing prototype electric cars capable of traveling up to 150 miles at a top speed of 70 miles per hour. However, a primary concern for all carmakers designing electric cars should be the dependence on fossil fuels for electricity used in recharging batteries. Alternative renewable energy sources should be developed in conjunction with any design that includes rechargeable batteries—in fact with *all* future car designs. Under consideration at BMW are cars powered by hydrogen and those that can use green plants as fuel.

It may require more significant environmental measures than those implemented by one company before the public perceives the auto industry as motivated by altruism. However, the leadership shown by BMW has the potential to make that collective impression change sooner rather than later.

The Three *R*'s in Furniture Making from Herman Miller

When a company is listed by *Fortune* as one of the five hundred largest U.S. firms, is named one of the country's three most ethical companies by *Business Ethics*, and is consistently at the top of many "best run" lists, it must be doing something right. When it is also included in many "environmentally aware" lists and is a recipient of the President's Environment and Conservation Challenge Award, it can be considered an exceptional model of good management and ethics. That exemplary company is furniture manufacturer Herman Miller Incorporated.

Known primarily for supplying offices around the world with clean and elegantly designed furniture, it is perhaps best known as the manufacturer of the Eames lounge chair. In fact the company has been the only licensed manufacturer of the chair since Charles and Ray Eames first designed it in the 1950s. It has been a strong and stable seller every year. But in 1989 Herman Miller decided it needed a change. Why tamper with a good thing? Because the Eames brothers specified that it should be constructed of rosewood—a hardwood that is found only in tropical rainforests.

In keeping with company policies that uniquely address social ills, employee concerns, and the environment, Herman Miller decided that only tropical woods obtained from sources that sustain the forest would be used in the company's products.

Since Brazilian rosewood was not available from such a source, the popular chair would be manufactured in cherry or walnut. "We share the growing worldwide concern about the tropical rainforests," said Richard H. Ruch, chief executive officer at the time. "Rainforests are a critical resource to people around the world, benefiting us ecologically and providing valuable raw materials and by-products to many industries. The rainforests will survive only if we add value to them by encouraging their productive use rather than their destruction," he said in 1990. Although this meant changing a long-standing tradition, the company has never avoided taking risks—or taking a stand for principles.

If it's true, as we hope to show in this book, that a comprehensive environmental policy can have a positive effect on the bottom line, then Herman Miller is tangible proof. The company has a wide range of initiatives that address the impact it has on the environment as a manufacturer. Herman Miller's "environmental activities have been developed and implemented throughout the organization by the initiatives of the employee-owners. Our success also demonstrates that environmentally responsible policies are financially sound and make good business sense," says Kermit Campbell, current president and CEO.

Concern from Within

Each initiative is indicative of Herman Miller's corporate belief that responsible policies arise from inside the corporate culture itself, not in response to outside pressures. And an important element in the company's success is that the employees have equity in it. They are instrumental in promoting changes within the company, even to the point of being encouraged to go over their bosses' heads about issues that concern them.

One formal means of communication is an annual company-wide survey that encourages workers to identify processes that need to be changed and to discuss current situations that may be preventing Herman Miller from attaining its goals. Many environmental ideas are suggested in surveys of this kind, as well as through the company's award-winning employee suggestion system.

The evolving environmental strategy encompasses such issues as the acquisition of source materials, the earth-friendly practices of suppliers and vendors, waste reduction through more efficient manufacturing and packaging processes, and even remanufacturing used furniture with new pieces to sell "as new." All initiatives are monitored by a cross-functional Environmental Quality Action Team, which serves as a clearinghouse for concerns and suggestions that can be shared among the various divisions and subsidiaries. To date, the most impressive component of the environmental program is the company's conversion of waste to energy.

When the oil crisis threatened to inflate the energy costs of manufacturing in the late 1970s, Herman Miller went ahead with a plan to build its own waste-to-energy plant, which would provide a large portion of its energy requirements by burning waste products for fuel. By 1982 this new cogenerator was supplying all of the central plant's heating and air-conditioning needs.

Housed in the company's Energy Center, it is basically an incinerator that creates steam by burning nontoxic waste that would have been sent to landfills. The steam produced in the process is sent through a turbine generator to create electricity, which in turn is distributed through the HVAC system to heat and cool the buildings. The company claims this conversion saves more than $450,000 annually in natural gas and other fuel costs, plus $70,000 in supplemental electricity the system produces. The process also saves the company $300,000 a year in landfill costs and tipping fees, for a total payback of $820,000 a year.

The system has proved to be so efficient that waste has been reduced to a minimum. Engineering plant manager Joe Azzarello says the process "has a ninety percent burndown ratio. Instead of taking a hundred cubic yards of waste to a landfill, we take ten." The resulting wood ash is all that remains to be landfilled, but plans are in the works to sell it to a local cinder block manufacturer. Not only will this complete the materials recycling loop, it will also save Herman Miller $500,000 in annual energy and landfill costs.

The generator's principal fuel was once several tons of corrugated paper from packaging and shipping containers, but now that waste is hauled away by a recycler. Wood scraps totaling more than 100,000 cubic yards per year constitute the majority of waste to be burned, and Azzarello says the plant will be modified to include sawdust in the near future. Currently sawdust poses a hazard when burned because of its highly combustible nature, but the engineering department is researching ways to safely incinerate it with other waste.

While there is still controversy surrounding the safe emissions from incinerator burning, Azzarello told *International Design* magazine that the Herman Miller facility is extremely safe because "we don't just burn any old junk—there are no plastics here." In fact during a test period, the emissions released by the cogenerator were 90 percent lower than those allowed by Herman Miller's Environmental Protection Agency permit.

The company's concern for pollution is also carried indoors. Herman Miller has been monitoring its manufacturing methods and materials over many years to ensure that no significant amounts of potentially hazardous gases are emitted from wood products, fabrics, foams, or plastics. This also involves facility management practices that dictate the proper number of air exchanges per hour via the heating, ventilating, and air-conditioning systems.

Natural Partnerships

When the company makes a decision about an environmental initiative, it thoroughly researches the implications and in many cases forms strategic alliances with other organizations that serve as consultants. This was particularly true during the changeover of the Eames chair from rainforest rosewood to more replenishable hardwoods. The company worked with both industry and environmental advocacy organizations not only to help document sustainable forest management practices and identify alternative hardwoods but also to find ways of protecting the balance of nature in the areas providing the wood.

When Herman Miller made a change in its packaging to minimize or reduce the amount of materials used, it contacted suppliers and worked with them to incorporate reusable packaging. In addition to protecting the environment from unnecessary packaging materials, these methods reduce the cost of cleaning up an installation. Alternative packaging materials include those made from recycled products, the use of blankets to wrap products shipped by truck, and the introduction of minimal packaging for large bulk orders. The company publishes a list of recycling businesses for its dealers and distributors to use in their areas.

Recycling has been an important element in the company's overall plan and includes such diverse materials as office paper, computer paper, fabric, foam, plastic bags, corrugated cardboard, vinyl, chemicals, and solvents used in production. Much is reused internally. About 350,000 pounds of fabric scraps accumulated over six months, for instance, was converted to insulation and matting for packaging. The company says that in one thirty-day period, the fabric program netted $3,000 in savings from unspent landfill and waste-hauling fees alone.

Even customers are part of the recycling efforts. To recapture products that are good enough to be reused, the company created a subsidiary division that purchases used equipment from customers when they decide to upgrade to newer lines. The AsNew Action Office production process disassembles and remanufactures parts from used furniture to create a product line that can be resold at substantial savings. Not only does this lessen the need for more virgin hardwood, it gives Herman Miller's product lines a longer life. "The point is that we don't want to see our products in the landfill after fifteen or twenty years of service," says corporate liaison Bob Johnston.

Herman Miller's environmental strategies were not born out of a need for quick fixes. In fact the types of initiatives implemented would not produce the sizable savings realized each year if they were done only for the short term. The company estimates that waste reduction alone saves more than $3 million dollars annually.

Employees Only Need Guidelines

Behind much of the program's success is the corporate philosophy itself, which is unique among companies of its size. Called "value-led" by *Industry Week*, Herman Miller's management approach sees employees not as laborers but as individuals whose personal development and self-fulfillment needs only to be unleashed by a supportive system of values.

While most executives indulged in unrestrained greed during the 1980s, Herman Miller chairman Max DePree was writing in his book *Leadership Is an Art* in 1989 that a company should give employees "space so that we can both give and receive such beautiful things as ideas, openness, dignity, joy, healing, and inclusion." He leveled harsh criticism at managers who "are at the leading edge of consumption, affluence, and instant gratification" and decried the prevalent "throwaway mentality that discards goods, and ideas, that discards principles and law, that discards persons and families."

With annual sales posted at $2 million in 1950, $50 million in 1976, and $804 million today, Herman Miller has grown steadily. When those figures are combined with the fact that even during the current recession the company has grown at twice the rate of the office furniture industry and has maintained a strong cash flow by reducing debt and operating expenses, it looks like Max DePree and the employees of Herman Miller may be onto something.

CHAPTER FOUR

Consumer Goods

From the Ground up
at Smith & Hawken

Founded in Palo Alto, California, in 1979, Smith & Hawken had the mission to supply local environmental activists with high-quality gardening tools. Today Smith & Hawken has grown to become a major national retailer in gardening tools and supplies, housewares, furniture, and clothing. In homes across the United States, people eagerly await the delivery of its popular, informative, visually spectacular, sophisticated mail-order catalogs.

"The purpose of Smith & Hawken," according to Paul Hawken, outspoken founder and former CEO, "is to change the way people see the world. We live in a society where most people cannot name five native plants within walking distance of their homes. If you don't know where you are, you don't know who you are. If you don't have a sense of place, you don't have a sense of life.

"We try to change how people see their immediate environment; right around their home, the dirt, the plants. We've sought to promote products and processes that are life affirming and sustaining, and that are not degrading, either to the user's immediate environment or to their source."

Known for the integrity of both its products and business practices, Smith & Hawken has built its success on a foundation of strong environmental ethics. The company's environmental director coordinates a three-pronged effort, described in what follows.

Environmental Partnerships

A portion of company profits are donated to environmental and horticultural organizations, including

- a donation to Conservation International for a debt-for-nature swap in the cloud forests of the Talamanca Mountains of Costa Rica;

- a $700,000 interest-free loan to the Trust for Public Land to protect the Lamoille Canyon in Nevada's Ruby Mountains from development;

- a $100,000 contribution to the Rainforest Alliance to help develop a teak certification program, an assurance that the teak used is from controlled farms, under which the company is now certified for all its tropical wood products;

- ongoing donation of tools and assistance to the San Francisco County Jail, where inmates learn organic gardening and grow produce to feed HIV patients and homeless people in San Francisco;

- memberships free of administrative charge to numerous horticultural organizations, including Seed Savers Exchange, Xerces Society, Sierra Club, American Horticultural Society, and the National Wildlife Research Center.

Product Efforts

- Recycled redwood: The company offers furniture and trellising made from recycled redwood taken from century-old disassembled wine fermentation vats.

- Tagua nut buttons: Many of its clothing items are affixed with buttons made from sustainably collected tagua nuts, which grow on palm trees in Ecuadorian rainforests. Production of these buttons provides people with an income and a reason for protecting a diverse and valuable forest.

- Project Colores: The company sponsors the efforts of a consultant to help unemployed women in urban Mexico combine their skills to form a self-standing cooperative that produces naturally dyed, hand-spun knitted garments.

- Endangered bulbs: To stem an active trade in endangered species, the company eliminated from its product line all planting bulbs that didn't have verifiable proof of commercial propagation.

- Natural pest management: The company offers an extensive line of beneficial insects for pest control and actively promotes organic gardening.

Internal Efforts

- Recycled catalog: Since 1990 many of the company's catalogs have been printed on recycled paper with postconsumer waste and a high percentage of de-inked fiber from paper that would have been thrown away otherwise. "The energy saved by using recycled paper in 1991," estimates Ted Tuescher, Smith & Hawken's environmental director, "is enough to power an electric car around the Earth at the equator over three hundred times." The company is also striving to use more vegetable inks in its catalogs and other printed materials.

Look into purchasing a re-inking device or service. Some nylon ribbons can be re-inked a hundred times. Ribbons can be returned to the manufacturer for reprocessing.

- Environmental audit: Each year the company conducts an environmental audit that is reviewed by the Coalition for Environmentally Responsible Economies (CERES). Smith & Hawken was the first signatory of the Valdez Principles created by CERES, which include sound environmental practices like sustaining natural resources, reduction and appropriate disposal of wastes, energy conservation, and other protective measures.

- Talking for nature: The company is a member of Working Assets's donation-linked telephone service, wherein a percentage of the cost of its long-distance calls is donated to various environmental groups.

- Junk-mail campaign: Starting in the fall of 1990, the company implemented a nine-point program aimed at reducing the amount of unwanted and undelivered mail it sends. This involved many computer changes so that customers receive only the catalogs they desire. The catalogs urge customers to contact the Direct Marketing Association to remove their names from that mailing list, the largest in the country, and $5 gift certificates are awarded to customers who send in duplicated labels.

- Recycling and reusing: Simply put, the company recycles everything that can be recycled, reuses everything that can be reused, and seeks alternatives to everything that poses a threat to the environment.

Nearly all its corrugated boxes are made of 100 percent recycled material, with 83 percent postconsumer fiber. Benefiting from new technology, these boxes require 17 percent less material even while they meet the same strength requirements. Most of the company's packaging material is uncirculated newspaper. The company banned the use of bubble wrap, which had the unexpected consequence of saving money. It also switched from plastic to biodegradable glassine for wrapping clothing and other products.

Another innovative Smith & Hawken touch, not seen by us in other environmental programs as comprehensive as Smith & Hawken's, is compost collectors in each of its kitchens for organic lunch scraps, which are then emptied into a main bin for use in gardens, naturally.

Nearly all toilets and shower heads are low-flow models, and wherever possible, sinks are fitted with aerators. The company blankets and maintains all water heaters at the energy conservation setting or at 130 degrees Fahrenheit. Every few months a few quarts of water are drained from the bottom faucet to remove sediment and increase tank life. Seven-day programmable timers are on nearly all thermostats.

Smith & Hawken uses low-voltage (incandescent) halogen lamps (fifty-watt MR16) for most task lighting. The reflectors on these lamps make them state of the art in energy-efficient incandescent lighting. They burn for 2,000 hours and thus outlast the 750-hour life of standard incandescent lamps.

The company's environmental literature claims that the forty-four compact fluorescent lights it has installed so far as replacements for

Examine ways to reduce the packing materials used in your shipping and receiving department. Shred paper for packing, use edible popcorn, or reuse materials received in packages from other sources. Include a note in every package informing the recipients of your environmental action and encouraging them to do likewise.

Installing water-conserving aerators on faucets and shower heads can reduce usage by as much as 50 percent, without a noticeable loss of force. Fresh water is a scarce resource and needs to be conserved.

incandescent lights will save more than $800 a year and will prevent the burning of enough natural gas to fill a Goodyear blimp. Compact fluorescents are miniature fluorescent lamps that use one-fifth the energy of incandescents and last ten times as long. New triphosphor compounds have significantly improved color rendition. Although more expensive, these lamps pay for themselves in energy savings.

Electronic ballasts that use 35 to 40 percent less energy are being installed in many of the company's fixtures with fluorescent tubes. These ballasts don't hum, and they raise light flickering far above perceptible levels. A ballast for two tubes costs about $15 (net a $10 utility rebate). Excluding installation costs, the ballast pays for itself in about twenty-seven hundred hours with two forty-watt tubes (about three hundred working days).

In some locations the company has installed below-the-sink water filters to replace the bottled water it used to receive. The filters save money and eliminate pollution from both plastic containers, which can leach into the water, and trucking from the source. Replacing the electric water coolers with filters also saves energy and avoids CFCs, which are used as coolant.

Branching Out

Smith & Hawken is dedicated to serving the communities in which it does business. Through its business practices, volunteer efforts, and charitable giving, it supports organizations, communities, and individuals and strives "to have a lasting and meaningful impact" in all it does.

Smith & Hawken lives up to its commitments in monumental fashion with an extraordinary number of environmental partnerships and community outreach programs.

- Habitat restoration: Two seedlings are planted for each tree used for paper pulp in the company's catalogs. In 1991 the company planted sixty-one hundred Douglas fir seedlings, another sixty-one hundred in 1992, and forty-five hundred in 1993. The seeds will be tended until they're self-sufficient.

- Kid's Art wrapping paper: Its Holiday '91 catalog featured recycled wrapping paper with holiday designs created by local schoolchildren and packaged by disabled workers at Northbay Industries in Novato, CA.

Smith & Hawken produced, printed, and marketed the wrapping paper and donated all profits to the Mill Valley Schools Community Foundation. Each year, Smith & Hawken incorporates a similar program to benefit a special group. In 1992, the company offered greeting cards designed by children.

■ Silk for Life: The company has donated tools to this organization, which is helping Colombian farmers triple their income by substituting mulberry bushes to harvest silk from silkworms instead of growing coca plants for cocaine. Its catalog also offers socks made with silk harvested and spun by the farmers.

■ Ancient Forest Protection Initiative: To support efforts to stem the rapid diminution of the Earth's original forest cover and the species living within them, the company has printed 100,000 copies of this initiative to be submitted to Congress by the Rainforest Action Network. Copies have been enclosed in customers' orders since the 1990 holiday season.

In addition to this list and other sustained development projects, the company recently sponsored a benefit to raise funds for the video "Rainforests: Proving Their Worth," which demonstrates the economic value of nontimber goods like fruits, nuts, oils, fiber, and botanical products. Trade in these goods offers people a way to earn an income from the forests without destroying them.

The Customer Has a Right to Know

"Smith & Hawken has a unique sensitivity to the ongoing relationship with its customers. What's more it treats them with respect," says the *Journal of the American Center of Design* (Spring 1991). "We've always assumed that our customers are intelligent people," says Hawken, "and that if given the right sort of information, they can make an intelligent choice." To serve that end, the company provides information on how to select tools that are both satisfying and inexpensive, tips on care and maintenance of tools, and examples of how one can positively affect the global environment.

It encourages customers to keep its catalogs, promising to carry products longer than other companies do, and it resists repackaging old catalogs to make them appear new, a common direct-marketing practice.

"Smith & Hawken is truly a business about design," commends the *Journal*, "worthy of the resources it consumes. It is one of those rare companies driven by its values, seeking profit only in empowering its customers."

Along with such items as "Bulldog Forks," "Wood Rim Riddles," "Scoons," "Marmande Tomato" and "Rouge d'Etampes" seeds, and the "Garden Beneficials Variety Pack," consisting of ten thousand trichogramma wasps, two thousand ladybugs, a thousand green lacewing eggs, five hundred red worms, and one praying mantis case, the recent Smith & Hawken catalog offers this sage advice: "Common sense should guide us," "Simplicity should reign," and "The Earth should be our teacher."

Ecollection d'Esprit de Corp.

In 1968 Susie Tompkins and Jane Tise formed the Plain Jane Dress Company. They made their first deliveries from a station wagon, with Susie's two young daughters traveling along in the backseat. Soon Susie's husband, Doug, became involved with the business, which was renamed Esprit de Corp in 1979. During the early 1980s Esprit became synonymous with a youthful California way of life. The pioneering clothing company bucked the system by ignoring the dictates of Paris and New York and producing a line of liberated, comfortable clothing. In turn this line produced an empire worth an estimated $500 million.

Susie's success had a hefty price tag. The marriage dissolved in a heavily publicized divorce case that involved a nasty fight over the jointly owned company. Through a buyout completed in June 1990, Susie Tompkins became the new owner with the help and support of three shareholders, Isaac Stern, Michael Ying, and Bruce Katz.

Once again, going against the trends, in a soft-market climate, Susie has launched her own "Susie Tompkins" label for the older, more sophisticated woman. "My work and my life are one and the same," says Susie. "I never finished high school, so I learned as I moved along. When you don't know the 'right' way to do something, you're less inhibited by dogma. I have always been interested in doing the right thing than in doing things right."

Like successful entrepreneur Anita Roddick of the Body Shop, Susie Tompkins credits travel as the single most important influence on her acquisition of the style and knowledge that led to accomplishments in business and in raising her social consciousness. Like Anita Roddick's line of natural cosmetics and toiletries, Susie Tompkins's line of clothing reflects an attitude of conservation.

The Esprit line of junior sportswear is sold in twenty-nine countries. The corporation distributes a wide number of apparel lines, including Esprit, Esprit footwear and accessories, and Esprit Kids. Early on the company gained recognition as an operation with a social conscience. It has continued its commitment to support causes and speak out on issues that are of global concern.

The Esprit and Susie Tompkins clothing lines appeal to sensible, responsible women who are interested in timeless chic rather than "power-fashion" flash. The clothing is about wardrobe building in classic shapes versus instant disposability. Her respect for herself and others is carried through in her concepts of clothing, her business, her lifestyle, and her business style. Respect for the environment is built into the package.

Gloria Steinem is quoted as depicting Susie as a fine example of "proving that values can be a bottom line as well as dollars." "Susie shows that the reputation of business can be redeemed," added Steinem in an article on Susie Tompkins in the September 1992 issue of *Metropolitan Home.*

Not everyone is enamored with Susie's heart-on-her-sleeve approach to business. She has run an ad with teenagers' ideas on what to do to save the planet. She opened her new line, not with a fashion show, but with a sermon by the Reverend Cecil Williams of Glide Memorial Church, San Francisco, on the unresolved problems of America's cities. Critics accuse of her running a New Age company, to which Tompkins responds that her company has always been a "lifestyle" company. In fact Esprit's mission is to be a company that lives its values. Esprit's motto is "Be informed, be involved, make a difference." This corporate culture is a reflection of the company's customers and its employees.

Employees get time off to do volunteer work, and they can apply to the company's foundation for grants for various organizations with which they are involved. She is credited with knowing how to empower others within her company and within the organizations she is active in.

Susie Tompkins's business style has evolved over two decades. Today environmental and social responsibility complement her energetic "business and life style" as well as the values of her customers.

Tompkins's company runs an "Eco Desk," overseen by Jennifer Carroll in the United States. Two other Eco Desks are located in Esprit's Düsseldorf and Hong Kong offices. The Eco Desks are Esprit's environmental and community affairs department, responsible for implementing the company's environmental audit, prepared by outside consultants at the Elmwood Institute, of all the company's factories worldwide. The audit covers concerns regarding use of energy, materials, and packaging. The desks are also responsible for coordinating paper recycling and waste reduction, and coordinating volunteers, community relations, and employee education.

Tompkins admits that compromises have been made. Because Esprit's fabrics are made with a high level of environmentally sound raw materials and processes, increased costs are incurred. In order to keep down the retail price, Esprit has had to incorporate use of some synthetic, petroleum-based fabrics. Every effort, however, is made to include postconsumer recycled wools, like the donegal tweed blazers that feature 87 percent postconsumer recycled material; the solid-cotton T-shirts in natural white, organically grown cotton that is unbleached, undyed, and resin- and formaldehyde-free; and the hand-knit cardigan sweaters of naturally colored wool with reconstituted glass beads, hand-painted buttons, and no mothproofing. Recycled wool and fabrics are obtained from companies that specialize in recycling material goods. The current goal of the company is to do everything in the best way it can, not in the most perfect and costliest way.

Call other companies. Share information, exchange ideas, work together. Especially if you are a small company in a large building, make the effort to communicate with your neighbors, share your cost-savings findings, and enlist the building management to promote your goals.

Like most concerned business owners, Tompkins has realized that making environmental changes is an ongoing process, not an overnight phenomenon. The cost of maintaining the environment needs to be worked into the cost of doing business as effectively as it can be. As long as day-to-day operations are continually audited, new ways to comply with one's goals will become evident.

This is one way of making the commitment affordable and realistic. Tompkins sees these times as serious times, but not oppressive or depressing. "We can be optimistic, because the changes we are making now are solution oriented," she says. Business has an opportunity to make a difference.

A September 1992 press release from Esprit outlined its innovations for the clothing industry with its Ecollection: "Fabric from trees...colors without dyes...buttons made from glass...tweed from hand-me-downs." Esprit has become the first major fashion line to incorporate rigorous environmental and social standards into design and production.

Nike Will Just Do It

Like Esprit, Nike is working on a developing a comprehensive environmental program. A $3 billion company, with fifty-five hundred employees worldwide, Nike's growth and its relationship to the fitness of its customers and employees are linked with the health of the environment. It aims to act aggressively through innovative actions to preserve, protect, and enhance the environment, working toward eliminating practices that cause environmental degradation. "We believe the environment is a partner for life, not a servant," says Nike in its collateral material.

From initiating the EPA's Green Lights Program (see Addendum for details) to the use of recycled and recyclable material in consumer packaging, Nike is making efforts to broaden the scope of its environmental commitment, according to company spokesman Keith Peters.

Keep initial expectations simple. Unless you have a small group or virtually everyone is committed, too stringent requirements at the beginning of the program will likely not work. Develop some programs with immediate results that encourage further participation and create momentum.

The company recently appointed Henry Chriss (the chemist who developed its regrinds system) to create an environmental action team and to write a corporate policy statement on the issues. Nike recognizes that putting its environmental house in order is a critical priority.

This has not stopped Nike from addressing some serious environmental issues or from taking action in its day-to-day operations. Already it has computerized energy management systems in all its U.S. facilities. Water use reduction measures are in place, and freon has been eliminated from the manufacturing processes. Nike packaging is made from recycled materials only. In-house, Nike promotes recycling in all its U.S. locations and offers appropriate training to all its employees. Nike has an active Bike, Run, Skate (BRS) program that encourages carpooling, the use of mass transit, walking, and biking.

Nike's well-promoted "Just Do It" fund supports local environmental protection organizations like the Environmental Federation of Oregon, the Conservation Alliance, the Nature Conservancy, Earth Share, and the Surfrider Foundation.

The company's most significant contribution to environmental technology is the innovative Nike regrind system, which allows waste material from the production process to be recycled into outsole material for new shoes. The result is reduced demand on nonrenewable resources, reduced impact on landfills, and reduced pollution, all without sacrificing durability. At present, Nike is not realizing profit from regrind, except in savings resulting from not landfilling, which is balanced by the cost of the investment in its equipment. However, down the line, the company expects the process will be a breakeven proposition. The challenge for Nike is to discover ways to incorporate postconsumer waste (recycled shoes) into the process.

Encourage staff to create car pools or to use public transportation alternatives. Offer some sort of recognition or incentive for this effort. This helps reduce air pollution while creating comradery among co-workers.

Like so many U.S. companies, Nike is pursuing the right course in recognizing the need to create and develop a mutually beneficial arrangement with the environment.

Mary Kay Cosmetics: Driving Pink
Cadillacs down a Green Highway

From the company that made pink Cadillacs the ultimate incentive for enhancing women's beauty comes a program that aims to "keep the country more beautiful." At Mary Kay Cosmetics in Dallas, Texas, the corporate philosophy has always been guided by the Golden Rule. Perhaps you could also say now that to "do unto others as you would have them to do unto you" extends to the earth as well.

For a manufacturer of thirty-eight product lines of skin care and makeup, with annual sales upward of $600 million, environmental awareness not only has the potential to heighten its already favorable public image but also has the potential to save the company money. The easiest place for Mary Kay to launch its environmental effort was in the area of recycling and waste reduction. It's primarily that approach that has fueled Mary Kay's environmental campaign since 1989.

Mary Kay Cosmetics started in 1963 as a visionary idea from a woman who, while she had a profitable career in direct sales herself, was tired of seeing most women settling for compromised achievements in the business world. Her plan was to create a company that would give women of all ages, cultures, and business experience the ultimate opportunity: to be in business for themselves and to set their own goals of success. Today more than 250,000 women, called "independent beauty consultants," compose the independent sales force for whom success is measured both by how much they sell and how many other women they recruit into the business. To some this pyramid style of direct sales is nothing new. But to this sales force, founder Mary Kay Ash is revered as the woman who has allowed their dreams to come true.

While the sales principles are taught almost by formula, new ideas and suggestions from the seventeen hundred employees and the worldwide sales force are always encouraged. It's only fitting that the environmental program was suggested by one employee in March 1989. In this case the employee met with related departments for further evaluation and expansion and finally presented the program to the company's president, Dick Bartlett. Being an avid environmentalist himself, he wholeheartedly supported it and encouraged all employees to participate.

From the beginning, the program has been based on a three-tiered structure:

1   Recycling of office paper and other materials.

2   Employees bringing recyclables from home (ostensibly to encourage the market for recyclers).

3   Designing and implementing recyclable and recycled product packaging.

To date, more than 8.5 million pounds of paper, corrugated cardboard, aluminum, plastic, and glass has been recycled. Revenue generated from these efforts is either donated to environmental causes, such as the Texas Nature Conservancy, of which company president Dick Bartlett is vice-chairman, or the Dallas Parks Foundation. Currently the payback on these combined initiatives has totaled more than $95,000.

The environmental program is managed by a Recycling Creative Action Team consisting of managers and employees representing ten departments from the corporate, manufacturing, and distribution divisions. Monitoring the costs and revenues is the responsibility of the project manager for distribution. To keep both employees and the general public aware of its efforts and progress, the marketing department publishes all results in an environmental fact sheet.

In many ways, Mary Kay Cosmetics is not only in the business of sales; it's also in the business of training. Educating employees about its environmental initiatives is therefore part of its corporate communications and two newsletters, *Applause* and *Heartline*. In the beginning, incentives to participate were offered in the form of movie tickets and free lunches. In 1989 they were the means for encouraging employees to bring recyclables from home to fill bins in the parking lot.

After the initial launch, however, the program had enough support that inducements were no longer necessary. The company states that now "employee pride in the program and the recycling habits formed since inception have continued to make it a success."

Within the corporate offices, those habits include separating all white paper, computer paper, and junk mail, as well as newspapers, magazines, and soda cans. Since August 1991 all polystyrene food service items have also been collected for recycling and crushed on site in a Dart polystyrene densifier. Mary Kay claims it was the first company in Texas to purchase this recycling machine, which prepares the plastic for remanufacture.

In addition to recycling waste, the company is also supporting the market for recycled goods. Currently 90 percent of its corporate letterhead and business cards are printed on recycled paper, and all products are packaged in recycled paperboard. Additionally, the program has reduced trash volume enough to save more than $30,000 annually in waste pickup costs. To add to that yearly savings, waste hauling equipment is leased monthly and paid for by the revenue generated from the sale of recycled paper, which is often in excess of expenditures.

On all corporate correspondence, soy-based ink has replaced the nonbiodegradable and toxic oil-based ink. According to Dave Armbrester, printing services buyer, "there's really no reason for Mary Kay to use oil-based inks anymore, especially since we're environmentally conscious."

Although the company does not now use recycled plastic for product containers, it does imprint the Society of Plastics Industry code on each bottle to help recyclers identify the types of resins used.

Manufacturing follows many environment-saving practices as well. The plant recycles all corrugated materials, paper, aluminum, and glass. Wastewater generated during production is treated to meet or exceed EPA requirements. All chemicals used to develop product formulas are disposed of safely, and all toxic waste is disposed of separately to avoid polluting the local water system. In addition, as soon as the 50-gallon drums that contain chemical ingredients are empty, they are sent back to suppliers to refill. Not only does this reduce the burden of waste, it eliminates the need for storage space.

Currently the company's skin and hair care products are processed by contract manufacturers. During a typical year, more than 11 million pounds of raw ingredients and up to 500 million individual component parts are purchased by Mary Kay buyers, to create more than 100 million product units.

While the company's main focus right now is in recycling and using recyclable packaging, it is the authors' hope that Mary Kay's researchers and developers will investigate new raw materials that will make their product lines nontoxic as well. Then the company will be in a leadership position as both manufacturer and distributor of biodegradable, recyclable, and earth-friendly goods. And it, too, will be part of the pyramid to environmental success.

Sebastian Products Provide
a Natural Balance

For John Sebastian Cusenza, the Brazilian rainforest is more than just a passionate environmental issue. To him it's also a source for renewable raw materials he can use to help create hair care products for his company, Sebastian International. His staff has been known to spend up to two years searching the Amazon for just the right combination of plants, herbs, and botanicals to create environmentally safe sprays, gels, shampoos, and dyes.

Besides looking to the rainforest for raw source materials, he is also dedicated to creating a sustainable economy for the Brazilian Kayapo Indians with the hopes that it may someday eliminate deforestation and resource destruction. You could almost say the company is an environmental organization in its own right—like many that have been established to promote greater awareness of issues such as rainforests. The company's mission statement indicates how far-reaching this concern is: "Sebastian International believes in the human spirit, in the domination of good will . . . towards all living things. Through beauty, we strive to preserve and improve the quality of life . . . for we can envision the world as a safe, caring, protective environment. One where plant life is as important as human life. And one where Planet Earth continues to be the ultimate purveyor of beauty."

So committed is John Sebastian to saving the rainforests that inside his corporate headquarters in Woodland Hills, California, he built a 2,200-square-foot model of a tropical forest, complete with hanging vines, a waterfall with fish and turtles, the fragrance of live orchids, and the sounds of monkeys and macaws. All at a cost of $237,000. It's his attempt to bring the sights and sounds of a thriving rainforest to a public that may only get to read about it. Visitors can walk through an exhibit containing extracts from rubber trees, artifacts from the Indian tribes, and a variety of facts and photos designed to entertain and enlighten.

A "barefoot" tour takes guests through a lush green jungle that gradually leads to a dying brown forest—bringing home a lifelike example of current neglect. At the tour's end visitors can join a question-and-answer session in a special theater, and children are given packets of seeds to plant in their own backyards. The exhibit is so popular that there is a three-month wait for tickets.

Undergoing its own environmental makeover during the past few years, Sebastian International has discontinued popular product lines and redesigned packaging in favor of exclusively biodegradable earth-friendly products.

The Road to Success

But John Sebastian wasn't always so high-minded. In fact twice in his life he struggled just to make ends meet. First was his family's exodus from his native Tunisia. When they arrived on American shores they had only $81 to spare and spoke virtually no English. A survivor even then, the young Sebastian earned money at various odd jobs, including working in his cousin's barbershop.

After attending barber school for nine months to pursue his new career, Sebastian got an assistant hairstyling job in Hollywood, coiffing hair for celebrities like Marilyn Monroe and Jayne Mansfield. Later he met up with the Lapin brothers, who started a chain of beauty schools and made him a partner as both manager and teacher. There he met Geri, a student who would become his wife and later chief product designer for Sebastian International.

The schools were sold and Sebastian was paid $18 million in stock—making him a millionaire at thirty-four. Unfortunately the new owners soon went bankrupt, forcing him and his wife to start over completely with a small salon of their own.

By 1974 business at Sebastian's salon took off. Geri had just invented a crimping iron that popularized hairstyling at home, and orders were rushing in. The couple, along with Sebastian's brother Tony, decided to formalize their partnership, and Sebastian International was born.

During the early 1980s all was going well and Sebastian took great pride in forecasting consumer trends. What he didn't see was that by 1985 his company would be outsized, outclassed, and unable to keep up with demand.

So he instituted a major operations overhaul and computerized all sales and inventory right down to the point of purchase at each salon. But even after making his business more efficient, he soon began to realize that business as usual would not survive the coming trends of the 1990s.

A Green Awakening

In 1987, fully three years before America began thinking green, Sebastian decided his company had to anticipate the public's concerns. "After all the materialism in the eighties, we foresaw that consumers in the nineties would look at what a company *stands for*, not simply what it sells," he told *Profit* magazine last year.

He remembered a trip he took in the 1960s to Brazil when his brother was the Peace Corps director there. Then it was considered a sin to harm the forest's delicate balance; yet now it was endangered. Finally in a position to do something about it, he made a commitment to help save the threatened ecosystem.

At the time, the cause's most visible advocate was rock musician Sting, who had just helped launch the Rainforest Foundation in New York City. Four years and two concerts later, Sebastian International had provided financial support to the tune of $350,000. Even now a portion of all products sold is donated to environmental and social organizations.

John Sebastian Cusenza has finally locked into a secure future. Over the past five years, Sebastian International has doubled annual sales, from $50 million to $100 million—during a relentless economic recession that has seen many competitors go under.

He attributes the company's staying power to its alignment with environmental and social causes. Customers can visit a salon carrying Sebastian products, for instance, and donate $10 to one of seven organizations that make up UNITE (Unity Now Is a Tomorrow for Everyone). In return they receive $15 in Sebastian products as well as $65 dollars' worth of coupons and discounts. Sebastian says Club UNITE was born out of a desire to give consumers the means to take a stand about issues that affect them personally and at the same time to reward them for their efforts. "Up until now, people came to salons simply to have their hair done. Club UNITE gives salons the voice to influence their clientele toward positive change. This is not about having another 'promotion.' This is a way of life," he says.

Securing the Vision

Sebastian knows that many companies are touting their environmental responsibility with token measures and marketing hype. So he's making sure the entire company is actively involved. He encourages employees to participate by sending them open-ended eco-questions like, "We as a company can make a better world for our children if we . . . ," to which staff members write their answers on butcher paper hung around the offices.

Recycling and reducing are two other priorities within headquarters. Office paper is separated and recycled, and corporate communications use recycled paper. In addition, employees are encouraged to type and photocopy correspondence on both sides of paper and reuse paper whenever possible for drafts and memos. To save energy, Sebastian has installed motion detectors that turn lights off when a room is unoccupied.

Employees are also enlisted to help lessen air pollution from commuter traffic in the Los Angeles area by taking part in the South Coast's Ride Sharing Plan. Among the many incentives to use alternative means of transportation are a $15 cash bus subsidy, excused tardiness, quarterly days off, monthly prize drawings, and free shampoo.

Planting the Seeds

But Sebastian is most excited about the future environmentalists that come through the company's rainforest each day. "It starts with the children," he says. "The best way to change behavior is to focus on the next generation."

To foster greater environmental awareness among the children of the world, Sebastian launched Little Green in 1990. It's an international campaign that includes a creative arts competition for kids between the ages of 5 and 15. Cosponsored by the Smithsonian Institution and featuring pop singer Paula Abdul as spokesperson, the campaign invites young people to write or draw their concerns about the environment—particularly the rainforests—using crayons, paint, watercolor, and collage. Entries are displayed in the company's rainforest exhibit, and four grand prize winners are given a free trip to the real rainforest in Brazil. The company claims that in its first year Little Green Creative Arts Project reached 2 million children representing four continents and inspired more than 100,000 entries. Abdul helps increase awareness of the program by writing a regular column for the campaign newsletter, *Planet Power.* In addition, her recent CD "Spellbound" includes a special card inviting listeners to write for more information on the program.

While an environmental campaign directed at children may seem to go a little beyond the business of a hair and skin care company, Sebastian is committed to helping consumers understand the earth's environmental distress call. "Our environmental policy is not applicable only when it benefits us," he says. "It applies across the board." He adds, "We in the business world have to stand for more than just our products' names. One of the solutions is to provide programs that inspire people toward personal and civic growth." Sebastian believes that the company's environmental campaign together with its rainforest tour will provide more information for discussion at school and home and will inspire a new generation of environmentalists and consumers to think "Sebastian" when they think of the earth.

No Such Thing as a Plain Cup of Tea

Celestial Seasonings had its beginnings in 1969 in Aspen, Colorado. There, Mo Siegel, then only nineteen years old, gathered wild herbs along the Rocky Mountains and made them into healthful teas.

A year later Siegel and his friend Wyck Hay produced their first blend, Mo's 24 Herb Tea, packaged in hand-sewn muslin bags and sold to a local health food store. Hay's brother, John, joined the partnership in 1971, and the threesome set up shop in an old barn outside Boulder. They expanded their markets to include all of Colorado, New Mexico, and the East Coast. The partners also began buying herbs instead of picking them. Slowly a national herb tea company emerged.

Red Zinger™ herb tea was introduced in January 1972 and was an overnight sensation; it remains one of Celestial Seasonings's best-selling teas today. Whereas herb teas were once widely thought of as appropriate for medicinal purposes only, Celestial Seasonings virtually created the market for herb teas as flavorful, healthful beverages.

Working closely with herb farmers from around the world, Celestial Seasonings solidified its source for obtaining ingredients. This concept attracted the attention of Kraft, which bought the company in 1984. Kraft's ownership brought Celestial Seasonings to the attention of new consumers and enhanced its lead in the increasingly popular herb tea industry. During this time the company introduced a gourmet line of traditional black teas. Coming full circle in 1988, Celestial Seasonings's management purchased the company from Kraft, reverting it to independent ownership, headquartered in Boulder.

Celestial Seasonings offers more than forty innovative products, cleverly packaged, and is the largest herb tea manufacturer in the United States, with products available in health food stores and grocery stores nationwide.

Despite its rapid growth, Celestial Seasonings remains true to its cottage-industry roots and dedicated to its "quest for excellence" in its product line and its commitment to customers.

Celestial, Earth-Wise Teas

Naturally that commitment includes a concern for the environment. Celestial's teas are all-natural, containing no artificial colorings, flavorings, or preservatives. Herb teas are made from many kinds of plants, leaves, flowers, roots, bark, and seeds. Buying ingredients from the global community increases the company's awareness that there are natural resources that require protection and sustained cultivation.

Most tea companies buy their ingredients already processed, but Celestial Seasonings purchases whole herbs directly from the growing countries to maintain the highest quality standards. Ginseng from China, blackberry leaves from Yugoslavia, and hibiscus from Thailand are a few examples. Company herbalists travel the world sampling and selecting entire crops for purchase.

From inception, by its very nature as an organic product company, Celestial Seasonings has implemented environmentally correct actions. It uses no strings, staples, or individual envelopes for its oxygen-bleached herb tea bags, which in turn prevents 2 million pounds of extra packaging from reaching landfills every year. A single sheet of unbleached wax paper lines each box of recycled paperboard in lieu of plastic or foil packaging. Herbs are fumigated using recycled CO_2 instead of the more commonly used ethylene oxide, a known carcinogen.

Celestial Seasonings's corporate mission statement outlines its intent to be a good corporate citizen and a catalyst for positive changes in the food and beverage industry.

Celestial Seasonings conducted a 1991 poll of food editors and writers at the International Food Media Conference held in Dallas and found that 98 percent thought that environmental responsibility was more than a passing fad. More than 50 percent concurred that consumers are basing their buying on a product's environmental qualities, such as lack of excessive packaging and use of recyclable materials. For a company that has been environmentally friendly all along, this was confirmation that their corporate ethic is well founded. "We are not green just to be commercial," says Angie Dorsey, public relations specialist for the company. "We've been environmentally responsible for over twenty years."

During the mid-1980s, when Kraft purchased Celestial Seasonings, company founder Mo Siegel left the company to found Earth Wise, a manufacturer and distributor of biodegradable household detergents and cleaners and 100 percent recycled ecological trash bags. Celestial Seasonings acquired Earth Wise in 1991, when Siegel returned to the company as chairman and CEO. "I'm thrilled to be back at Celestial," said Siegel in a press release issued to announce the acquisition. "I love the company and see Celestial and Earth Wise as a dynamic growth opportunity. Celestial's emphasis on the health and well-being of its consumers is even more timely today than when we founded the company in 1970. The big winners are our customers, who want healthful and environmental products."

"I'm excited about teaming up with Mo again," added Barnet Feinblum, the president of Celestial Seasonings who organized the buyback from Kraft. "Celestial is well positioned for the 1990s. By combining our energies and experience, we can better focus the company to promote the health and welfare of our planet." In a $100 million herb tea market, this partnership has ensured Celestial Seasonings a leading market position, outselling all competitors combined.

A Leader in Environment

Mo Siegel is one of Colorado's best-known entrepreneurs and a leading spokesman for natural food and environmental products. His hang-loose approach to business encourages a lot of employee participation. There's a shower at headquarters for employees who bike to work and a track for noontime runners and rollerbladers. The corporate uniform is T-shirt and jeans. Siegel is known to wear a tie, shorts, moccasins, and ankle socks.

Before returning to Celestial, with the $10 million he acquired from the Kraft buyout, Siegel helped to found Omega Technologies, which grows algae containing Omega 3, a chemical that helps prevent heart disease. He also worked with John Denver to start Windstar Foundation, an environmental group. In addition to Earth Wise, he also started the Jesusonian Foundation to further the teachings of Jesus.

On the advice of Mother Teresa, who, upon his visit with her, poked him in the chest and advised, "Grow where you're planted," Siegel returned to the competitive corporate world that offered him "so much fun."

This corporate competitiveness combined with spiritual guidance has resulted in a highly comprehensive environmental campaign. A grass-roots environmental committee composed of employees has been established to oversee corporate recycling of paper, aluminum, glass, scrap metal, cardboard, and burlap. Companywide efforts include duplex copying, composting of unused tea, a corporate library to eliminate duplicate subscriptions, recycled typewriter ribbons, and recycled paper goods, including computer, photocopy, writing, and toilet paper, among other ecological choices for the office.

China and silverware grace the lunchroom; no paper plates or throwaway coffee cups litter the lounges. Employees plant live

Christmas trees on the grounds during spare moments and are cultivating a six-hundred-herb garden. Celestial Seasonings also offers its employees socially responsible investment choices through a company thrift plan.

A number of international programs have been implemented. The company's interaction with farmers around the world to establish sustainable agricultural programs is one facet of its global environmental outreach. The farm programs have resulted in a cross-fertilization of ideas between different indigenous people. Throughout their interaction with various farming communities, Celestial has implemented an integrated pest management system to help free farmers from dependence on chemicals.

National programs include working directly with American wildcrafters, independent pickers of herbs and teas who use nonindustrial methods to gather materials, to enhance the wildcrafters' botanical expertise. Celestial also has a toll-free hot line for the public that offers information about recycling, packaging, and environmental responsibility.

These days when I receive a letter or memo that requires a short reply, I return it to the sender with a handwritten note jotted in the margins. I also turn manila file folders inside out to reuse them. Whenever possible, I use the routing slip system or leave short messages on voice mail. Electronic mail is another way to communicate and save paper and postage.

Since Celestial Seasonings's product line is environmentally sound by nature, it has to make fewer adaptations in order to be ecologically correct. Yet certain elements of processing and packaging do pose challenges. Oxygen-bleached tea bag paper to eliminate dioxin from the earth's water supply is one solution the company employs. Innovative, solution-oriented research (to improve tea quality, and the packaging and environmental qualities of the product) is conducted at the company's labs. When Celestial gets letters from tea drinkers asking why the tea bags don't have tabs and strings, it answers with a letter informing customers that such decisions have resulted in a savings of 2 million pounds of paper. Contrite letters of apology usually follow such correspondence, with a typical response being "Sorry, I never thought of that." Education remains a key component in Celestial Seasonings's endeavors, beginning with its entertaining, enlightening, and decorative tea boxes.

Its health-conscious focus offers Celestial natural promotional tie-ins, including a number of bicycle races: the Red Zinger Mini Classic for children (which was sold to its director for $1, and later sponsored by the Adolph Coors Company); a women's Olympic bike team captained by silver medalist Rebecca Twigg; a men's amateur cycling team, winner of four championship titles; and top European racers and American Greg LeMond's winning team. In addition to its sponsorship tie-ins, Celestial has established the Best Buddy Program to benefit traumatized children in Colorado. Such conscientious support and comprehensive environmental efforts have been recognized with honor-roll status in corporate social responsibility according to the consumer guide *Shopping for a Better World*.

Of the company Feinblum presides over, he has this to say: "Celestial always has been, and probably always will be, a living, breathing experiment in modern management. Our premise is employee participation and involvement, and it is reflected in our management style: no time clocks, no dress codes, no reserved parking spaces. Dignity of the individual is part of our belief statement."

CHAPTER FIVE

Chemicals
Pharmaceuticals
Plastics
Petroleum

Merck & Co. Operates by the "Butterfly Effect"

In 1960 physicist Edward Lorenz used the butterfly as an example to explain the complex mathematical calculations in a meteorological problem on which he was working. Lorenz theorized that even the fluttering of a butterfly's wings could affect huge weather systems for several weeks, reaching to the other side of the world. His theory is known as the "butterfly effect." As this seemingly innocuous action can greatly influence the weather, so can individual acts have a tremendous impact on the environment, observes Merck & Co., citing the butterfly effect as "one important reason Merck made a corporate commitment to environmental excellence."

Merck & Co. is a worldwide research-intensive health products company that discovers, develops, produces, and markets human and animal health products and specialty chemicals. Headquartered in Whitehouse Station, New Jersey, Merck employs nearly thirty-eight thousand people, about half of them outside the United States. With origins that reach back to Germany in 1668, Merck was established in the United States in 1891 and rapidly became known for its achievements in pharmaceutical science.

In 1993, for the sixth consecutive year, *Fortune* magazine named Merck the most admired corporation in the United States. While very proud of that recognition, Merck is cognizant that true leadership requires more that just a good reputation. Because Merck's business is concerned with enhancing health and well-being, the company believes it must prevent any aspect of its operations from undermining this mission. This is embodied, declares Merck, in "our commitment to conduct our business worldwide in a manner that will protect the environment as well as the health and safety of our employees and the public."

Strategic Planning

In 1990 Merck formalized its commitment to environmental excellence with the publication of the company's first public environmental statement outlining its policy and setting forth its objectives. Periodic reports review Merck's progress toward meeting the goals of its five-year environmental strategic plan.

In an annual report Merck asserts that "no law or regulation required us to make these commitments." Instead Merck was motivated by its "fundamental mission to the health and well-being of society only a healthy environment can provide." Yet in other company literature, Merck concedes that "though reduction of waste was not often the driving force for initiating process improvements, yield enhancement, and raw material charge reductions, it is a natural consequence of these efforts."

Develop an environmental policy statement to set the standards for your program.

To fulfill the intent of its environmental policy, Merck set its broad-based objectives to

- minimize the release of chemicals into the environment that could affect health, deplete the ozone layer, or contribute to acid rain, the greenhouse effect, or any other global environmental problem;
- seek, through research, innovative routes to waste minimization and resource conservation;
- minimize the generation of wastes and seek self-sufficiency in treating and disposing of wastes;
- apply in its research, manufacturing, office, and vehicular fleet operations energy and resource conserving practices;
- promote resource conservation through innovative package design and the use of recyclable materials.

Meeting SARA

While Merck is targeting all waste for reduction, special goals have been set for the reduction of those wastes that are listed under the U.S. Superfund Amendments and Reauthorization Act (SARA). While the company is not required to reduce emissions under SARA (only under the Clean Air Act [CAA]), Merck's goals far exceed SARA suggestions and CAA mandates. Using the company's 1987 release levels reported to the EPA as a point of reference, Merck made a voluntary commitment to

- reduce air emissions of carcinogens, known or suspect, by 90 percent by the end of 1991;
- eliminate these air emissions entirely or apply the best available technology by the end of 1993;
- reduce all environmental releases of corporate toxic chemicals by an average of 90 percent by the end of 1995 (applying to all direct releases as well as the transfer of materials for off-site treatment or disposal).

At the April 1992 annual meeting of the stockholders, Merck chairman Roy Vagelos announced that as of 1991, the company had achieved its first goal on schedule and was well on its way to reaching the second. By the end of 1992, Merck reduced all worldwide releases of toxic chemicals by 50 percent from 1987, putting the company comfortably closer to its third goal.

Refuse Resolution

The toxic waste reduction program in Merck's chemical manufacturing organization, which is the source of most of the company's emissions, provides a good illustration of how the corporate strategic plan works at the division and plant levels. The strategy requires the division, individual plants, and every salaried employee with a job directly or indirectly related to manufacturing to set their own targets to achieve corporate goals for the years 1991 through 1995.

Within Merck's bulk manufacturing organization, there are eight plants and two manufacturing vice-presidents, each held accountable for the success of action plans for waste minimization at all eight plants. The central environmental resource staff plays a coordinating and supportive role to ensure that divisions are heading in the right direction.

Preeminent in the company's environmental hierarchy are source reduction, recovery/recycling/reuse, and waste management, in that order. While much of Merck's waste consists of nonhazardous materials such as paper, cardboard, aluminum, glass, metal, and sludge from its waste treatment plants, some is chemical and hazardous. Most of the latter consists of used solvents, such as ethyl alcohol, acetone, and methyl alcohol, used in Merck's manufacturing processes to dissolve the chemical building blocks that are reacted to make its human- and veterinary-health and specialty products. The recovery process typically involves boiling a waste stream, condensing the purified vapors, and collecting the liquid. This can recover up to 90 percent for reuse. The rest must be disposed of as hazardous waste.

Additionally, Merck's manufacturing division has established an aggressive program for the reduction of packaging components to conserve natural resources and landfill space. Projects already underway in Europe will reduce by 10 percent the amount of aluminum and foils entering the environment and the size of cartons by 20 percent. In the United States cotton wadding has been eliminated for trade and sample bottles. In Europe, where sizes and shapes of tablet packaging are numerous and often unique to each market, this division has undertaken a packaging standardization initiative. Conversion to uniform blister packages and high-volume carton printing significantly increases production flexibility to deal with unexpected changes in sales demands while it saves money and reduces waste.

Minimizing by Modification

In order to create products and manufacturing processes that are environmentally sound from the outset, Merck is focusing on front-end changes rather than on end-of-pipe treatment techniques. A company can realize the greatest return on investments for modifications made at the process development stage of a new product. Minimizing waste at the outset, thanks to this new, more efficient machinery, saves enormously on disposal costs.

Source reduction makes even more sense for Merck, given its concentration on pharmaceuticals, since the Food and Drug Administration must approve any significant changes made midstream in the manufacture of a drug. Once clinical efficacy of a drug is established, any modification of processes to produce that drug must be approved by the FDA. Getting approval is a time-consuming, expensive effort.

New processes at Merck are evaluated not only from the standpoint of yield and product quality but also from their environmental impact and safety. What solvents will the process require? What waste will be created? What will be the impact of waste streams on the treatment facility into which they will be discharged? In its "stewardship" role, Merck takes "responsibility for the total life cycle of the materials we use and the products we manufacture."

Corporate Connection

Merck fosters open lines of communication with the communities in which its facilities are located by participating in community environmental committees, responding directly and promptly to any expression of public concern, and providing public officials and the community with the information needed to understand the potential environmental impact of Merck operations. The public has access to a plethora of printed materials offered by Merck, which also sends frequent releases on its activities to the media. Merck has been featured in numerous articles hailing its environmental and sound business accomplishments.

As a member of the Chemical Manufacturers Association (CMA) Responsible Care Program, Merck participates in CMA's outreach efforts to address public concerns about the chemical and pharmachemical industries' impact on the environment as well as on public health and safety. CMA runs ads in magazines such as *Time* and *Life* inviting readers to call a toll-free number to learn about the environmental performance of companies in their locations. Few take advantage of that invitation. Merck, which fields its own calls, reports that "for the most part the questions have been friendly inquiries about local Merck plants."

The absence of inquiries is not indicative of lack of concern, however. The public is not tolerant of companies who damage the environment in any way and is particularly anxious about chemical spills. Merck has established and maintains emergency response systems at facilities that make, handle, or store hazardous materials and provides technical and material assistance in emergencies to appropriate public agencies. To ensure safety in the transportation of chemicals, Merck has what it calls its Transafe Program, which makes it "partners with the communities." Merck sets guidelines for and monitors its motor and rail carriers and warehouses that store its products in its concern for the safe transport of these chemicals. This program, points out Merck, was already in place by the time the CMA had developed a transportation initiative.

While company management assumes overall responsibility for safety, health, and environmental protection, employees are encouraged to support their site's recycling, waste minimization, and safety programs and are urged to make suggestions for waste reduction, better chemical handling, process changes, or any other environmental improvements. Additionally, employees are asked to practice good environmental procedures at home by recycling news-papers, bottles, and cans; by using more fuel-efficient cars, heating and cooling systems, and other household appliances; and by plant-ing trees around homes to reduce the load on furnaces and air condi-tioners and to absorb carbon dioxide.

In Partnership with Nature

An excellent illustration of Merck's dedication to its environ-mental policy is its new corporate headquarters at Whitehouse Sta-tion in Readington Township, New Jersey. By all accounts, the company went to extraordinary lengths to preserve the site, which spans 460 acres of woodland, wetlands, and fields. "Using a scalpel rather than a bulldozer," Merck achieved what was once thought impossible: the construction of a 900,000-square-foot hexagon-shaped building and a 700,000-square-foot underground parking garage with mini-mal impact on the natural environment. Merck has received several awards in recognition of its environmental sensitivity in developing the site.

After considering more than two hundred architects to design its complex, Merck selected Kevin Roche, renowned for creating de-signs that blend into the surroundings. Despite the size and scope of the project, much of the site remains in its original state: a five-acre forest, now standing in the center of the hexagon, was virtually untouched; wetlands remain undisturbed, thanks to the rerouting of roads or bridges, which go over rather than through them. Even the trees and shrubs that were in the path of construction were uprooted, tagged, balled, and moved to an on-site nursery. Some thirteen hun-dred shrubs and trees, of thirty-five different species, some as high as 40 feet, were nurtured for nearly three years until they could be returned to their native environment as part of the site's natural land-scape plan.

The building design incorporates energy-saving features such as sunshades to minimize heat penetration in the summer and an air-conditioning system that uses water as a cooling agent instead of freon, a pollutant. Since the facility houses administrative offices, the principal waste product is paper, which is recycled. Still not fully occupied by mid-1993, the facility nevertheless produced 2.8 tons of trash every day, of which 2 tons were recyclable. Still unique among businesses, a 17,000-square-foot center for the children of employees sits on the northeastern corner of the property. Residential in design, the center is home away from home for 190 children ranging in age from six weeks to six years.

Saving the Rainforests

A pioneering agreement between Merck and the Costa Rican Instituto Nacional de Biodiversidad (INBio) could serve as a model for halting the destruction of the rainforests. Thanks to a $1 million initial grant from Merck, INBio is attempting to catalog Costa Rica's tremendous biological wealth with the goal of preserving it and putting it to work for society. In exchange for the grant and a percentage of the royalties of any new medicines developed, INBio has given Merck the rights to use the plants, animals, and chemical entities found in the Central American nation's tropical forests. Given the high odds against developing products through pharmaceutical research in general, the company may not have any royalties to give. However, if they do hit on a solution, the return will be far greater than all the failed projects combined.

Scientists believe that Costa Rica possesses more biological diversity per acre than any other country on earth. They estimate that this tiny nation contains between 5 to 7 percent of the earth's species—about half a million—most of which are unknown to science. There are as many species of birds in Costa Rica as in all of North America. Because of its geographical location and topography, it is much more than a rainforest, having every major tropical habitat.

Under the terms of the two-year agreement, Merck is funding a new extraction lab at the University of Costa Rica and training local people to collect samples and perform extractions. INBio will provide Merck with plants, insects, and microorganisms collected by the institute. Merck will evaluate these species for pharmaceutical and agricultural applications. The potentially mutually beneficial arrangement between Merck and INBio could encourage "chemical prospecting" for plants and animals in other wild areas throughout the world that may be made into useful products.

Natural substances as a source for drugs is not a new concept for Merck. Indeed the pharmaceutical industry was rooted in the use of natural compounds, mainly derived from medicinal herbs. Based on this tradition, the industry is willing to explore natural substances, even though plants and insects are more difficult to work with in the development of drugs.

By finding new ways to use forests without destroying them, countries such as Costa Rica can better protect their natural resources. Costa Rica will use the Merck royalties to support conservation. A January 1992 *New York Times* article declared that in the Merck/INBio venture "everybody wins: the world gets new drugs, the pharmaceutical companies earn profits, and people in the tropics are justly compensated." Merck was hailed by most of the national media for this unprecedented agreement.

What's Next?

Once viewed by most companies as a drag on corporate competitiveness, environment, health, and safety management are now seen as a means of enhancing business. As firms seek to cut costs and improve product quality, productivity, and public image, executives are discovering how their sensitivity to environmental trends can translate into competitive advantage and new opportunities. As an industry leader, Merck, too, recognizes that by developing environmentally sound technologies and products, it is assured a lofty position in rapidly expanding markets.

The trick is preventing what has been accomplished from eroding as a company expands. Merck is achieving that goal. However, the company knows that much remains to be done and has committed itself to long-term as well as global actions for maintaining the momentum.

Chevron Corporation "Smart"-ens Up

The approach toward environmental protection at Chevron Corporation can be summed up in one word—*smart*. At Chevron, however, this is not so much a word as an acronym for a program that became the basis for its overall policy—"Save Money and Reduce Toxics."

Until the mid-1980s, Chevron was not so much initiating environmental reform as it was responding to regulations and to the demands of environmental groups. That is not to say that Chevron had not already launched a series of very effective initiatives. But, despite tremendous progress achieved by Chevron in such areas as reducing refinery emissions and improving the quality of the water it discharged, the pressure for a more ambitious policy continued. In response to outside pressures, SMART was introduced in 1987. It was created primarily to reduce waste but has been expanded to focus on reducing air emissions and water pollution.

Going on the Offensive

SMART was designed as a way to monitor achievements in waste minimization and management practices companywide and to provide a forum for exchanging practical ideas. SMART was then the most advanced environmental policy in the global oil industry. It had emerged after a meeting of environmental specialists from throughout the corporation, who were looking for ways to "reduce what you generate, recycle what you can, treat what remains, and properly dispose of what's left." In Chevron's labs, refineries, and processing plants, as well as in marketing, production, and transportation facilities, the search was on for ways to improve processes and operations while reducing, if not eliminating, hazardous waste.

Vividly demonstrating that Chevron had every intention of paying much more than lip service to its principles, the board of directors established a permanent Public Policy Committee in the spring of 1990 to monitor and evaluate environmental issues as well as other broad social and political concerns that could affect the company. Environmental protection and ecology are high on the list of these issues, among which are reducing emissions to air and water and meeting cleanup requirements for contaminated sites. Chaired by Bruce Smart, former chairman and chief executive officer of the Continental Group and former undersecretary of commerce for international trade, the committee is composed of Ken T. Derr, Chevron chairman of the board, and four outside directors and is charged with making recommendations to the board.

Within five months after the committee was formed, Chevron issued its *Report on the Environment: A Commitment to Excellence*, a comprehensive document detailing everything from past brushes with regulatory agencies to a full-scale description of policies, performance, compliance, responsibilities, programs—current and planned—and future goals.

Pollution prevention at the source is the company's primary goal. Chevron is analyzing its business decisions, operations, and products to find ways to eliminate or curtail pollution. Specific objectives include

- reducing the amount of waste generated and recycling what's left;
- finding nontoxic alternatives to toxic materials and processes;
- devising safer operating procedures to reduce the number of petroleum spills, chemical releases, and other accidents;
- using resources more efficiently;
- ensuring that pollution reductions in one area don't transfer pollution to another.

Risky Business

Basic in Chevron's new policies is the emphasis on risk management—identifying and prioritizing potential problems, determining the probability of problems occurring, exploring alternative solutions, and taking action where appropriate. Chevron is taking the initiative to find cost-effective solutions before either a controversy or a compliance problem develops. While the concept of risk management had not appeared in Chevron's policy manual prior to 1990, employees quickly embraced it and have applied it effectively since it was implemented.

Stockholders, too, have expressed their support of Chevron's environmental policy and programs. At the 1991 annual meeting, 98 percent of its stockholders voted in favor of the company's philosophy and policy for safety, fire, health, and the environment, outlined in its brochure titled *Strategic Management in the Environmental Era*. In this publication, Chevron pledges to put its new policy into effect and to lengthen the list of environmental success stories by

1 conducting and periodically updating training programs to help employees understand how the social,

political, and legal aspects of society's environmental values affect its business;

2 expanding corporate environmental compliance reviews to include assessing and managing risks in addition to maintaining legal compliance;

3 promoting the integration of regulatory issues into the business-planning and decision-making process;

4 promoting the search for economic solutions to environmental, health, and safety concerns by rewarding employees for finding creative and economic ways to correct operation problems and identifying what expenditures today will increase competitiveness tomorrow;

5 communicating the success of its environmental, health, and safety programs to the public.

Smart and Profitable

SMART also aims to benefit the company's bottom line. In its first five years, Chevron facilities reduced disposal of routinely generated hazardous waste by 60 percent and saved more than $45 million in disposal costs. Another example of savings from this proactive policy is the replacement of old underground gasoline tanks at service stations with double-walled fiberglass tanks when such tanks were not required. Each fiberglass tank costs $25,000 to $50,000, whereas fixing a leaking tank and cleaning up the resulting contamination costs $250,000 or more.

Throughout its various facilities, Chevron is saving from $9,000 annually to hundreds of thousands, even millions, of dollars by implementing and sticking to SMART programs, many of which started as employee suggestions.

An Infrastructural Partnership

Early in the development of its environmental policies, the company discovered, as did The Boston Park Plaza Hotel, that employees in the field—those who work in the refineries and plants and are thus closest to operations—provide the best resources and the most creative ways to achieve environmental goals. To motivate management to meet the growing environmental responsibilities, more than fifty seminars were conducted for Chevron's approximately three thousand managers over the course of one year (1991–92).

The seminars outlined the company's policy, summarized environmental laws, addressed trends in public opinion, and stressed the responsibility for managers to comply with all corporate policies, procedures, practices, and laws that apply to their assigned duties. This mandate applies to all Chevron employees.

All managers are required to include environmental considerations in all business decisions. No one in the pecking order is exempt. Each operating company has a compliance staff to support environmental and safety efforts. Several corporate staffs provide additional information, technical support, and compliance monitoring. The vice-president for environmental affairs recommends policy changes and directs the implementation of programs and guidelines. Outside consultants are brought in to give independent opinions of the company's environmental compliance audit process and to compare it with others in the industry. In all, Chevron employs more than five hundred full-time workers in environmental, health, and safety areas.

Chevron recognizes that involvement by its employees, from top-level management to frontline personnel, is critical if it is to achieve the rigorous environmental goals it has set for itself.

Judging from a survey conducted in 1991, Chevron's employees are just as committed to the company's environmental policies as the top echelon that established them. Of the six hundred polled, 85 percent rated themselves as "identified with the term *environmentalist*," with more than a third of that 85 percent "of the most ardent variety."

A company that practices environmental action encourages voluntarism, exercises teamwork, promotes empowerment, and champions the minimization of government regulation.

Nearly nine hundred Chevron employees and members of their families demonstrated how ardent they really are by helping to restore a hundred woodland acres in Yosemite National Park in 1991. They gave many weekends to accomplish this task. Backing up their actions, Chevron contributed $200,000 to the park. In Pascagoula, Mississippi, employees created a twenty-five-acre intertidal marsh to replace wetlands that had been displaced by a refinery expansion project. Transplanting native grasses and trees to guard against erosion, they developed new wetlands that are home to fish, shrimp, crabs, mussels, birds, reptiles, raccoons, and deer.

Employees also get involved in the preservation of endangered wildlife. Near Stillwater, Montana, where Chevron mines platinum and palladium, employees aided in efforts to learn why the bighorn sheep population is declining, helping local officials tag and place radio collars on the sheep as well as on mountain lions that sometimes prey on them. They also provide the sheep with medicated feed and salt blocks to combat parasites. Chevron reseeded and fertilized a large portion of the sheep's winter grazing and was subsequently honored by the U.S. Forest Service.

Community Contact

Earning the public trust is not easy, acknowledges Chevron, but it is critical. It requires candor and a willingness to acknowledge concerns. Conceding that living next to or near petroleum and petrochemical operations is "not entirely risk free," Chevron invites the public at large and environmental groups into its facilities to learn about operational risks, safety measures, and emergency plans. Discussions and formal negotiations are encouraged for settling unresolved issues. Open lines of communication with the public and special interest groups through tours of facilities, company publications, and frequent press releases are an integral part of Chevron's policy.

In another demonstration of its goodwill, Chevron contributes more than a million dollars each year to environmental, public interest, and safety groups. The company also sponsors the Chevron Conservation Awards, an annual program that recognizes the achievements of citizen volunteers, environmental professionals, and not-for-profit as well as public agencies. "National Geographic" specials on public television are partially underwritten by Chevron.

Protecting People and Property

Earning public trust is easier when the public is confident that Chevron's operations and products do not and will not compromise the safety or health of its neighbors, employees, and customers. Sound facility design, a responsible operating philosophy, thorough training, and individual accountability all play critical roles at Chevron in meeting this commitment.

Occupational injury and illness cases among Chevron employees are consistently lower than the industry average. Company toxicologists and epidemiologists study potential long-term health risks by tracking health exams, test results, and reasons for absence. Employee illness patterns are surveyed, and similar studies are conducted for the general population. Long-term studies over the last 40 years at larger refineries reveal mortality rates among employees from all causes combined, including cancer, to be lower than in the general population.

"Deeply concerned about fire safety," Chevron has beefed up its system for identifying and correcting "process hazards"—areas of operation where equipment or procedural failures could result in fires, spills, or the release of hazardous chemicals. Company facilities have upgraded emergency procedures, operator training, and mechanical protection systems. Managers of oil fields, refineries, marketing terminals, chemical plants, and mines must participate on safety committees, and all employees must attend regular safety meetings to supplement job training and be brought up to speed on specific issues. All work areas are inspected regularly.

Safety programs are conducted that jointly train employees and others in the communities where Chevron does business. For example, a rail tanker car called the Safety Train has been transformed into a rolling classroom and travels from state to state to teach employees, fire departments, and other public emergency-response units how to handle tanker cars carrying petroleum products and other hazardous materials. Similar educational efforts have been intensified to ensure that outside contractors operate safely when working at company facilities.

Chevron operates a twenty-four-hour Emergency Information Center (CEIC) for initial telephone contact in emergencies related to its products and facilities and to respond to health, safety, and environmental questions. The telephone number appears in the material safety data sheet, on some product labels, and is also on file at poison control centers and hospitals throughout the United States. The Chemical Transportation Emergency Center (CHEMTREC), a twenty-four-hour hot line operated by the Chemical Manufacturers Association (CMA) to provide immediate information to police and fire departments during chemical emergencies, uses CEIC as its initial contact for Chevron transportation emergencies.

While preventing accidents is Chevron's first priority, the next is to respond quickly, responsibly, and effectively when accidents happen, a fact of life, asserts Chevron. Following the Alaska oil spill in 1989 and other accidents, the public became skeptical of the petroleum industry's ability to prevent and respond to spills and releases. Chevron's intensified efforts to strengthen its spill prevention and response programs are all geared toward dispelling this skepticism. In addition to stepping up training of employees in crisis communication skills, Chevron belongs to and provides major financial support for approximately fifteen major U.S. petroleum industry spill response and equipment cooperatives. The company is also involved in creating an industrywide group that will coordinate cleanup efforts in the event of a major U.S. spill. This group will spend more than $500 million by 1995 to establish cleanup staging areas and research programs.

Jumping off the Drawing Board

Using SMART tactics, Chevron is reducing or eliminating many air-quality problems, cutting water pollution, and avoiding soil and groundwater contamination. Although the largest refinery in the Los Angeles Basin, thus the largest single generator of air emissions, Chevron's El Segundo refinery has the best record among plants of similar size in terms of citations received. At the St. James, Louisiana, chemical plant, the company voluntarily installed improved seals on storage tanks to reduce benzene emissions to below state standards. At the Richmond, California, chemical plant, emissions of methylene chloride have been reduced by approximately 65 percent from 1988 reported levels. Chevron Chemical has pledged to reduce by 50 percent its level of Superfund Amendments and Reauthorization Act (SARA)-reportable air emissions by 1995.

Use of chromium as a corrosion inhibitor in water-cooling towers is being discontinued nationwide even though only California requires the ban by law. At the Richmond refinery, the company has curtailed freshwater usage by 30 percent since 1986 by recycling and reducing its use of cooling water. Although Chevron had to spend $2.6 million for equipment changes to accommodate reclaimed water, it will realize cost savings by buying "used," treated water from a local water district.

An important lesson for businesses: Companies' sincere willingness and efforts to remedy their polluting practices can help avoid the courts.

One of the problems Chevron acknowledges along with its successes in its report occurred in 1989 at the Perth Amboy refinery in New Jersey. Inaccurate testing results and a period of unusually heavy rain caused the facility to exceed permitted wastewater discharge levels. Local environmental groups and the state sued.

The refinery has since complied with permit levels and has reached a tentative settlement with the environmental groups, but rulings on state charges are still pending. In 1988 Chevron settled another suit alleging wastewater permit violations at the El Segundo refinery. By installing a new system that captures storm water in two 170,000-barrel holding tanks until it can be treated, the facility is now in compliance.

Considerable time and money has been spent restoring Chevron's plant, terminal, and service station sites that have been contaminated with oil, chemicals, or waste. Through the Tank Integrity Program, Chevron has removed, replaced, or upgraded more than 90 percent of its U.S. underground tanks since 1981 at a cost exceeding $140 million. Chevron also employs sophisticated systems to monitor its pipelines. A substantial reduction in leaks was achieved in Texas, for example, by replacing 190 miles of an older pipeline.

Many of Chevron's actions are voluntary, aimed at preventing future environmental problems. Others are the result of agreements negotiated with state or federal agencies. Chevron faces additional cleanups in conjunction with Superfund, a statute enacted by Congress in 1980. Superfund allocates tax money for identifying and cleaning up contaminated and hazardous-waste disposal sites in the United States. Companies such as Chevron must contribute funds through a tax based on production volumes for crude oil and chemical products. Even though companies may have conformed to existing laws and regulations when using disposal sites, they nevertheless must share in cleanup costs.

In the early 1990s U.S. industry was still generating 300 million tons of hazardous waste. To reduce their share, Chevron's U.S. refineries are recycling many spent catalysts instead of dumping them in landfills. In many locations bulk containers for chemicals are being reused whenever possible, and vendors are urged to take back their empty drums for refilling. Unused chemicals are returned to vendors at a savings of up to $1,000 per drum over disposal.

Oil and gas production facilities and refineries are using high-speed centrifuges and filter presses to separate oil and water from solids to recycle the oil and reduce the volume of waste sent to landfills. Huge refinery units called cokers are used in California, Mississippi, and Texas to turn oily sludge into useful products. Employees at the El Segundo refinery are pioneering a process for fully recovering valuable hydrocarbons from hazardous waste for return to the crude oil stream, resulting in a 55 percent reduction of waste since 1986. In 1991, the EPA added twenty-five chemicals to its original hazardous waste list of fourteen. Still, Chevron has been able to reduce its hazardous waste by 70 percent overall.

Using the Used

Reducing nonhazardous waste is also an important part of Chevron's conservation agenda. Paper recycling is a prime target. At Chevron's San Francisco Bay Area facilities alone, nearly 80 tons of paper is recycled each month, sparing 16,000 trees annually. A major producer of plastics, Chevron is working to solve plastic waste problems and is investigating ways to turn plastic products such as bottles and bags back into basic chemicals for reuse. Chevron continues to provide funding and technical support to the American Plastics Council, which explores options for reducing, recycling, and disposing of plastic waste. Chevron is one of eight companies in the National Polystyrene Recycling Company, whose goal is to facilitate the recycling of 25 percent of all U.S. disposable polystyrene by 1995.

Other efforts include conserving energy in the making of petroleum products and in office buildings as well. Several of Chevron's refineries are upgrading their utility systems to save as much as 100,000 to 300,000 barrels of oil per year per refinery. Collectively Chevron's recently installed cogeneration units, turbines fueled by natural gas to produce electricity, can generate enough power for a city the size of Denver.

Hi Neighbor

Alongside many of Chevron's facilities, animal and plant species, many endangered, survive and thrive. Habitat restoration and employee-awareness training are two of the programs sponsored by Chevron to protect its animal and plant neighbors. At its Pittsburgh & Midway Coal Mining operations in New Mexico, extensive efforts to restore mined lands are underway, including reintroducing ponderosa pines, developing new seeding methods to aid regrowth of natural vegetation, and introducing innovative erosion-control methods. In 1988 the company donated valuable water rights to Colorado's Gunnison River to the Nature Conservancy, a group that preserves wild areas.

An Eye on the Future

Chevron is well aware that its work is far from over. If anything, its successes have spurred it to redouble efforts. Areas to be tackled with greater energy are cleaner automotive fuels and fuel systems than are currently in use. Lower-emission gasoline and a new diesel fuel have already been introduced, and an experimental project at eight California Chevron stations is underway using methanol fuel in a fleet of government cars and trucks.

Other important pollution-prevention research efforts at Chevron focus on better methods for treating oily waste, new technologies for recycling and reusing wastewater, improved leak-detection technologies for above-ground storage tanks, and the use of microbes to treat oil-contaminated waste.

SMART is not just a flash in the pan to appease regulatory agencies and environmental groups. Its premise is intended to guide the company through the 1990s and beyond. As flea market shoppers know, one person's junk is another's treasure. Environmentally, as noted in Chevron's SMART brochure, "One company's waste stream can sometimes serve as another's feedstock."

Amoco's Environmental Policy
Spans Broad Issues

"The pro-Earth drive of the 1990s (for developing environmental so-lutions) will be more inclusive and far more successful than the confrontation-filled campaigns of previous decades," observed Richard M. Morrow, former chairman and chief executive officer of the Amoco Corporation in a special environmental issue of the company's quarterly magazine, *Span*. As a self-proclaimed leader of the international, pro-environmental cause, Amoco is candid about the varied reasons for pursuing environmental excellence in addition to the obvious ecological benefits.

First stressing that Amoco is made up of people—employees and stockholders—who want to "breathe clean air, drink safe water, and eat foods grown in good soil," Morrow also pointed out the potential contribution to profits. "Increasingly, consumers' buying patterns endorse environmentally solid performance and shun the products of companies that are perceived as indifferent, negligent, or worse," he said.

Amoco believes that its loyalty to the environment will help to attract the most talented and committed workers, greatly enriching the ranks of its company. Investors, too, will be drawn to a company that conducts itself with environmental responsibility.

Moreover Amoco recognizes that taking the initiative in environmental issues puts the company in a position to participate in crucial decisions that establish public policy and priorities. Environmental legislation will proliferate in the 1990s, and Amoco wants to be a part of that process. This involvement is reflected in Amoco's participation in and support of the tough environmental codes developed by the Chemical Manufacturers Association and the American Petroleum Institute.

Amoco considers itself fortunate for not having to choose between good business and environmental leadership. According to Amoco, outstanding environmental performance is a natural consequence of the business philosophy that steers its pursuit of earnings. While this philosophy is conservationist in the sense that waste is not tolerated, notes Amoco, it also encompasses the premise that enhanced profits are synonymous with conserving resources and reducing environmental damage.

Due Process or Not

While recognizing the need for government regulation in safeguarding the environment, Amoco voices an objection to those regulations that are "excessive, ill-conceived or unreasonable—bad for business and often environmentally counterproductive." Some government requirements for how money will be spent is another sore spot with Amoco, which believes that more could be accomplished if the same amounts were deployed in programs that would maximize the environmental benefits.

A "waste-not" approach to environmental performance will be most effective if it can be accomplished under government policy that is both smart and capable of operating in harmony with free-market incentives, contends Amoco. A better government policy, suggests Amoco, is one that takes into account all consequences of a regulation and aims at balancing goals to allow the most cost-effective use of resources. Amoco urges fairness to all competitors and built-in rewards for those that demonstrate good environmental performance.

Frances Cairncross, environmental editor for *The Economist* and author of *Costing the Earth: The Challenge for Governments, the Opportunities for Business* (Harvard Business School Press), appears to agree with at least some of this theory. In a June 1992 article in *Across the Board*, Cairncross advised that "governments need to look for the most cost-effective ways of regulating and not push regulating to the point where returns diminish sharply."

Earth, Wind, and Fire

Often more demanding than governmental requirements, Amoco's overall corporate standards for environmental quality, product safety, and the health and safety of the workplace and communities surrounding its facilities are prominently listed in the many brochures and periodicals produced by the company:

- To conduct activities in a manner consistent with appropriate safety, health, and environmental considerations.

- To manufacture and market products and furnish user information on them in a manner consistent with appropriate safety, health, and environmental considerations.

- To establish and maintain corporate controls, including periodic reviews, to ensure that the company's policy is being properly implemented and maintained.
- To work with all levels of government in the furtherance and development of appropriate public policies supportive of environmental quality, product safety, and occupational health and safety.
- To comply with applicable environmental quality, occupation health and safety, and product safety laws and regulations.
- To design, construct, and operate facilities in a manner to protect the environment and the health and safety of employees and individuals in surrounding communities.
- To safeguard employees' health through appropriate medical programs.

To oversee all of these ambitious goals, Amoco's board of directors created a committee composed mainly of nonemployee directors and chaired by a nonemployee director, Robert H. Malott, former chairman and CEO of the FMC Corporation. Other members represent academia and a wide range of business and research pursuits.

Setting the Standards

With its eye on "setting the standards by which the competition measures its own performance," Amoco employs some six hundred environmental, health, and safety professionals who represent a wide range of disciplines, including chemical, environmental, and safety engineering; hydrogeology; chemistry; biology; meteorology; toxicology; industrial hygiene; and public health. Its determination not to find any of its facilities on any future "most hazardous" list and other lingering memories of spills and accidents are, perhaps, even greater motivators for keeping one step ahead.

Since 1986 federal law has required all United States companies to make public the amounts of certain substances they emit from each of their locations. From this information a list is compiled of the five hundred most hazardous sources of emissions. In 1989 Amoco's Texas City refinery was among those given that damaging distinction because of its estimated emissions of chromium compounds, which are used in cooling water treatment. The company no longer uses chromium for this purpose at any of its refineries. The specters of Amoco *Cadiz* as well as explosions at its New Castle, Delaware, and Whiting, Indiana, facilities still haunt Amoco. The company is aware, now more than ever, that an aggressive environmental policy is the best exorcism for these ghosts.

Reduce or Remediate?

Most companies have come to realize that environmental protection is more effective and less costly if they avoid producing pollutants at the outset of operations rather than trying to reclaim them from the end process. Amoco, too, now subscribes to the general waste-minimization hierarchy: reduce waste generation as much as possible, recycle or reuse whatever one can of what's left, treat residuals to reduce volume and hazard, and dispose of what's left in an environmentally acceptable fashion.

Now with a formal waste minimization program, Amoco is constantly researching new technology and modifying old processes to minimize waste. Its chemical company, for example, reduced its hazardous waste disposal by 87 percent in 1989, based on 1983 figures, despite the manufacture of significantly higher volumes of chemicals each year. Amoco Chemical's Chocolate Bayou plant near Alvin, Texas, achieved a 55 percent reduction in waste generated per pound of production.

In 1990 Amoco Chemical Company announced its long-term goal to eliminate hazardous waste from all of its more than sixty facilities worldwide. Designating 1988 as the base year for measuring progress in waste reduction, Amoco Oil Company set its sights on a 50 percent decrease in disposed refinery waste by 1994. Amoco Production Company has inventoried thousands of its sites since 1988 and now is using the data to help evaluate a variety of new techniques to expand its waste minimization projects. One focus is on recovering larger volumes of usable hydrocarbons from all waste streams, including tank bottoms, emulsions, and various other solids and liquids.

In another breakthrough, Amoco Production Company developed a comprehensive program to evaluate the efficiency of closed-loop mud systems and is working on the development and use of more environmentally acceptable muds. These programs are now being used successfully to design new drilled solids removal systems, reducing drilling waste volumes by more than 60 percent in some U.S. drilling operations while also cutting drilling costs.

A joint Amoco-EPA study was completed in 1991 at its Yorktown, Virginia, refinery, one of six Amoco refineries operating in the United States, identifying criteria and setting priorities for emissions reduction. Amoco and the EPA determined the releases from the refinery, measuring their amount and composition. Their findings revealed that the more economically efficient reduction programs cost 20 percent of the required alternatives while being more effective. Between 1992 and 1994 Amoco will spend more than $100 million to reduce hydrocarbon and benzene emissions at Yorktown, more than it has to, says Amoco, but the effort will be more cost effective in the end.

Many of the battle plans for Amoco's war on waste are initiated by its Waste Management Committee, established in 1988. The work of this sixteen-member committee includes auditing the commercial facilities to which Amoco supplies waste for recycling, treatment, or disposal. Since this auditing process began, only about half of the disposal sites inspected have passed muster. Members also prepare an annual waste inventory, evaluate the effectiveness of its programs, and establish guidelines. The committee reports its findings and suggestions for improvement to the corporate Health, Safety, and Environmental Coordinating Committee.

Don't assume that the commercial facility recycling your company's waste is handling it correctly. Organize a committee, or hire a consultant, to audit the recyclers or treatment plants once in a while. Ask for a tour of the facility, or request a copy of its licensing report or external inspection report, before you decide to use it.

A Future in Plastics

Since the volume of all plastics before compacting amounts to between 20 and 24 percent of all garbage in landfills (16 percent after composting), recycling is critical. Contrary to public assumptions, plastics are among the easiest materials to recycle, asserts Amoco, one of some two hundred companies reclaiming millions of used plastic containers for conversion to paintbrush bristles, traffic signs, toys, floor tiles, wastebaskets, plastic lumber, and many other useful items. In fact Amoco holds a major interest in Obex, a Connecticut-based company that makes plastic lumber from commingled plastics.

As of 1990 about 20 percent of soft-drink bottles made of poly-ethylene terephthalate (PET) were being recycled for use in making textiles and fibers, appliance handles, and fiberfill for pillows, cush-ions, and ski jackets. However, only 2 percent of milk and juice con-tainers made from high-density polyethylene (HDPE) were being recycled. Amoco, along with other companies, is developing technol-ogies for reclaiming a wider variety of plastic materials, including polystyrene foam, vinyl, polyethylene films, and mixed plastics.

Polystyrene is used in fast-food containers such as trays, cups, and sandwich boxes, which several local governments are seeking to ban. In reality fast-food packaging accounts for less than one half of 1 percent of the weight of materials in landfills and no more than one-third of 1 percent of the total volume of the average landfill's contents. All the expanded polystyrene foam that is thrown away each year in the United States accounts for no more than 1 percent of the volume of landfilled garbage.

Amoco envisions an even "more significant" recycling pro-gram for these materials as a better alternative to banning them. Already most foam is blown into egg cartons, meat trays, coffee cups, packing material, and molded forms for packaging electronic equip-ment. Amoco established the world's first polystyrene recycling fa-cility, Polystyrene Recycling Inc. (PRI), in Brooklyn, New York. A subsidiary of Amoco Foam Products Company, PRI turns foam fast-food containers into polystyrene flakes that can be sold to manufac-turers of insulation board, plastic lumber, and other consumer goods.

Polyethylene can also be converted to usable energy through incineration. A pound contains more than twice as much energy as a pound of high-quality coal, although incinerators still leave about 10 percent to be placed in landfills. More than a hundred waste-to-energy incineration facilities operate in the United States, and more are planned but meet opposition in some communities. Amoco maintains that technology has advanced so far in recent years so as to minimize emissions in modern waste-to-energy in-cinerators. Virtual elimination of emissions is what these commu-nity residents are seeking before giving the green light to incinerators in their backyards.

Leaner and Meaner

Recycling plastics, though, is the second part of a four-part integrated solid-waste management system advocated by the U.S. En-vironmental Protection Agency (EPA), as well as by Amoco Chemical

Company and the chemical industry's Council for Solid Waste Solutions, of which Amoco is a founding member. Source reduction is the first part—simply create less disposable material in the first place.

PET bottles, for example, replace heavier glass bottles and have become even thinner since they were introduced. Polyethylene trash bags, too, have become leaner (and stronger), as have Amoco's Applause drinking cups, "now smaller in volume and thinner than polystyrene-bead or paper cups." Amoco says it has reduced the amount of material going into all of its foam products by 40 percent.

To Market, to Market

Finding markets for secondary materials that once would have been discarded is another breakthrough for Amoco. Its chemical division now sells waste atactic polypropylene, spent aluminum chloride, polypropylene scrap, spent caustic, waste terephthalic acid, and wastepaper. The Whiting refinery sold 6,832 tons of a spent catalyst to another company that can use this in place of conventional raw materials.

Exchanging wastes is another form of waste management in which several of Amoco Oil's refineries are participating. It now appears that one facility's overflow can be a source of energy for another. For example, 879 tons of a spent catalyst generated at the Yorktown refinery was sent to Amoco refineries in Whiting, Indiana, and Casper, Wyoming, because, unlike Yorktown, they have units that are capable of using a lower-grade catalyst.

Energy conservation programs that include the installation of cogeneration units at several Amoco locations not only produce enough electricity for the company's own facilities but an excess that is sold to local power companies. Amoco estimates annual savings on its electricity costs in the hundreds of millions, not to mention some 200 trillion BTUs of energy compared with 1972 figures, when Amoco Corporation and its subsidiaries formally began energy conservation programs.

A pilot program Amoco conducted at thirty-two Illinois service stations in 1990 could serve as a model for the rest of the country. Motorists were encouraged to take their used motor oil to one of the participating service stations for recycling. Amoco's refinery in Whiting, Indiana, reprocessed the oil into new products or used it as fuel for the refinery.

According to the EPA, at least 180 million gallons of used oil are discarded improperly each year by do-it-yourself oil changers. If all of that were recovered and converted to fuel oil, it would supply the whole nation for about five days. Collected and burned to produce electricity, the discarded oil could yield enough power to supply about nine hundred thousand homes for a year.

Open Doors

Intensive environmental efforts and open-door policies appear to go hand in hand, and Amoco is among the many companies that embrace this partnership. Not only does it invite the public and the government to give their input, it also promises to disclose to employees and the public incidents relating to its operations that cause environmental harm or pose health or safety hazards.

Whistle-blowers, employees who report dangerous or illegal conditions in the workplace, are assured that there will be no repercussions for their actions. In fact they are encouraged to call the company's attention to any threatening situations, which Amoco pledges to report to the proper government authorities "if such situations are significant."

The one aspect of Amoco's plan not included in its printed literature is employee participation in its development and implementation. Only one quote by Roy L. Hutson, manager of environmental affairs and safety for Amoco Production Company, makes reference to "enlisting the help of each employee to minimize the impact of our exploration and production operations on the environment." That's because employee value and enthusiasm in this area is a given, claims Amoco, pointing out that while management can dictate, employee cooperation on every level is critical to the success of any plan.

Always Prepared

A Crisis Management Program was implemented in 1990 to make sure that the company is aware of potential catastrophes and is prepared to deal with them. This includes major explosions, chemical releases, and natural disasters. While no one wants an emergency, says Amoco, "one can occur even though exemplary efforts have been made to prevent it." Cooperation between company facilities and community agencies is necessary to respond effectively, notes Amoco, which sponsors periodic programs to foster this cooperation.

As a member of the Marine Spill Response Corporation (MSRC), Amoco is among the oil industry leaders working together to deal quickly and efficiently with catastrophic oil spills. Despite the lessons of the past, no one is yet ready to guarantee that it can't or won't happen again. Five regional MSRC centers would have a response capability for oil spills of up to 216,000 barrels, approximately the size of 1989's Exxon *Valdez* spill. Amoco and its subsidiaries are members of a number of other consortia that are trained and equipped to prevent oil spills or to minimize their impact if they do occur.

Safe and proper use of its products is another concern addressed by Amoco. The company provides material safety data sheets printed in several languages to explain the safe and correct use of Amoco's thousands of products, even though these instructions are required only for hazardous substances. Toxicological evaluations of its products are performed by the Illinois Institute of Technology's independent Research Institute; the products are then analyzed by Amoco's own toxicology staff to determine the kinds of protection needed for employees and customers. A Product Classification and Labeling Committee has the power to require any restrictions or conditions on the sale of a product or to prohibit the sale entirely.

Amoco admits to animal testing for providing "reliable health information" about its products, although "not when there is a realistic alternative." Tests involving animals are conducted in a dedicated contract laboratory that is inspected and fully accredited by the American Association for Animal Care. Openly apologetic for the necessity of these tests (many nonanimal tests are not recognized by the general scientific community or government agencies), Amoco continues to search for alternative methods and supports other agencies in their efforts.

Fueling the Future

According to an Amoco report, America's petroleum refineries fill 43 percent of the national demand for energy, 65 percent when natural gas is counted. Yet, claims Amoco, the 193 refineries in the United States supply this huge share while contributing very little to the nation's total air pollution. Additionally, since 1970, airborne lead is down 95 percent, sulfur dioxide is down 17 percent, and carbon monoxide emissions are down 25 percent even though vehicle miles traveled have increased 25 percent.

Although Amoco acknowledges that alternate fuels such as compressed natural gas, methanol, and ethanol will have roles in improving the nation's air quality even further, the company believes that a combination of reformulated gasoline and modified engine designs is the dominant factor in improving air quality. The company urges the government to allow the competitive marketplace the freedom to decide which fuel or fuels will meet regulations for improved air quality and not mandate the use of any fuel that could discourage searches for solutions that would be better in terms of cost, efficiency, or environmental benefits. While conducting what it terms a "major research program," Amoco is also a member and supports the efforts of the Clean Air Working Group, a broad-based national coalition of small and large businesses and trade associations that promotes cost-effective means to improve the quality of America's air.

Global Responsibility

Increased involvement by U.S. business in helping to formulate the global environmental philosophy would have a major impact on how the world community deals with U.S. commerce and industry, stresses Amoco. The company is developing new international environmental and safety policies for Amoco Corporation and its subsidiaries. This new company policy will meet the legal requirements of all of the forty nations in which it now operates, including the United States. Most significant in this approach, asserts Amoco, is that "the natural environment does not recognize national borders. Our job is to do everything required to protect, preserve, and—where and when necessary—clean up our environment."

Monsanto Takes the Pledge

A worldwide company employing some thirty-two thousand people, Monsanto is composed of the Monsanto Company and four subsidiaries: the Chemical Group, the Agricultural Group, Searle (prescription pharmaceuticals), and the NutraSweet Company (food products). A fifth—Fisher Controls International, makers of industrial process control equipment—was sold in 1992.

Make your environmental program an effective part of your marketing and public relations campaign. Environmental concerns influence consumers' purchasing decisions. Today's consumers, aware of the global environmental crisis, are demanding environmental correctness in all products and services. The seriousness of your program is conveyed to your vendors and employees. Plus, it can serve as a means to transfer information to others in your industry and to illustrate the common need for rethinking business practices.

As with most industrial companies over the last decades, Monsanto has been conditioned by governmental command-and-control regulations. Now Monsanto is primarily motivated by the realization that environmental improvement "is essential for any company that seeks society's endorsement for products and practices." Based on that reality, Monsanto is reengineering processes to avoid making waste in the first place and to save valuable raw materials and energy. This not only achieves environmental improvement, notes Monsanto, but "presents yet another opportunity for competitive cost reduction."

Monsanto continues to be listed among the largest emitters of toxic chemicals in the United States, though Monsanto argues that "none have caused an immediate hazard." But Monsanto has pledged "to do what's right for the environment." In its annual environmental review, Monsanto outlines its pledge to

- reduce all toxic and hazardous releases and emissions, working toward an ultimate goal of zero effect;

- ensure no Monsanto operation poses any undue risk to employees and communities;

- work to achieve sustainable agriculture through new technology and practices;

- ensure groundwater safety;

- keep plants open to communities and involve the community in plant operations;

- manage all corporate real estate, including plant sites, to benefit nature;

- search worldwide for technology to reduce and eliminate waste from operations with the top priority being not making it in the first place.

Pollution Control

By mid-1992 Monsanto was well on its way to living up to its pledge. Air emissions of toxic chemicals were reduced by 66 percent, and the company was quickly closing in on its goal of achieving a 90 percent reduction by the end of that year. As with many companies, Monsanto was spurred on to more voluntary programs when good results were achieved, both environmentally and financially. A broader voluntary program to reduce effects on air, land, and water by 70 percent by 1995 was adopted. Targeted for reduction are approximately 240 million pounds of chemicals, at the source whenever possible.

One by one, Monsanto's facilities are showing improvement at an impressive rate. The Sauget, Illinois, plant reduced air emissions of toxic chemicals 66 percent between 1987 and 1991, from 3.8 million pounds per year to 1.3 million. In 1991 Sauget also began operating a wastewater pretreatment system that removes 1.8 million pounds of organic chemicals from the plant's wastewater each year. Of this, 1.2 million pounds is recycled and reused, the remainder destroyed in an off-site treatment facility.

The manufacturing process for Saflex, used to reinforce automotive windshields, has been modified. Now thousands of pounds of scrap material once put in landfills are being recycled. In Muscatine, Iowa, 3,500 tons of fly ash, generated during the combustion of coal to make steam, is now used in the manufacture of cement. Not so long ago this material was bound for landfills.

Working toward zero waste, Monsanto applied some new important technology at the Luling, Louisiana, plant in the manufacture of an intermediate chemical, phosphorus trichloride. Because of these improvements, manufacturing capacity was doubled while toxic air emissions were reduced by 82 percent and total waste generation by 50 percent at that site by 1992. Also accomplished at Luling are completely automated unloading and loading operations and the company's first enclosed phosphorus trichloride loading system, reducing air emissions and eliminating the possibility of accidental releases from leaks.

Conservation Cuts Costs

Demonstrating once again that what is good for the environment can also be good for business, a comprehensive program to use, recycle, and eliminate hazardous waste by 1995 lists as one of its successes a system at the Searle plant in Augusta, Georgia, that eliminates the off-site transport and destruction of 600,000 gallons of waste solvent per year. Millions of dollars are saved by eliminating these disposal costs and the need to buy fresh solvent.

Also in Augusta, engineers at NutraSweet continue to optimize the reuse of flammable process waste as fuel in plant boilers. In Alabama a Waste to Profits Quality Improvement Team at the Anniston plant developed technology to burn approximately 2 million pounds of solid waste as fuel, thereby reducing annual costs of waste disposal and natural gas usage by more than $1 million.

Team Work

While Monsanto concedes that its more recent environmental practices and procedures have not yet been recognized and accepted by all of its businesses across the corporation, it cites numerous success stories to demonstrate that most of its people are "working to turn the vision of the Monsanto Pledge into reality."

One employee at the Greenwood, South Carolina, plant established a resource council to support environmental programs in a seven-county area. Employees of the Fisher Controls plant (still a Monsanto subsidiary at the time) reduced hazardous waste generation by 92 percent, compared with 1988 figures, and cut toxic air emissions by 72 percent. They also developed programs for recycling, customer and community awareness, and emergency preparedness. Some plants cosponsor environmental activities on Earth Day.

Members of the Utilities Team at the W. G. Krummrich plant in Sauget, Illinois, found an innovative way to turn scrap tires into fuel for the plant's steam-generating boilers. By using a blend of coal and scrap tires, they developed a lower-cost fuel that burns cleaner than coal alone. More than a million tires were used in this manner in 1992, safely and economically, ridding the earth of a blight that breeds insects, poses fire hazards, and does not degrade in the environment.

To recognize the contribution of its people toward environmental, safety, and health improvements, the Monsanto Pledge Awards were created. Four employee teams are honored annually, one in each of four categories: pledge performance, innovation, marketplace, and community service. Each award includes a donation of $25,000 to the environmental group or project designated by the winning teams.

Involving the Community

The public has an inherent distrust of any chemical-based operation, and Monsanto is working diligently to earn confidence. Merely pledging to conduct safe, environmentally responsible operations is not enough, acknowledges Monsanto. Its approaches to building "community partnerships" are keeping plants open to scrutiny, involving the community in operations, listening to their concerns, and finding the best solution to problems.

In addition to having formed fourteen community advisory panels, which Monsanto says are "changing the way plants and their neighbors communicate with one another," Monsanto facilities throughout the country are implementing programs to bring their neighbors into the fold. In Pensacola, Florida, some six hundred came to call and were greeted by volunteer firefighters from the community who had attended a day of emergency training at the plant. They passed out printed materials produced by the plant giving background information on the operation, emergency telephone numbers, the plant manager's telephone number, and an outline of environmental programs. This was the first of regularly scheduled plant open houses.

The Greenwood plant helped to found an Environmental Resource Council, a coalition of businesses, hospitals, schools, and other organizations, to keep up to date on and respond to demands of increasingly complex environmental regulations. One of the council's self-imposed functions is to arrange for the pickup of household wastes from homes in a seven-county area.

Monsanto employees are encouraged to give freely of their time and skills to local communities. In Springfield, Massachusetts, Indian Orchard plant workers participated in river cleanup projects, an energy efficiency exhibit at the local science center, an emergency community planning committee that raised money for emergency equipment, and a wildlife area survey that was done in conjunction with a local affiliate of the National Audubon Society. A sales representative created the Southern Iowa Herbicide Education Program to address farmers' concerns about runoff of herbicides and fertilizers into groundwater and drinking water.

In 1992 Monsanto published its annual environmental review for the second time, and the company intends to produce one each year complete with an updated section of charts and statistics to track its progress toward pollution prevention goals. Press releases on programs are periodically placed in newspapers. Slide shows are put on by plant managers for their communities. These and future efforts at becoming part of the community, declares Monsanto, are essential to earning the continued right to operate.

At the Root of New Technologies

The earth's population of 5.3 billion has doubled in the past forty years and is expected to grow by more than 3 billion by 2025. Farmers will have to produce more food in the next forty years than has been grown since agriculture began. Monsanto is striving to help them meet that need. Production of high-quality, safe, abundant, and affordable food supplies must, however, be accomplished through environmentally sound methods. To that end, Monsanto's plant sciences researchers are developing genetically improved food and fiber plants, ones that have natural defenses against pests or viral infections.

During 1991 large-scale field tests were conducted on cotton plants that make their own natural insecticide. The plants protect themselves by producing a protein that is lethal when ingested by undesirable insects such as the cotton bollworm but does not affect honeybees and other beneficial insects and is harmless to people, animals, and the environment. In addition to increasing farmers' yields at lower cost, this innovation could greatly reduce the amount of insecticides needed to produce cotton. Field research programs were also conducted on soybeans, corn, tomatoes, potatoes, canola, and sugar beets.

Reaching for a Star

A voluntary Protection Program at thirty Monsanto facilities in the United States is striving for "star" status, an honor bestowed by the Occupational Safety and Health Administration (OSHA) on facilities that develop safety programs and practices far beyond those required by law. Monsanto boasts that its injury and illness rate is already about one-third that of the chemical industry as a whole, but it is accelerating efforts to ensure that all facilities pass OSHA's rigorous audits. Its safety commitment extends to contract employees, visitors, and anyone on Monsanto property.

Moreover Monsanto is strengthening programs to ensure the safe use, handling, and transportation of hazardous chemicals. An employee team has produced videos demonstrating safe methods of loading and unloading materials. It also holds safety meetings at every U.S. customer location and outlines to community emergency response organizations safe methods of responding to a spill or a fire.

Results achieved at the Pensacola, Florida, plant are now serving as a model for other Monsanto operations. Through a comprehensive safety training program and continuous audits of performance, an 82 percent reduction in injuries and illnesses was achieved in a five-years period. Pensacola was the first manufacturing operation in the state of Florida and in Monsanto to achieve star status from OSHA. Zero incidents and zero accidents are Monsanto's vision.

Communing with Nature

Natural habitats around the country are being preserved or restored with the help of Monsanto agricultural products. A good example is the Prime Hook National Wildlife Refuge in Delaware, where Rodeo herbicide helps control a reed called phragmites, which threatens to choke marshlands important to thirty thousand migratory ducks.

Near Soda Springs, Idaho, where Monsanto mines phosphate ore, the source of chemicals used in products ranging from soft drinks to telephone cords, it carefully replanted and reclaimed hundreds of acres around its Henry Mine. The land has been restored in harmony with the natural surroundings. These efforts were recognized in 1991 by the U.S. Bureau of Land Management with its Partners in Public Spirit Award, the highest it bestows.

Employees from the Columbia plant in Tennessee turned the former manufacturing site into a five-thousand-acre wildlife sanctuary that includes large blinds for wildlife observation by the public. In St. Charles, Missouri, a group of employees volunteered to create an eleven-acre environmental education park and helped to raise more than $150,000 in grants and aid. Called the Henderson Forest, the park was designed to grow almost 140 native and indigenous woody plant species and is a wildlife habitat supporting several species of birds and animals.

Beyond the Limits of the Law

Now driven more by public sentiment than regulations, Monsanto is moving its operating procedures well beyond what the law requires. It is proving that manufacturing efficiency and environmental protection go hand in hand. "It's the right thing to do," concludes Monsanto in one of its reports, "a sound business strategy that will promote more efficiency, less waste, and higher-value products for our customers."

Ciba Has Tradition and Vision

How can a conglomerate as large as Ciba keep up with environmental concerns? "How can it not?" asks Richard Barth, chairman, president, and CEO of Ciba-Geigy Corporation, the U.S. subsidiary of Ciba-Geigy Limited of Basel, Switzerland. "Ciba is one worldwide company that has always taken its environmental responsibility very seriously."

Ciba's policy under its Vision 2000 plan "requires a reasonable balance between our economic, social, and environmental responsibilities." The company says it is "continually striving to operate without adversely affecting the environment and to conform with all applicable laws and regulations, while ensuring the prosperity of our enterprise beyond the year 2000."

Operating worldwide in the areas of pharmaceutical, biological, and chemical specialties, Ciba-Geigy Limited employs ninety-two thousand people in more than sixty countries. The company offers products and services to customers in health care, agriculture, and the manufacturing and industrial markets. Headquartered in Ardsley, New York, Ciba's U.S. arm employs seventeen thousand people and records more than $4 billion in annual sales.

Economic use of natural resources, optimal production processes, workplace safety, waste minimization, responsible disposal of unavoidable waste, and safe, environmentally compatible products have traditionally been, and will continue to be, Ciba's primary objectives. All of these points and more are outlined in Ciba's *Principles for Environmental Protection in Production*, an international environmental policy that applies to all Ciba companies worldwide. Among its top priorities is solving environmental problems at the source.

Environmental protection measures are a positive challenge and not a hindrance to its operations, asserts Ciba. The company says that its overall strategic business direction is aimed to "reduce the impact of our products on the environment, whether in research and development, production or eventual disposal, and to conduct business in a socially responsible manner by keeping employees, neighbors, customers and the media fully informed of what we are doing."

Open to the Public

Ciba reports its commitment to environmental practices in company publications, and updates are periodically released to the press. Company representatives speak often at public conclaves to share information on its policies and practices. In addition, a number

191

of Ciba divisions and production facilities have established advisory panels that directly involve local citizens in ongoing Ciba activities.

Perhaps even more significant is Ciba's open communication with the general public. "Historically our industry has tended to keep a high fence—literally and figuratively—between ourselves and neighbors," concedes Joseph T. Sullivan, Ciba-Geigy Corporation vice-president. "We said, 'Chemistry is complicated. They won't understand it. And besides, our processes and technology are confidential.' We've learned the hard way that that doesn't always work."

Ciba's difficulties with the international environmental group Greenpeace in 1984 at Ciba's Toms River, New Jersey, plant is an ideal example of how problems can be exacerbated when a company resists dialogue with the public. Treated wastewater from the Toms River plant used to be discharged through a ten-mile-long pipeline to the Atlantic Ocean. Considered "a symbol of environmental abuse" by the public, the wastewater "would meet drinking water standards (with the exception of salts)," maintained Ciba, "and repeatedly was proven to be harmless to marine life and bathers."

When the pipeline sprung a leak a few months later, Greenpeace members occupied the plant's 165-foot water tower for two days in a highly publicized attempt to call attention to the ocean discharge. The hole had been quickly repaired, but the hue and cry continued. Understandably concerned over what was seeping into neighborhoods along the pipeline's path, the public looked to Ciba for answers. Many felt that the information they received was incomplete and, in some cases, inaccurate.

Anti-pipeline sentiment persisted although Ciba insisted that it far surpassed the requirements of the most stringent discharge permit of its kind in the country and that countless scientific studies revealed that the treated wastewater was harmless. Ciba eventually closed the pipeline at the end of 1991.

Earlier, in 1988, public opinion had prevented the construction of a proposed pharmaceuticals facility at one of Ciba's locations. Ciba now concedes that a more forthright approach to the public's concerns at the outset could have fostered better understanding and cooperation for existing and future projects. "Public involvement, not exclusion, is the name of the game for the future," promises Ciba.

Now much more sensitive to the very serious credibility gap that the chemical industry faces between the environmental protection efforts it undertakes and the perception the public has of the industry, Ciba involves the public in managing its environmental safety practices. The company encourages the public to learn about Ciba facilities in their communities, inviting concerned citizens and groups to visit its operations, to ask questions, and to make suggestions. The company has found that even in the most controversial situations, inviting people in and explaining what the plant does, thus showing its facilities and "human faces," the reaction is invariably positive. "Openness," asserts Ciba, "promotes discourse, discourse promotes dialogue, and dialogue promotes compromise and understanding."

Keeping up the Guard

The best way to avoid public consternation is to prevent incidents from occurring. Ciba is scrupulous about policing itself. Comprehensive audits are periodically held at all U.S. facilities to ensure that each is complying with environmental, health, and safety laws as well as with company policies and standards, which frequently exceed the requirements of law. Company auditors meet with site management, interview employees, and tour the facility. Audits take from a few days to as much as two or three weeks.

Findings are presented by the auditors to site management, which is required to develop a formal action plan addressing each finding. Quarterly progress reports are required. All of these reports and findings weave their way through the hierarchy, from the divisional and corporate managers right up to the CEO. The audit programs are periodically evaluated by outside experts to ensure "they are state-of-the-art."

Our Brothers' Keepers

Ciba participates in many efforts that promise to have positive effects. When the Chemical Manufacturers Association (CMA) introduced Responsible Care, the chemical industry's performance-based initiative, in 1988, Ciba quickly joined with other CMA member companies to implement the program's six "Codes of Management Practices."

Responsible Care illustrates by performance that the industry is committed to handling products and the environment in ways the public will accept. "It's not an easy standard," points out Dr. Sullivan, "because the public's requirement today is simple: Zero defects. We continue to be challenged, well aware that institutionalizing the environmental ethic is not optional in our industry; it's a requirement to achieve public acceptance and survival."

The six codes of Responsible Care, listed here, establish performance standards for the broad scope of industry activities.

1 Community awareness and emergency response to ensure preparedness and to foster the community's right to know.

2 Pollution prevention to promote industry efforts to protect the environment by generating less waste and reducing pollutant emissions.

3 Process safety to prevent fires, explosions, and accidental chemical releases.

4 Distribution to reduce the risk that the transportation and storage of chemicals pose to the public, carriers, customers, contractors, and company employees and to the environment.

5 Employee health and safety to protect the people working at or visiting CMA member-company sites.

6 Product stewardship to promote the safe handling of chemicals at all stages, from initial manufacture to distribution, sale, and ultimate disposal.

Committees were set up in various Ciba facilities to evaluate where improvements according to these codes could be made and to monitor implementation. At the Additives Division "AddCare" was established as part of the division's increased customer focus. Its intention is to develop more environmentally preferable chemical processes, products, and product packaging.

At the McIntosh, Alabama, site a Responsible Care oversight committee was formed, assigning a chairman and a work group for each code. These groups wrote detailed, comprehensive work plans that serve as models for other Ciba facilities. The St. Gabriel, Louisiana, plant has a twelve-person Responsible Care committee, which includes representatives from each department or area. Committee members at St. Gabriel meet each week to review progress and provide recommendations on such issues as community outreach efforts, risk communications to employees and the public, and the sharing of safety information with the government and the community. Their efforts quickly resulted in a number of improvements, including the development of a system to eliminate fumes during drum loading.

For areas of particular concern to a number of divisions, generic action plans were developed that could be fine-tuned by local coordinators for their specific business units. Since CMA survey data indicate that the general public's single greatest area of concern has to do with the transportation of chemicals through U.S. communities, high priority was given by coordinators to the distribution code.

The CMA codes were augmented in 1991 when the Corporate Governance Committee of Ciba's U.S. board of directors initiated a project to establish baseline expectations and procedures to be applied throughout the U.S. company in the areas of health, safety, and the environment. With the cooperation of division, corporate, and plant representatives, this work was embodied in an updated *Corporate Health, Safety and Environmental Policies and Procedures Manual.* The manual informs employees of Ciba's requirements in these areas in order to make these standards an integral part of designing, manufacturing, distributing, using, recycling, and disposing of Ciba products.

Reduction at the Source

Until recently the focus of environmental concerns and solutions was on the end of the production process. Today Ciba continually assesses its chemical processes, using advanced scientific methods to identify ways to improve the beginning stages of production, which reduces the amount of waste generated at the end.

Tighter controls at the design stage is critical, Ciba believes. This is particularly true of facilities that produce many different products, such as the McIntosh site, which makes over three hundred. Adapting new processes in the production of fluorescent optical brighteners, for example, has achieved a significant waste reduction. By elim-

Pollution is waste. Prevention at the source saves money, material, and time.

inating some steps during production, 48,000 pounds per day of sulfuric acid waste is no longer generated, and the production of 33,000 pounds per day of iron sludge, a nonhazardous solid waste that must be sent to landfills, was eliminated.

Ciba Vision Corporation in Atlanta, Georgia, producers of contact lens and lens care products, achieved a 70 percent reduction by 1991 in its emissions of freon, a fluorinated hydrocarbon used to process contact lenses. Aware of the public's concern over the destructive effects of freon on the upper atmosphere, Ciba Vision is working toward the eventual elimination of all freon use.

195

Also high on the public's concern list were the health risks from heavy metals and solvents used in pigments. In response Ciba developed pigments that reduce risk to the environment while maintaining the efficacy of the product. In 1987 Ciba invented an organic red pigment, Irgazin DPP, for automobile paints, the first to be introduced in twenty-five years. DPP contains none of the heavy metals, such as lead, cadmium, or barium, that are hazardous to human health.

Another product for the auto industry was developed by Ciba and is used in automotive defrost grids and "blackouts" around windshields to protect adhesives from degradation. It can be dried through ultraviolet light instead of traditional methods of heat to drive off excess solvents. This high-solids coating has low emissions.

Investments in Our Future

Ciba is making significant investments so that its facilities nationwide will be model plants that lead the chemical industry in safety, environmental protection, and quality as well as economical production. The company invested more than $500 million in environmental protection improvements and cleanups in the United States between 1985 and 1992.

In 1992 Ciba's Toms River, New Jersey, plant was honored by the National Environmental Awards Council with a Renew America Certificate of Achievement for its efforts in reducing wastewater in the dye-standardization process. The project is known by the acronym SWEAT (Standardization Without Effluent at Toms River) and uses ultra-filtration, reverse osmosis, and high-pressure cleaning technology in this process. Wastewater was reduced from 400,000 gallons per day to an average of 4,500—nearly a 99 percent reduction. Additionally, about 200 pounds of dye per day is recovered. This was the second award for the Toms River site from the council. In 1990 Ciba was recognized for the significant improvements made to the plant's wastewater treatment facility.

Between 1985 and 1990, Toms River expended over forty man-years of research and spent $25 million to meet the requirements of the most stringent wastewater discharge permit ever issued in the United States. Requirements were met two and half years ahead of schedule. In recognition of its achievements, Toms River was presented with the Excellence in Industrial Wastewater Treatment Award from the New Jersey Water Pollution Control Association.

At the McIntosh, Alabama, site, $70 million was committed to building a state-of-the-art wastewater collection and treatment plant.

In addition, air emissions at that facility were reduced 44 percent in 1991 due to process changes and the installation of additional control devices. In the spring of 1992, Delta, the Textile Products Division's $70 million dyes manufacturing facility, was dedicated in a public ceremony held at the St. Gabriel, Louisiana, site. Delta's cutting-edge technologies provide for both reduction of waste at the source and the reuse and recycling of waste materials.

Through process changes and improved engineering controls, the St. Gabriel plant achieved a 42 percent reduction in its total Title III air emissions within three years (1987–90). Emissions of toluene, its major Title III compound, were 90 percent eliminated by 1992. In addition, operation of a new vent gas combustor at St. Gabriel has reduced carbon tetrachloride emissions by about 50 percent. At St. Gabriel a new biologically activated sludge wastewater treatment system was completed in late 1992, which will further reduce discharges to the Mississippi River. State-of-the-art incineration units for both St. Gabriel and the McIntosh production sites will be installed by the end of 1993 at a cost of $69 million.

Surpassing EPA Goals

Ciba's divisions and plants decreased the company's overall SARA Title III emissions by more than 30 percent between 1990 and 1991. This brought down total emissions since 1988 by 46 percent—from 11.1 million pounds in 1988 to 6 million pounds in 1991. Another 5 percent in SARA emissions were decreased in 1992. Ciba's Health Tecna Aerospace Company (part of the Composite Materials Division) received an Air Quality Environmental Excellence Award from the Association of Washington Businesses for reducing its SARA III emissions by 65 percent since 1989, making it one of four finalists for the 1992 (Washington State) Governor's Award for Outstanding Achievement in Pollution Prevention.

By the fall of 1992, Ciba surpassed the initial goal for emissions reduction identified in the Industrial Toxics Project (ITP), a voluntary environmental program, commonly referred to as the 33/50 Program, established by the U.S. Environmental Protection Agency (EPA) in 1991. Ciba exceeded the 1992 goal of a 33 percent reduction by installing dust collection systems to recover and reuse lead, cadmium, and chromium in pigment production, installing refrigerated condensers that recover solvents during chemical manufacturing, and practicing preventive maintenance with special emphasis on leak detection and repair on all manufacturing equipment containing seventeen targeted

ITP chemicals. These replacements and adjustments eliminated more than a million pounds in releases of chemicals on the 33/50 list and reduced waste in areas not specified under the program. The use of tetrachloroethylene was totally eliminated. EPA's goal is a 50 percent reduction by 1995 of the seventeen 33/50 chemicals.

A Common Goal

Employees, too, actively implement Ciba's environmental policies. Both knowledge of and compliance with Ciba's updated *Corporate Health, Safety and Environmental Policies and Procedures Manual* is required of all Ciba-Geigy Corporation employees. Companywide education and awareness sessions are conducted to convey both the message and the spirit of the new manual. The company encourages initiative and self-responsibility among its employees.

For example, in the Pharmaceuticals Division, headquartered in Summit, New Jersey, workers who are closest to waste problems are encouraged to help solve them. Five waste minimization teams were established within the division, focusing their solutions on key stages in the production cycle, from packaging and printing to disposal of nonusable products. These teams are developing innovative techniques to eliminate waste.

Sorted, recycled office paper is a precious commodity. When we recycle a ton of paper, seventeen trees and 3 cubic yards of landfill space are saved. Recycled paper is used to make other paper goods.

In fact the Additives Division and its packaging supplier Bonar Incorporated of Ontario, Canada, won the first Ron Hayter Award for environmentally responsible plastic packaging. On the premise that less is more, a rubber-reinforced polystyrene package that disappears upon use was developed. When a 25-pound sack of Ciba's best-selling Irganox 1076 antioxidant is added to the production process, the bag dissolves and releases the chemical into the polystyrene mixture. The soluble package minimizes user exposure to dust, and there's no container to throw away.

An extensive paper recycling program, where employees separate office paper, magazines, newspapers, and computer paper, has salvaged hundreds of tons of paper. Thousands of tons of other recyclable materials have been gathered as well. For example, at the Ardsley, New York, headquarters, more than 90 tons of paper, 3,000 pounds of glass, 14 tons of scrap metal, and 2,000 wooden pallets were recycled in 1991, while the McIntosh, Alabama, facility recycled 87 tons of paper.

The Pharma Division's Environmental Awareness Team went one step further by retrieving twenty-five thousand sheets of outdated company letterhead from the recycling bin. Convinced that the paper could do more good "as is," they looked around and found an area school that needed paper for lessons. The team's conviction that there's more than one way to recycle paper was most appropriately demonstrated.

Even the workers who are not active participants in creating and implementing environmental programs at Ciba's many facilities have gotten into the act. Conferences for "nonenvironmental managers" bring them up to speed on all efforts, from waste reduction at the source to postproduction resource recovery, as well as on all the acronyms for the myriad programs. Involvement, even at this level, gives these "nonenvironmental" types a better handle on their personal responsibilities in this critical area. A videotape and written materials from one such conference held for employees in New York and New Jersey is in great demand at other Ciba locations throughout the country.

Waste Full

Although the recycling or elimination of everything used is the goal of the future, Ciba still has to deal with the reality of waste management now. Its teams of scientists and engineers are striving to develop innovative technologies to ensure that wastes that can't be eliminated or recycled are managed safely.

These efforts resulted in the development of the Volatile Organic Substance Capture and Treatment System, for which Ciba Corporation was issued a U.S. patent in 1990. The system is used in Ciba's high-tech wastewater treatment facility at the Toms River plant and eliminates 97 percent of all volatile emissions from the facility, exceeding the most stringent requirements for wastewater treatment in any state.

In 1985 Ciba received the first U.S. permit for an above-ground hazardous waste landvault. Built at the company's chemical plant in McIntosh, Alabama, the landvault offers the most appropriate means currently available to Ciba for handling a variety of wastes. According to a spokesman for Molten Metal Technologies, an environmental consulting firm in Waltham, Massachusetts, while a landvault may not be the most sophisticated way of handling waste, it is an effective means of storing extremely pernicious waste for which there is no other available means of elimination, such as incineration or landfilling. Landvaulting has a very long shelf-life, from tens to hundreds of years. Ciba, as a responsible, environmentally cautious company, regularly monitors the safety of its landvaults. Ground and surface waters are protected from waste contamination since a landvault is double lined and totally enclosed. Construction of a second landvault at McIntosh was completed during 1992.

Working to reduce the number of pesticide containers disposed of each year, Ciba's Plant Protection Division introduced its first recycled, refillable plastic pesticide container in 1992. The 60-gallon Field Pak can be refilled and used for about five years, at which time it is recycled to make a new Field Pak. Ciba is the first pesticide company to recycle old pesticide containers into new ones.

In 1988 Ciba's Additives Division redesigned its packaging to make it environmentally sound. Its "supersacks" are large bags that can hold medium-volume product shipments. Each supersack used removes eleven to fourteen fiber drums from the waste stream. The companywide Packaging Task Force works closely with such organizations as the American Plastics Council and the Society of the Plastics Industry.

Reaping the Harvest

One by-product of Ciba's manufacturing process at the St. Gabriel, Louisiana, facility no longer has to be disposed of at a secure landfill. Since 1985 area farmers are encouraged to take, free of charge, this calcium carbonate compound called RECAL II to reduce the acidity levels of their soil, a major problem in parts of the South. More than 600 tons of this lime grit waste is produced each year at this facility.

Crop yields improved significantly where RECAL II was applied at normal rates. In four years about ten farmers in the East Baton Rouge Parish saved about $75,000 on lime costs on 840 acres, not to mention the cost savings from their more efficient use of fertilizers. The RECAL II program has proved to be one of Ciba's best and most innovative success stories.

Farmers benefit in a variety of ways from Ciba's research and development programs. The herbicide Beacon is one outstanding example. Unlike traditional herbicides, Beacon is highly active at low-use rates—about three-quarters of an ounce per acre, compared with pounds per acre of older products. This means less chemical load on the environment.

The product is packaged in premeasured, water-soluble packets called Accupaks. A carton the size of a child's shoe box holds five resealable bags with five Accupaks in each, enough to treat fifty acres of corn to control problem grasses. The water-soluble packets dissolve in the spray tank, leaving no chemically contaminated waste to dispose of.

Call of the Wild

Wildlife species are living in harmony with their Ciba neighbors. In fact Ciba continues to foster relationships between its plant sites and local and environmental organizations and agencies to provide guidance and financial support for sound wildlife management practices. In 1989 the McIntosh site was presented with the Mobile Bay Audubon Society Annual Award for its efforts to safeguard human health and environment.

The Toms River plant gives financial support to Trout Unlimited, a national conservation organization, for studies of Toms River water quality and trout-stocking activities. In addition, twelve thousand seedlings and saplings were planted with assistance from Ocean County and the Boy Scouts of America. This facility provides a habitat for a number of wildlife species, including deer, fox, and bluebirds.

Safety First

Ciba also has a commitment to the safety of its two-legged neighbors. Its facilities are well prepared to deal with any chemical emergency. Preparedness plans are in place and regularly updated. Mock emergencies are staged to train local fire and police departments.

Ciba's McIntosh plant is an industry leader in safety, the recipient of the 1988 National Safety Council's Award of Merit. In 1989 the plant became only the 64th industrial site out of 5 million in the U.S. to receive the coveted OSHA "star" designation. To qualify, the plant had to pass a week-long inspection. A near-perfect safety and health program is required for this prestigious stamp of approval.

While Ciba has its own corporatewide program to handle all emergencies, it is tied into a network of organizations that provide standards and other services for the industry. One such is a transportation emergency service called TERS (Transportation Emergency Response System), based in Greensboro, North Carolina. TERS gets technical advice to the scene of a spill within six to ten minutes and includes a staff of technical, communications, and security experts who are on call twenty-four hours a day.

Ciba's transportation emergency system is tied into CHEMTREC, a voluntary chemical industry–sponsored service based in Washington, D.C. This service is designed to provide immediate information to freight carriers and public safety officials at the scene of an emergency. To minimize potential risks inherent in transporting and storing chemicals, Ciba's Agricultural Group ships only to those dealers with "diked" bulk storage tanks. For those dealers who do not have this specialized equipment, Ciba provides special cost incentives to upgrade safety equipment or diking facilities at their sites.

Another voluntary program established by the chemical industry in 1985 in which Ciba participates is CMA's Community Awareness and Emergency Response. This program helps local communities prepare for chemical emergencies.

Safety first is also the standard for Ciba's products, particularly for the Plant Protection Division, whose pesticides and insecticides could have far-reaching ramifications. All must be harmless to humans, must avoid any chemical contamination of the environment, must specifically attack the targeted pest without affecting other plants or animals, and can be used in minute amounts. Ciba has abandoned projects where the risk of application or potential damage to the environment appears, as it says, "unreasonably high." Ciba ceased marketing the cotton insecticide Galecron, for example, because its instructions for use were not always followed, thus health risks could not be excluded.

Ciba is a prime example, despite its size and scope, of how a company can operate with high regard for the atmosphere and for the bottom line at the same time.

CHAPTER SIX

How to Add a Green Lining to Your Business

Guidelines and Checklists

Environmental Evaluation: Self-Assessment

Reviewing the case histories outlined in this book and determining the common elements of each program, we have created an outline to help businesses begin their own environmental programs. It offers guidance about assessing areas of significant environmental impact and pinpointing the steps necessary to implement initiatives and proceed accordingly.

Whether the program is initiated at the grass-roots level from employees or at the top management level, the CEO has to endorse the corporate challenge. From that point, line-management develops function-specific environmental objectives and systems to coordinate with the corporate commitment and policies. A total-quality management approach should then be adopted to evaluate the effectiveness of the program.

Corporate Commitment

The first step in any program is to determine the breadth and scope of the commitment in a written statement. This document answers the following questions: What elements will you make your priority? What goal you have set, or in what ways will your participation positively affect environmental quality?

In this statement you should recognize environmental management as one of the highest priorities, as playing a key role in sustainable development. You need to establish policies, programs, and practices for conducting operations in an environmentally sound manner and to acknowledge the cooperation and shared commitment of top management with company staff in order to achieve the goals and fulfill the commitment.

Rate Your Objectives

Self-assessment will vary with each industry, as some are more regulated than others and some businesses are more prepared than others to make a commitment on a grander scale.

Once you have determined what your goals are, examine each operation you have targeted and determine how far removed you are from your ultimate goal. After you have reviewed that list, you can determine which of these operations can be tackled easily with quick results. This is an important step because it helps stimulate morale and encourage participation. These actions are the fruit at the bottom branches of the tree, easily reached. Combined with these easy pickings should be more difficult accomplishments with far-reaching impact. Weigh the importance of the effort relative to the importance of the commitment. This will allow others to understand the significance of each initiative and will provide a basis for future assessment and a means by which to measure progress.

For example:

1 Review regulatory compliance policies.

2 Review the system that is currently in place to comply with regulations and rate current activity.

3 Determine what is needed to improve expectations or exceed requirements in order to meet corporate commitment goals.

Repeat process to evaluate voluntary actions, as follows:

1 Integrate environmental policy with operating practices.

2 Rate present action and determine what improvements can be made to meet corporate environmental commitment.

Repeat process with business strategies, as follows:

1 Evaluate and rate business strategies and conduct in terms of environment and cost effectiveness, since these two often go hand in hand. Less waste saves money.

2 Identify ways in which business can be conducted to save money and reduce impact on the environment. Implement procedures.

Repeat this method to determine management of the program, for example:

1 Select staff members who will be held responsible for legal compliance.

2 Rate the performance of personnel to determine who may be given responsibility for monitoring the performance of each department.

3 Select a monitoring team from that body of predisposed individuals. A Green Team can be composed of enthusiastic volunteers. This team serves as backup to your management team and provides, in effect, checks and balances. Staff and managers should be evaluated in light of corporate environmental standards as one other aspect of their overall performance evaluations.

Ultimately, however, management is accountable for the successful implementation and renewal of environmental policies.

Goals for the program should be periodically rated, as follows;

1 Identify the goal and determine the system by which it is being met.

2 Rate the performance of individuals or the progress of the project.

3 Establish means by which performance can be improved, recognized, or maintained.

Once you adjust to this system, you can measure and account for all corporate environmental action, including corporate policy, individual actions like pollution prevention, source reduction, and line management's effectiveness in meeting objectives. You can then make adjustments accordingly. This system also helps to create a record of your program—it origins, its progress, and the effectiveness of actions taken. This record provides a means of transferring the information to others, within the company when a division head changes or beyond the company when business colleagues want to see how you are doing it.

Employee Education

Look to department heads to conceive methods of educating, training, and motivating employees to conduct business in an environmentally responsible manner. Make employee-geared materials and incentives a priority for your program.

Outreach

Advise and educate your customers, vendors, and local community regarding the goals of the company and the shared responsibility of the community at large to adopt similar commitments to the environment. Such outreach programs empower consumers and enable them to make their own choices by encouraging alignment with companies committed to environmental action.

Vendors, Contractors, and Suppliers

Promote the adoption of similar principles by your vendors or suppliers. Encourage and, where appropriate, require them to align with your environmental goals. When they do comply, recognize the accomplishment.

Foster Dialogue

Openness and dialogue are key components to a successful environmental program. Dialogue among employees and management should be encouraged. Every program we examined had significantly boosted the morale of its employees. This increased self-esteem was directly attributable to the empowerment cultivated by making a difference. Allow employees to adopt programs; allow customers and consumers to participate in active ways.

Furthermore, anticipate and respond to concerns about the potential hazards and impact of operations, products, wastes, or services.

Transfer of Technology or Knowledge

Contribute to the transfer of environmentally sound technology, ideas, information, and management methods throughout the industry and public sectors. When you find ideas that work well, don't keep them to yourself. Other businesses can benefit by not having to reinvent the wheel.

A Common Cause

Remember that the health of the environment is a shared responsibility. One company alone cannot make a significant contribution to a better environment. But like-minded companies and organizations aligned with one another can. Therefore, contribute to and support the development of public policy as well as business, government, and educational programs and initiatives that will enhance environmental awareness and protection.

Eco Logical Solutions™ Five-Phase Checklist for Environmental Integration

PHASE ONE: INITIAL ASSESSMENT

1 Walk-throughs of all operations and facilities
2 Meetings with key personnel to identify areas of concern
3 Management team
4 Finance
5 Regulation compliance
6 Operations facilities and grounds
7 Marketing and sales
8 Health and safety
9 Administration

PHASE TWO: GENERAL EVALUATION

10 Document outlines environmental issues by area
11 Voluntary and regulatory initiatives are identified
12 The assessment will identify these specific areas of environmental concern:
   a Source reduction
   b Material reuse
   c Recycling and waste management
   d Environmental health
   e Construction/development
   f Hazardous materials elimination
   g Water quality and conservation
   h Lighting/energy conservation
   i Public and employee education
   j Communications outreach

PHASE THREE: COMPREHENSIVE IMPLEMENTATION PROGRAM

13 Implemented and integrated across all operations
14 Consulting team is highly visible and active on your premises

15 Initiatives balance economic realities with environmental responsibilities

16 Education and communications strategies are
created with a positive context

17 Internal education strategies are multilingual and
multidimensional

18 External communications are unique and developed
to generate positive publicity

PHASE FOUR: MEASUREMENT

19 Measurement tools are established to monitor
achievements

20 Results are measured against future environmental
goals and used to support your communication effort

PHASE FIVE: ONGOING CONSULTATION

21 New services, products, procedures, and resources
are reviewed in order to maintain a viable long-
term commitment to the campaign

Environmental Management Systems Audits

FRANK J. PRIZNAR

*The following material is suitable for those businesses with strict regula-
tory guidelines.*

*This information was prepared by Frank Priznar, the founder of the
Institute of Environmental Auditing, located in Alexandria, Virginia. The author
is a registered environmental assessor and the author of over thirty-five articles
and publications addressing the issues of environmental management.*

Improving environmental performance is an important consideration
for business because of legal, economic, and social pressures to protect the environment. This affects organizations of all sizes, whether
they are commercial, nonprofit, or governmental. The concept of
"sustainable development" is commonly used to define an acceptable
environmental objective for organizations. With respect to business,
sustainable development means ensuring that operating activities
meet the needs of stakeholders while guaranteeing the viability of
continued business in future generations. For the environment, this
means that current uses of the environment do not prevent similar
uses by future generations.

209

To achieve sustainable development status, organizations must deliberately and continually integrate environmental objectives into their normal business plans. This requires integrating these plans into daily practices. Although steps taken to achieve sustainable development should be integrated into the organization's management system, the parts that center on environmental management, when taken together, can be considered the environmental management system.

The need to understand how well an organization's environmental management system functions is clearly important for executives and managers. They simply cannot make wise decisions without good information. However, because so many others can be affected, such as local communities, suppliers, and vendors, the pressure to make wise environmental decisions is vital for business success. To assure themselves, and other stakeholders, that wise business decisions are being made, and that environmental issues are accounted for, an environmental management systems audit should be completed.

The environmental management systems audit is helpful in three ways. First, it can define the suitability of current environmental management systems. Second, it can identify established areas of environmental management systems that do not meet expectations. And finally, it can provide some indication of the effectiveness of the environmental management system in fulfilling the organization's environmental policy.

The material that follows describes what an environmental management system typically consists of and outlines what specific areas can be audited.

Environmental Management Systems

Many organizations have prepared guidelines that recommend what elements an environmental management system should include. Elements that are generally common to these guidelines include the following:

1 A policy statement covering the overall relationship of the organization to the environment and a commitment to environmental management and its level of priority.

2 Conservation and protection of natural resources.

3 Reduction of waste and avoidance of excessive consumption.

4 Legal compliance.

5 The promotion of the adoption of environmental principles by suppliers, customers, and others who have a relationship with the organization.

6 The development and support of innovative technology, products, and services that contribute to the preservation of the environment or minimize environmental damage.

7 The integration of environmental issues into overall management and decision making.

8 Employee education and public information.

9 The measurement of environmental performance and continual improvement of policies, programs, and performance.

10 Cooperation with governments, other organizations, and the community.

11 Commitment to action.

The operation's acceptance of these goals can become the basis of environmental management system expectations, against which an audit can be conducted.

But accepting these elements as the basis for an environmental management system is less important than emphasizing prevention of environmental harm in the first place. There are further guidelines to address this need. The environmental management system should

- identify and assess the environmental effects of existing or proposed activities, products, or services;

- identify and assess the environmental effects of potential accidents and emergency situations;

- identify relevant regulatory requirements;

- enable priorities to be identified and pertinent environmental objectives and targets to be set;

- facilitate planning, control monitoring, and auditing, and review activities to ensure that the policy is both complied with and remains relevant;

- be capable of evolving to accommodate changing circumstances.

Because each organization is different, not all of these guidelines will necessarily apply; but they are useful for focusing priorities.

Environmental Management Systems Audit

An environmental management system audit is critical for measuring the effectiveness of internal systems. It can also satisfy external stakeholders that the organization is sincere about its environmental policies and goals and wishes to operate according to an accepted standard. Because there is no generally accepted standard for environmental management systems at this time, it must usually be developed by each organization to fit its unique context. The audit, although measuring each organization according to its self-imposed standards, should nevertheless be guided by some de facto criteria:

1 Environmental policy. This should be clearly defined and documented. It should be relevant, understood at all levels, publicly available, and oriented toward pollution prevention and sustainable development. It must include a commitment to meet regulatory requirements, to continue improving environmental performance, to provide for the setting and publication of environmental objectives, and to publish regularly updated environmental reports.

2 Management responsibility. This should be defined and documented, with specific information on authority, interrelations of key personnel, and lines of communication.

3 Environmental impacts. These should be identified and recorded through a formal process that includes regulatory and policy issues on the environmental aspects of an organization's activities, products, and services.

4 Environmental objectives. These should be established, maintained, and communicated to all levels of the organization.

5 Environmental management program. This should be established and maintained and should include schedules, designation of authority, and expected mechanisms for accomplishing goals.

6   Environmental manual. This should describe the company's policy, objectives, program, roles, responsibilities, the interaction of system elements, and emergency procedures.

7   Operational control. This should be established so that responsibilities are defined at all levels to ensure that control, verification, measurement, and testing are adequately coordinated and effectively performed.

8   Environmental management record. This should be maintained in order to demonstrate compliance with requirements of the environmental management system and to track progress toward environmental objectives.

9   Environmental management system audits. These should be a regular occurrence to determine the suitability of the environmental management system and to detect any nonconformance with environmental management program expectations and policies.

10 External communications. These should represent fair and true information and be communicated to interested parties on matters related to environmental management, policy, performance, and impacts.

The environmental management system already outlined should also guide the audit. Successful audits will show organizations where there is room for ongoing improvement, which will vary among organizations according to economic or other circumstances.

For More Information

Further information on environmental management systems audits is available from the Institute for Environmental Auditing, Suite 660, 1725 Duke Street, Alexandria, VA 22314.

Eco-Ideas for Your Office and Company

The following suggestions are offered to help you integrate environmental solutions into your everyday business practices. Remember: Daily change creates long-term effects!

It is important not only to recycle but to reduce consumption at the source. Here are some directions to help your company with a source reduction plan.

Rethink creatively

Reduce at the source

Recycle and purchase recycled products

Reuse

Recycling

Develop a waste-stream audit for your company. Look at every department and identify waste. Using your eye and simple methods, calculate the volume of each item:

Glass

Paper
- white
- computer
- mixed

Plastic

Polystyrene

Cardboard

Newspaper

Tin

Steel

Outline the procedure for disposal of each item from purchase to Dumpster. Identify the location of all trash receptacles and calculate whether or not there is space available for additional receptacles.

Create a source reduction task force to identify areas of the company where waste can be cut back.

Office White-Paper Recycling

Start with one recycling initiative and integrate it into your operation before tackling several areas.

Contact a recycler or wastepaper dealer to see if it offers services to help your company establish a white-paper program.

Don't spin your wheels. Contact other local companies to get the names of successful recyclers who can handle your company. Compare the number of employees and the size of the facilities to get an indication of what is in store for your company.

Establish an interoffice task force that will develop the program, monitor its progress, and establish recycling goals. Include a facilities maintenance person on the team as well as line employees and management.

Enlist the help of your purchasing agent to target best prices for recycling bins and to secure contracts with waste haulers.

Look at different styles of recycling containers to create a system that fits with the decorating motif of your office.

Create signs and educational information that speak to all employees involved with recycling. This may include translating information in different languages so that all employees can feel a part of the program.

Rethink

In your offices you can also do these:

- Create an incentive program for soda can collection. Collect cans and place money earned toward an office gathering. Ask management to pitch in and match collected funds.
- Prepare documents single spaced whenever possible.
- Reduce margins where appropriate.
- Edit before printing.
- Prepare a sign at the office copier reminding workers to use both sides.
- Load laser printers with used paper for internal memos or first drafts.
- Choose a service agent for your printers who supplies recycled laser cartridges.
- Use a central bulletin board or E-mail for posting notices instead of distributing individual copies.
- Share documents, publications, telephone directories in the office. Ask the phone company to distribute fewer books to your office and to arrange to recycle old books.

- Eliminate fax cover sheets and use fax Post-its instead.
- Cut up used paper and use the clean side for phone messages.
- Keep cloth bags in the office for employees to share when buying office supplies.
- If your wastebasket is used for dry waste, eliminate the plastic garbage bag liner.
- Eliminate the use of polystyrene pellets when packing or shipping. Look for alternatives like newspaper, shredded paper, cornstarch pellets, or edible popcorn. Include a note with each package explaining your choice.
- Turn off all lights at the end of the day. Investigate energy-saving office equipment for overnight low power.
- Control thermostat from one location so that employees don't change setting.
- Work with your local utility to investigate energy-saving incentive programs. Contact the EPA regarding its Green Lights Program for more information.
- Offer employees car pool programs and public transportation incentives.

Reuse

Before recycling, consider creative ways to reuse items in your company and offices.

- Use 55-gallon drums for basement trash receptacles.
- Use glass jars to hold small items, such as nuts and screws, in engineering and facilities departments.
- Give away old equipment that you would usually toss into the Dumpster, such as phones, to shelters or other nonprofits.
- Repair mechanical items and reuse instead of tossing away.

Other Eco-Suggestions

- Create a maintenance program for upkeep of all equipment for longevity and less wear and tear.

- Use bicycle couriers whenever possible.
- Create a smoke-free environment by setting aside a less frequently used space for employees who choose to smoke.
- Keep plants at desks to help purify the air.

Create a Green Team

- Ask employees to create an environmental task force, preferably composed of enthusiastic volunteers. It also helps to choose people who are in key positions: purchasing, engineering, management.
- Create a suggestion box for all employees to use. Give away a rainforest crunch bar or eco-gift each month to the person with the best suggestion.
- Set readily achievable annual goals and monthly tactics for the Green Team. Recognize the team for its efforts and voluntary contributions.
- Discuss obstacles, alternatives, and solutions at regularly scheduled Green Team meetings.
- Implement new programs with task force participation.
- Allow team members to participate in community environmental workshops and activities on company time as a benefit for their participation and actions.
- Request that division heads and management respect the environmental obligations and added responsibilities of Green Team members.
- Communicate Green Team efforts with the rest of your staff through an environmental newsletter or a column in your existing internal organ.

The Power of Purchasing

Purchasing is one-stop shopping and a great way to cut back on waste. Purchasing agents have the power to persuade vendors to think green and can establish guidelines requiring green products. Purchasing agents can also replace throwaway items with reusable ones, such as refillable pens and pencils

refillable laser toner printing cartridges

recycled, recyclable envelopes with metal clasps

re-inkable or multistrike typewriter ribbons

erasable wall calendars

washable towels

reusable cups, plates, and flatware for employee kitchens

recycled office products

recycled paper products, stationery

reusable mesh coffee filters (small offices)

unbleached coffee filters (large offices)

oversized mailing labels to cover preaddressed envelopes

products with less toxic inks and dyes

reusable envelopes for interdepartmental mail

labels that cover old names on interdepartmental mail

Use purchasing power to ask vendors to use minimal packaging and reusable shipping containers. Establish a one-for-one shipping pallet program with all vendors. Here are some other ideas.

- Buy items in bulk.
- Increase use of durable and repairable equipment and supplies.
- Consider buying or leasing laser printers that can make double-sided copies.
- Use computer programs that allow for faxing direct from computers to eliminate printouts.
- Consider buying or leasing fax machines that use plain paper.

Communications

Make all these new procedures work with a strategic communications campaign.

- Communicate your efforts in multiple languages.
- Create a logo and campaign slogan to tag all environmental actions.

■ Try a combination of any of the tactics below or create new ones to broadcast the information and promote the program.

> bill stuffers
>
> posters
>
> brochures
>
> one-to-one training
>
> small-group training
>
> incentives
>
> awards and recognition
>
> management training and presentations
>
> lapel buttons
>
> encourage others by your actions
>
> step back and watch your results

CHAPTER SEVEN

Eco-Marketing

Environmental Marketing

It's not easy being green.

KERMIT THE FROG, "Sesame Street"

The notion of a partnership between business and the environment is generally greeted with suspicion by environmental groups and the general public, despite the fact that such a union is desirable for both parties. This suspicion is based in part on the enormous gap between the concerns of the consumer and the interests of business.

Most heavily industrialized businesses are in fact dealing with, not ignoring, their environmental issues. But many are afraid of going public with their results, expecting criticism for what they are not doing rather than appreciation for what they are doing. Their reluctance is not unfounded. Many environmental organizations have fault-finding task groups whose sole purpose is to cast blame on companies in violation of legislation or of expectations.

This is precisely why companies need to reach out and inform the public of their ongoing environmental initiatives. Every step is part of a goal. There is a tremendous need for a bridge between business groups and environmental groups. Finger-pointing is just as counterproductive as unsubstantiated claims. Only a transfer of knowledge and dialogue will bridge the chasm between environmental responsibility and economic necessity.

Through marketing, complex environmental issues can be made accessible to various consumers groups, including the young children's and the student markets. As environmental issues are incorporated into curricula, from preschool to graduate school, the subject matter becomes an integral and lasting component of everyday existence. Sponsoring educational programs, therefore, becomes an important tool for educating future consumers.

Likewise business leaders often share consumers' concern for the safety and well-being of their families and environmentalists' concern for the protection of wildlife and the conservation of nature. Because industry is viewed as the greatest contributor to pollution and to the degradation of resources, businesses need to associate with their communities and share their problems and concerns. Sponsoring community goodwill projects is another way business can bond with its community.

Consumers' attitudes are affected by the environmental crises closest to home. As environmental issues expand in reach and scope and individual regions discover environmental problems in common, the greater the number of people are affected, and the greater the outcry. This personal impact becomes a great motivator to do, and demand that others do, the right thing.

The media, too, are a force to be reckoned with. They are also a business with a product to sell. The media know that sensationalism and disaster sell. If they feel that their audience is interested in environmental issues, they will comply. Environmental columns and reporters have sprung up at every major publication. If the public is to be properly informed, it is imperative that business acquaint the media with its particular issues and concerns as well as its programs and services. The dissemination of information should be a shared responsibility, in this case, between business and the media. The public's challenge to business to solve environmental problems is not enough. The public must be part of the solution by listening and learning about the complex issues that the business community faces and by supporting its environmental achievements.

Business leaders, consumers, and activists have the same goal: a cleaner, safer world. From the business point of view, however, demands from environmentalists sometimes appear to be unrealistic. From the other perspective, it often appears that the business community is not addressing environmental concerns expeditiously. A spirit of partnership needs to be nurtured among these groups. One crucial way business can foster this is through effective communication directed to the appropriate groups.

In this portion of the book, we address the need for a crisis management marketing plan and present guidelines for green marketing, advertising, publicity, and public relations. We have included contributions from people actively engaged in this type of work and have relied on our own strategies and experiences at The Boston Park Plaza Hotel to formulate recommendations.

Crisis Marketing

Whether or not your company regularly deals with large volumes of hazardous substances, you run the risk of environmental contamination. An incident could involve commonly used materials like chlorinated solvents. The crisis could be a fire that results in environmental damage to a community. Today these common industrial accidents are viewed seriously by the media and the public. Your company is vulnerable. Being prepared to respond to an environmental emergency should be an essential task in all businesses.

An environmental crisis could include

- accidental release of toxic materials into rivers or sewer systems due to a fire;
- inappropriate disposal of waste;
- accidental spillage;
- uncontrolled toxic atmospheric releases;
- contamination of water supply from underground storage tank leakage.

Let us stress again that you needn't be in a dangerous industry to be vulnerable to environmental contamination and public scrutiny. Most companies use some hazardous materials, and any company can have a fire. In addition to saddling you with cleanup costs and increased insurance premiums, an environmental crisis and adverse publicity could result in public sensitivity to your product, which, in turn, could result in decreased market share.

The environmental risk management tools available are

- identification of the environmental issues;
- evaluation or field audit for assessment of crisis potential specifically at your company;
- abatement techniques.

Once these things are identified, it is important to make all top management and press-relations personnel aware of them. Representatives who are not properly prepared can show the company in a poor light, which may have long-term implications and ruin your company's credibility.

A crisis management plan combined with a communications strategy can be designed to minimize the negative effects of an environmental crisis. Be proactive rather than reactive.

First, create a high-level crisis management team to develop a strategy for dealing with local authorities, the community, the media, and employees. Rank the severity of each potential incident, its likelihood, and possible solutions.

Be ready to conduct an immediate investigation of the crisis and to relay information to the public and employees through public address and informational releases. Test your plan occasionally to ensure readiness.

Components of an Environmental Emergency Response Plan

Outline the purpose and objectives of the plan.

Identify environmental policies and philosophical approaches.

Outline geographic boundaries potentially affected.

Identify a corporate environmental emergency response task force.

Identify internal structures that are ready to respond.

Identify which response procedures are in place.

Devise the means of notification.

Determine how damage and off-site impact will be assessed.

Inventory emergency response equipment and its location.

Determine means of waste disposal and state and local waste management requirements.

Identify cooperative sources.

Identify postincident activities.

Devise long-term monitoring or restoration plans.

Review possible litigation.

From an environmental viewpoint, an effective plan should define corporate policies and operational guidelines that can be quickly and effectively implemented to direct all phases of crisis response. This will minimize the effect of accidents on the environment and human health.

The communications strategy must integrate corporate planning, regulatory requirements, resource inventories, response strategies, and training programs. Be factual, comprehensive, and flexible so that in the case of an actual crisis, the plan can be implemented realistically. Plans should be maintained and updated as procedures, personnel, and regulations change.

An inappropriate, inept reaction could cause another crisis in itself. Being viewed as an irresponsible corporate citizen can lead to a loss of reputation and public confidence.

Green Marketing

Every green marketing firm or public relations agency has an approach tailored specifically to each client. We have asked certain agencies active in the environmental marketplace to share examples of the techniques. The details of their programs address positioning, imaging, selling, and publicity.

Green Marketing

JACQUELYN A. OTTMAN

President, J. Ottman Consulting, New York, New York

Just a few years ago, superconcentrated laundry detergents gathered dust in a Denver test market. Paper towels made from recycled content were rejected as inferior, even unclean. And extra packaging added perceived value to consumer products. More was more, whiter was better, and disposability was king. But all of this is rapidly changing. A new marketing age has arrived.

With garbage piling up in our communities, forests disappearing at an alarming rate, and the air getting harder to breathe, a revolution is underway to halt the misuse of our planet's resources. This revolution is taking place at our nation's supermarkets, drugstores, and mass merchandisers. With the growing legions of consumers concerned about the quality of their lives, "less" is now becoming "more," and purchasing decisions are increasingly being swayed by the impact that products have on the environment.

From now on, companies that don't respond to "green" issues with safer and more environmentally sound products risk falling out of sync with the consumer. And for marketers who do heed the consumer's call, opportunities abound. Sales at Church & Dwight, makers of Arm & Hammer baking soda, have grown from $16 million to $500 million thanks in part to a timely and thorough response to the trend. Concentrated laundry products cut down on waste and are more profitable than full-strength alternatives. With a product that is kinder to the environment as well as to people, 3M has expanded the market for paint strippers.

While the opportunities are enormous, so, too, are the challenges. Among them:

- no clear method exists for comparing the environmental impact of one product against another;
- most consumers are reluctant to make tradeoffs in lifestyles and product purchasing in their quest for a cleaner planet;
- misperceptions abound, representing the potential for unproductive public policy-making and significant risks to industry in the form of unnecessary and costly changes in products and manufacturing processes;
- there are no uniform national guidelines for communicating commonly used environmental marketing terms. The FTC has issued voluntary guidelines for terms such as *recycled, recyclable,* and *biodegradable,* but these are not legally enforceable, and they do not pre-empt stricter guidelines put forth by individual states, such as New York, California, and Rhode Island. Without uniform guidelines, the environmental message of national marketers cannot be heard, and the potential to confuse consumers is great;
- industry, seen as the culprit in creating environmental blight, has low credibility in communicating environment-related messages, and a backlash from environmentalists, regulators, and the press currently exists.

The companies that stand to gain the most from consumers' newfound environmentalism will adopt proactive thinking, integrating environmental planning into overall business strategy. They will develop products that balance consumers' concern for performance, quality, convenience, and affordability with minimal environmental impact. And they will communicate their environmental initiatives to all corporate stakeholders with credibility and effectiveness.

Yet before greening their marketing activities, they will green their companies; as Hubert H. "Skip" Humphrey III, state attorney general of Minnesota and principal author of Green Report II, has said, "Green your operations and the products will take care of themselves. Green your products and the marketing will take care of itself."

Following are ten strategies that forward-thinking, committed companies can use to ensure continued markets for their products and an abundance of opportunities to leverage environmental strategies as a source of competitive advantage.

Jacquelyn Ottman's Ten Winning Strategies for Succeeding in the Age of Environmental Consumerism

1 Do Your Homework

Understand the full range of environmental, economic, political, and social issues that affect your business.

2 Get Your House in Order

Start with a commitment from the CEO. Empower employees to develop environmentally sound products and processes.

Enlist the support of independent auditors.

Integrate environmental issues into your marketing planning.

Turn your brand managers into "environmental brand stewards" responsible for achieving corporate profit objectives with minimal environmental impact. Require an environmental assessment in all business reviews.

Communicate your corporate commitment and project your values.

3 Be a Leader

Be proactive; set standards for your industry.

Foster cooperation among competitors.

4 Build Coalitions with Corporate Environmental Stakeholders

Educate consumers on environmental issues and how to solve them. Help teachers educate young people.

Work with legislators and government agencies to develop balanced legislation and regulations.

Share information with environmental groups and solicit their technical support.

Inform the media of your environmental initiatives.

Help retailers address consumer needs and reduce waste through the creation of special promotional programs and co-sponsored recycling programs.

5   Develop Products That Balance Consumer's Needs

Combine high quality, convenience, and affordable pricing with environmental soundness.

Enlist the support of your suppliers, vendors, and retailers to accomplish these objectives.

Minimize the environmental impact of products and packaging at every stage of the product life cycle.

Take the high road. Strive to use leading-edge technologies, materials, and design. Practice source reduction—meaning use fewer materials or toxins whenever possible.

6   Empower Consumers

Help consumers understand the environmental benefits of your products and packaging.

Address the diversity of green consumers. Reward environmentally active consumers for their commitment, and motivate passive green consumers with easy, cost-effective substitutes to existing products.

7   Underpromise and Overdeliver on Your Environmental Marketing Claims

In keeping with the FTC guidelines, don't overstate, exaggerate, or mislead.

Use claims that are specific and supported by reliable, scientific evidence.

8   Establish Credibility

Position product initiatives as part of your ongoing commitment to the environment.

Use third parties, such as environmental groups, regulators, and educators to add credibility and impact to your messages.

Promote the concept of "responsible consumption" whenever possible.

9   Minimize the Environmental Impact of Your Marketing Programs

Use recycled paper and soybean inks. Cut down on unnecessary mailings.

10   Think Long-term

Monitor shifts in consumer attitudes, legislative trends, and changes in natural resource availability that could affect your business.

(Reprinted with permission from *Green Marketing: Challenges and Opportunities for the New Marketing Age* [NTC Business Books, 1993].)

Green Marketing: Promotion and Publicity Tips for Green Businesses

JANET BRIDGES,

Partner, Gaia Communications, Santa Monica, California

In the years since we established our environmentally focused public relations firm, the Gaia Communications partners have talked with hundreds of green businesses. We've talked with small businesses and large ones, start-ups and those well established.

Our experience reaffirms that there are no shortcuts to the successful promotion of any business—whether it's a new green enterprise or a veteran mainstream corporation.

For Green Companies

Green businesses have a built-in advantage for promotion and publicity because the media have, in the past, demonstrated their interest in green products and services. Nevertheless businesses in the green niche must continuously strive for innovation. The competition for media attention has become tremendous.

For example, it's no longer enough to create cruelty-free cosmetics in the personal care products industry—the leaders in the field are now using rainforest botanicals and even this isn't *that* new anymore. Who knows what the next new thing will be?

Another example: environmental catalogs and environmental stores. Though extremely important for wider distribution of green products, as a concept, such catalogs and stores are no longer new. Entrepreneurs with ideas for starting similar businesses need to build in a constant stream of innovative products so there will always be something newsworthy about the store or catalog.

Our experience also tells us that entrepreneurs who start green companies without a budget for at least a six-month media and advertising campaign are starting off at a real disadvantage. They will probably be wasting their money if they invest in media relations and advertising for a shorter period because six months of intense promotion is barely enough time for a campaign to take hold and begin producing results. This is not an easy time in economic history to start a business. Those who decide to proceed in the face of significant odds should have everything possible going for them.

If you don't have past experience in publicity, promotion, and advertising, or aren't married to someone who does, don't kid yourself into thinking you can be successful without spending the money it takes to hire professionals. When you put together your business plan, get quotes from local public relations and advertising firms for everything from complete programs to short-term projects to consulting services.

A do-it-yourself approach to PR and advertising is possible to some extent—with a professionally prepared press kit and good graphics. But if you are going to execute the program yourself, don't spread yourself too thin with other duties. Make sure that enough of the other administrative and management responsibilities are covered by other people to give you time to do the marketing tasks. The little-red-hen approach doesn't work for start-up companies—green or not. You can't do it all, all by yourself.

Greening Established Businesses

Established companies that decide to go green have many advantages over start-up green companies, including established customer bases and, it is hoped, positive profiles as good corporate citizens.

Green programs cannot be a perfume to cover the smell of dirty corporate laundry. If used that way, they'll backfire, because they invite greater scrutiny from the public, the media, and environmentalists.

If a company does have an image problem, the only way we recommend an environmental program is if it comes straight from the president or CEO's office and is part of comprehensive internal audit, reevaluation, and a long-term improved community relations plan.

As an example, the Chevron "People Do" advertising campaign may convince some people that Chevron is a good environmental citizen; but it doesn't convince many media people and environmentalists, who view Chevron's fines for dumping in California coastal waters as an indication of a company that is far from enlightened.

For an established company, publicity opportunities can come in the form of announcements of new internal green programs, new

> It would be far better for Chevron to emphasize what it is legitimately changing and compare that with what was done in the past in order to educate the public and media about its current corporate commitment.
>
> Across the board, whitewashing is not a quick fix. Communication with an educational element will eventually be heard. Past sins can be forgiven. No one expects business to say that it has always been right, but everyone expects business to change accordingly. It won't happen overnight, but legitimate, time-proven claims will be heard and appreciated.

green products, tie-ins with environmental organizations, or promotions, such as tree seedling giveaways.

Reductions in raw materials, waste, water, or energy use or achievements of recycling goals are other possible subjects for news releases—in fact all the areas covered by an internal environmental audit.

Promoting a company's green ethic can take many forms. The broad scope of public relations—internal relations, community relations, media relations—all suggest ways to inform employees and customers that the company is one they can be proud of.

But first everything has to be on recycled paper; and the higher the postconsumer content, the better. In fact some companies are producing recycled paper for their annual reports from the very same white office paper they recycled. The purchasing department should have special instructions to look for every affordable opportunity to buy recycled. If recycled products don't meet your specifications, talk to your vendors, let them know what you want. But all letterhead and stock for internal and external communications should definitely, absolutely, be on recycled paper. Recycled bathroom tissue and paper towels also make important statements.

Packaging is another vital area of your community environmental relations. The packaging of your product should be reduced to a minimum, and it should include as much postconsumer recycled content as possible. The packaging you receive from vendors should be recycled as much as possible. If you find it difficult to recycle, let the vendor know. After all, the vendor wants to keep your business.

Your place of business is a great place to hang signs stating your environmental philosophy and showing your progress toward waste- and energy-reduction goals. The signs not only communicate to customers but also reinforce employees' behavior.

The example set by management is also extremely important for internal and community relations. Does the CEO recycle his soda can, or toss it absentmindedly into the trash with the expectation that his secretary or maintenance person will remove it for recycling? Not good. The efforts of upper- and mid-level management to recycle will loudly broadcast the sincerity of the message.

Other ways to demonstrate that your company is more than superficially green is to encourage managers and employees to volunteer with local environmental groups, to stay up to date on local and national environmental issues, and to participate in letter-writing campaigns. Giving employees time off to testify at nearby public hearings on related issues and policies can have a big payoff in benefits to your local environment as well as to your company's environmental profile.

Finally, watching local and national media coverage of environmental business issues will help you shape your own green marketing efforts. By endeavoring to understand issues from the media's vantage point, that is, what's news, what's not, you will become increasingly savvy and gradually be able to anticipate where and when the approaching waves of public environmental interest will hit. When that happens, your company and your products can be there, making you one of the environmental success stories the media love to report.

Ten Tips for Promoting Your Green Business

1 Don't put all your promotional eggs in one basket; use a combination of approaches, such as sending out press releases, tying in with an appropriate nonprofit group, attending trade shows and conferences, getting involved in community events, and using direct-mail marketing.

2 If you don't want to hire an outside PR professional, assign someone in your organization to the task and make sure that person has the time and the resources to do the job right.

3 Establish relationships with the journalists who cover your beat. Ask them what they are looking for in a story, and be available if they want to pick your brain for a story that you may not necessarily appear in. Always call a journalist back immediately.

4 Make a commitment for the long haul. Building credibility with the press takes time. A steady stream of releases and follow-up phone calls at regular intervals are the best ways to ensure the coverage you want.

5 Always have on hand materials prepared about your business, written in journalistic—not sales brochure—style, for the media: bios of the principals, a background piece about your company, and fact sheets about your products or services.

6 Come up with original news hooks on a regular basis. See what the press is reporting on and try to fit into the pattern.

7 Get involved in community activities and let the media and local groups know what you are doing.

8 If you stick your neck out by trying to get media attention, make sure it doesn't get chopped by a negative revelation. Your whole operation must be a model of environmental correctness.

9 Solicit ideas from your employees. Since they work for your company, they probably already have an environmental ethic—and some innovative suggestions. Keep them informed about your environmental programs.

10 Keep up with the news about your industry. Subscribe to trade journals and other publications. Some of your best promotional ideas may be inspired by what you find out.

Mullen's Philosophy on Green Marketing

SUSAN SCHUMAKER,

Vice-president of public relations, Mullen Agency,

Wenham, Massachusetts

As a full-service communications agency, Mullen is involved in all aspects of its clients' businesses, from strategic planning to green marketing. Brand building is one thing common to all of Mullen's efforts on behalf of clients.

Evaluating the Merit of a Green Marketing Program

The Mullen Agency advises clients who wish to promote their green marketing efforts to be certain that these are comparatively worthy of promotion. Questions to help determine soundness might include (1) Do your efforts exceed regulatory compliance? (2) Is what you're doing unique in the industry? How does your investment compare with that of your competitors? (3) Is your program supported by the president and senior management of the company? (4) Does what you're doing enhance the brand's positioning?

If the answer to one or more of these questions is no, you may want to reconsider marketing your environmental efforts for the time being. Jumping on the green bandwagon simply for the sake of following a trend doesn't contribute to brand building. Having a program that is outstanding in your industry or that can teach others how to be more environmentally responsible merits external marketing. Otherwise such marketing may backfire.

People are increasingly savvy about environmental issues. The worst thing a company can do is not practice what it preaches, not put money where its mouth is. A scrutinizing public will be the first to hold a company to its written and oral standards.

Mullen helps its clients sort through the pros and cons before formulating a public message. Industry standards are researched so that the client has a yardstick against which to measure itself. Once the agency and client agree to proceed with a green marketing program, Mullen develops a positioning that is consistent with the overall brand message.

Implementing a Green Marketing Program: Two Cases

Mullen had already developed a brand positioning for Timberland, a manufacturer of leather footwear, apparel, and accessories based in Hampton, New Hampshire. As summarized by its ad tag line, "Boots, shoes, clothing, wind, water, earth and sky," Timberland is a company that makes products to be enjoyed in the outdoors while meeting Mother Nature's many challenges. The company therefore has a vested interest in preserving natural resources, and it wanted to make a substantial investment in this cause.

In cooperation with Timberland, Mullen's public relations group determined that the Wilderness Society, the leading national land preservation organization, would be a good match philosophically with the company. Coincidentally, in 1989, the year Timberland decided to approach this organization, the Wilderness Society was commemorating the twenty-fifth anniversary of the signing of the Wilderness Act. This milestone provided ample opportunities for Timberland's involvement.

For starters, Timberland made a significant financial commitment—more than half a million dollars—to the Society. Most of this funding was used to underwrite a major commemorative "Wilderness America" photography exhibit, which has toured throughout the United States, reaching more than 2 million people. The purpose of the exhibit was to heighten awareness and appreciation of the country's remaining wilderness land and to educate future generations about the importance of preserving it. A catalog and poster crediting Timberland's involvement accompanied the exhibit. Mullen was responsible for press relations in each city to which the exhibit traveled.

Timberland's financial support of the Wilderness Society has also enabled the publication of *Saving Our Ancient Forests: An Action Guide*, a book on forests of the Pacific Northwest. Another effort involved the production of a "Citizen's Action Kit," composed of prewritten postcards expressing concerns about preserving these ancient forests. These preaddressed postcards to President Bush were mailed to Society members and Timberland customers and distributed through Timberland stores. More than a million postcards were mailed to the White House.

Timberland devotes two pages in every edition of its magazine, *Elements: The Journal of Outdoor Experience*, to an issue of importance to the Wilderness Society. Readers of *Elements* are encouraged to get involved by calling or writing the Society for further information.

Timberland has also set up concept corners in its retail stores and departments as a tribute to the Wilderness Society. This and other Timberland efforts have substantially increased membership in the Wilderness Society. Timberland has invested millions of dollars in the Wilderness Society since the program began.

Timberland is genuinely concerned about preserving the great outdoors. Without wilderness land, there would be no appropriate places for Timberland's rugged footwear and clothing to be put to the test. Its commitment to the Wilderness Society is a way for Timberland not only to preserve its business but also to give back to the land that has helped build its prosperity.

Timberland's approach is to educate through an already established organization, better known as an affinity program. In the case of Veryfine, by contrast, the company itself serves as the role model and educator from which others can learn.

Based in Westford, Massachusetts, Veryfine Products (profiled in chapter 1 of this book) manufactures the leading brand of single-serve juice sold in convenience stores. The company also manufactures fruit juice and juice drinks for the vending, grocery, and food service segments. As a company in the beverage industry, Veryfine has a tremendous amount of waste associated with its business, from water to fruit pulp to packaging.

As discussed in greater depth earlier in this book, Veryfine recycles 96 percent of its solid waste. The company has gone beyond regulatory compliance in virtually every area of its business. Its latest accomplishment in the environmental area is the construction of an $8.5 million water purification plant. This facility is so advanced and so superior to any other built to date that representatives from the Massachusetts EPA visited it to learn how such a system works.

With the commitment and encouragement of its president, Sam Rowse (who is the grandson of the company's founder), Veryfine has successfully made the environment a topic that every employee lives and breathes. An employee recycling committee, for example, meets weekly to determine further ways the company can promote environmentalism internally. Whether it's buying pen refills instead of new pens or using a more environmentally friendly hand soap, the employees at Veryfine will continue to uncover the best possible methods and products.

After more than a decade of implementing its environmental program internally, Veryfine has decided to take a leadership role in educating other businesses based on its experience. Serving as a case study for this book is just the beginning.

Environmental marketing programs aimed at educating others about the importance of recycling and conservation include a speakers bureau, which coordinates opportunities for Sam Rowse and others in the company to present the Veryfine case study to business and academic audiences.

For younger audiences, Veryfine sponsors "Garbage Is My Bag," an interactive recycling skit performed at elementary schools by a character known as Dr. T, who has a Ph.D. in garbology. The program includes a take-home worksheet on recycling that kids complete with their parents.

Another education program involves a letter-writing campaign to keep Veryfine's brokers and distributors informed about the company's environmental efforts. The hope is that the personal message delivered by Sam Rowse will inspire them to educate retailers, who in turn will help spread the message to consumers.

An intensive media relations program targeting print and broadcast news media will be implemented to spread the word about Veryfine's environmental programs. Profiles on Veryfine's environmental efforts as well as bylined articles from Sam Rowse are included. A special environmental press kit is used as a means to inspire this type of coverage.

An advertising campaign highlighting Veryfine's success in reducing waste and recycling has been created. The series of ads feature an oversized photograph of a fruit on the left side of the spread and the tiny seed of the fruit on the right side to dramatize how little waste there is in the process of making Veryfine juices.

In the case of Veryfine, the sincere desire of president Sam Rowse and other senior managers to have the company serve as a corporate role model for recycling and environmentalism serves a higher purpose than self-promotion. If other companies can be convinced that there are both financial and employee morale benefits to be reaped from such a commitment, Veryfine will have achieved its goal of educating others.

Timberland and Veryfine represent two fairly different approaches used by Mullen to market its clients' environmental efforts. Both programs, however, are consistent with the brand positioning and image established for these successful companies. As an agency devoted to building the businesses of clients, Mullen is proud to take an active role in marketing the socially responsible actions of its clients whenever appropriate. By helping to further its clients' businesses through green marketing, Mullen also has the added advantage of contributing to the betterment of our world.

The Boston Park Plaza

Tedd Saunders was very cautious about rolling out the publicity campaign that eventually brought The Boston Park Plaza international recognition.

Suspicious himself, as a consumer, of green marketing approaches used by others, he was adamant about not leaking word of his environmental work-in-progress until it was firmly in place. Eighteen months passed before the first release was mailed to the trade media expounding the virtues of the program and encouraging others in the hospitality industry to incorporate environmental initiatives into their operations.

To Tedd publicity was an extension of the public outreach component of his program. He never dreamed that the response would be so far-reaching and would result in increased business directly attributable to the publicity campaign, nor did he expect that his independent efforts would receive such phenomenal media attention. Today it is something the hotel strives for in its continued effort to pass on the message to its constituency, its peers, and to other businesses outside the hospitality community. Comprehensive environmental actions were then and still are news.

Experience has allowed us to simplify the techniques we used and to lay down a guideline that others can follow.

Tedd's Take on Environmental Marketing

1 **Don't be in a hurry.**

Make sure your claims have substance and can be backed up with documentation. Have all your ducks in a row by having information prepared in advance that will address the concerns of your critics as well as your customers. Anticipate healthy skepticism while maintaining your positive convictions.

2 **Don't attempt to whitewash your problems.**

This is commonly called greenwashing. If you have an environmental problem, don't try to mask it by buying a few acres of rainforest. Face the problem head-on, fix it, or validate it.

3   Consider all the consequences of your actions.

Examine all the possible environmental ramifications throughout the entire life cycle of a new product, package, or action. When you are implementing an initiative or designing a product, consider everything from the use of natural resources in its creation to its method of disposal at the end of the line.

4   Support your community.

Align your efforts with benefits to your neighborhood, environmental activists, and the international community. It is often best to begin to promote activity in your backyard and expand your support to include national and worldwide institutions that bring attention to environmental problems.

5   Form alliances.

Work with groups both critical of and supportive of your claims and make efforts to work together to resolve issues. This action is generally more favorable than attempting to circumvent dissent. These groups may in fact provide helpful information.

6   Create logical sponsorships.

Sponsorships are effective ways to deliver your message to the public. Your choice of sponsorship should support your particular environmental efforts.

7   Make the necessary changes to your business now.

Given the newsworthiness of environmental responsibility, why wait to "clean up"?

Tools We Used

PRESS KITS: This kit was designed specifically for the program. Printed entirely on recycled paper, the kit's cover bore a reusable, detachable note card with a photo of planet Earth and a plastic envelope with a shower cap inside.

It asked the pithy question, "Would you be willing to give up this (the cap) to save this (the earth)?" signifying the hotel's decision to offer fewer amenities in an effort to reduce waste. Inside the kit was a release identifying the program, environmental facts, and the results of surveys conducted at the hotel. The kit was simple, direct, and informational, projecting the qualities inherent in the efforts being made at the property.

NEWS RELEASES: A steady flow of information is sent to the media to keep them updated on activities at the hotel as well as changes in the industry as a whole.

ALLIANCES: American Lung Association, New England Aquarium, Boston University, Earth Day, EPA, Hotel & Motel Association are a few examples of the types of organizations and business groups the hotel has worked with to promote environmental awareness.

NEWSLETTERS: These are used to keep both employees and clients aware of and educated about the progress the hotel is making in environment and other areas.

EMPLOYEE PROGRAMS: One example is Green Day, which is held on one Thursday a month with activities in the employee cafeteria. Other programs are used to maintain enthusiasm and to help employees practice environmental responsibility in their homes as well.

RECOGNITION FOR EMPLOYEES: Environmental awards for excellence in participation in the environmental program are issued to outstanding employees each month.

AWARDS: These are industry and environmental awards. Preparation for these awards is extensive but has proven valuable. The hotel has received several outstanding honors.

CUB CLUB: The hotel's family package is geared toward children. Each child is given a sapling for planting, in a reusable tube that converts to a bird feeder. There are eco-elements in the package collateral, including tips on how to enjoy Boston naturally.

SEMINARS, WORKSHOPS, AND SPEAKING ENGAGEMENTS: Tedd Saunders and Liz Kay speak at many local, national, and international gatherings in an effort to transfer information to various groups.

CONTRIBUTIONS TO OTHER WRITTEN WORKS, CASE STUDIES, SCHOOL PROGRAMS: Boston University's School of Management, under James Post, studies the hotel in its role as an industry leader on environmental responsibility. We have provided information to authors writing on the environment and have provided articles to industry and university publications on the environmental issues facing the hospitality industry.

Currently in the planning stages, a few new elements of the program include an eco-information phone, which will be placed in the lobby of the hotel, and a voluntary fund-raising effort that will have a matching contribution component and that is intended to benefit environmental organizations.

After two years of using public relations exclusively, the hotel has recently begun a limited placement of ads promoting the program. One reason for doing this is that the program has provided the hotel with a new, recognizable element that can be incorporated into its image-building efforts. The second reason is to take advantage of the increasing popularity of "eco-tourism," expanding the definition of the term to include the efforts hotels are making to provide concerned consumers with alternatives wherever they travel.

Green Meetings

Once you have launched a promotions campaign to unveil your company's environmental actions, you want to ensure that as many of your actions as possible reflect your commitments.

This effort can easily be extended to include the way your company prepares its meetings for shareholders, clients, sales staff, and so on, even when presentations are made outside the office.

We have all seen stacks of unused promotional materials left on exhibit floors, hundreds of discarded foam-backed signs and plastic name badges left behind on exhibit tables. With some simple rethinking and creative solutions, this waste can be eliminated.

More and more, meeting planners are demanding that their host hotel or convention center address environmental issues. A joint survey conducted by American Society of Association Executives and Meeting Planners International in early 1991 found that 56 percent of all meeting planners considered "green meetings" a priority. Mariyana Stamie, director of conferences for the Association of Records Management and Administration, has a list of environmental concerns for her conferences that includes the distribution of leftover food to local shelters and the provision of recycling containers on the exhibit floors.

The availability of these services affects her site selection decision. Stamie has also made all break sessions, up to eighty per conference, smoke-free. She recognizes that her demands can not only cut back on waste but also contribute to a more efficient conference. Her conference has taken on a new quality. And, what is more, Stamie has been empowered to effect change in the attitudes of everyone around her as well as on the exhibit floor.

Convention centers are responding to the demands of meeting planners. At the Moscone Convention Center in San Francisco, a concerted effort to recycle paper, glass, and aluminum has been implemented. John Adams, director of facilities for San Francisco Convention Facilities, says, "Although it takes some investment and tremendous operational support to create a successful recycling system, it will save money in the long run." Adams also feels that it is the shared responsibility of each exhibitor to reduce waste and to operate efficiently in order to achieve the overall goal of a green meeting.

Chicago's McCormick Place employees saved more that 2.9 tons of paper from April to August 1990, resulting in environmental and cost benefits—the latter due to lower trash bills. Conferees are now being asked to pitch in on recycling efforts by participating in full-scale separation of cups, bags, brochures, and other recyclable materials found on the trade show floor.

"If the client is concerned about green issues, we're prepared to handle them," says Nick Walker, special services manager at the Washington State Convention and Trade Center. The center has a comprehensive recycling program that responds to requests of planners who want to hold environmentally friendly events. He typically offers paper, cardboard, aluminum can, and badge recycling.

"It's becoming more prevalent that show managers and planners request environmentally friendly food service, utilizing glassware instead of foam cups or paper as well as recycling services," says Walker.

In order to help your company keep up with this trend, here are some easy ways to plan for green meetings.

Simple Guidelines for Conducting Green Meetings

1 Early on in the planning process, think through and list all printed materials that you will produce for your conference. Don't forget invitations, posters, signs, manuals, brochures, exhibit floor directories, and follow-up materials. Try to bid out the entire project with one printer. Purchasing a higher quantity of paper will allow your printer to buy in rolls instead of cut paper stock, dramatically reducing price. This will offer you a better opportunity to purchase recycled stock instead of virgin paper.

2 Check with the conference facilities manager to identify what is recyclable for the specific site, and clearly communicate that paper stock and recyclables are available to exhibitors and attendees early in the planning stages. Create an eco-page in preliminary materials to help integrate these initiatives during the planning and budgeting stages.

3 Giveaways should be environmentally sound as well. Consider a reusable plastic mug with logo and eco-message. Ceramic and glass products make excellent reusable gifts. Exhibitors can give away seeds, saplings, plants, and small trees. You can put your logo on recycled Frisbees. And attendees can take all their gifts home in a reusable cloth bag bearing your logo.

4 Cut back on throwaway coffee cups, plates, and utensils. Consider those cups alone and five thousand people at one conference. . .

two coffee breaks per day . . . and a five-day conference: fifty thousand cups saved from landfills and Dumpster fees. Some convention centers will not allow glass or china on the floor, but remember that recycled plastics last forever. With every eco-step you take, do not forget to tell attendees why you made the choice. Education is a key element to environmental awareness at all levels.

5 Choose foods that can be distributed to local shelters or soup kitchens. Take the time to set up a plan with the site to handle this logistic. Decide who will pay for transport; sometimes only a $10 taxi fare is needed. Require a receipt for transportation to the shelter.

6 Suggest that nonrecyclable colored paper not be used and that two-sided copies be used whenever possible. Have receptacles available for all badges, preferably reusable badges. If using sticky-back labels, encourage participants to reapply them for as long as possible before disposing of them. Have collection containers located throughout your meeting space to separate glass, paper, and cans, and encourage participants to recycle.

7 Do what you can within your budget, yet try to stretch your environmental goals in just one area as an extra green-meeting challenge. Do something you can have fun with, and be imaginative in expressing your environmental concern, like snacks from a manufacturer that donates proceeds to environmental causes or a coupon or pass to the local aquarium, park, science museum, or other eco-attraction.

Sample Press Release

Tips on Writing News Releases

The purpose of a news release is to report newsworthy and verifiable events. Opinions are news only when they come from people whose positions make them relevant to an issue.

Opinions about the quality of one's personal endeavor ("We're the greatest thing since sliced bread!") are more appropriate to advertising. The exception to this would be a news release announcing the presentation of an award, when the opinion would be substantiated by the award itself.

News releases are written in journalistic style, or "inverted triangle" style, so called because the opening paragraphs will answer the questions *who, what, when, where,* and *why.*

They are written in the past tense. The writer assumes the persona of a reporter and "reports" on what the spokesperson said (past tense)—even if the writer *is* the spokesperson!

News releases should be short—never more than two pages. They should be double-spaced.

The contact person's name and phone numbers (both home and business) should go at the top.

The first information—called the dateline—tells the city from which the information is being released and the date.

The title and affiliation of each person quoted must be included with the first quote from that person. If additional quotes from that person follow, only the last name needs to be used, though some newspapers (the *New York Times*, for example) always refer to the person quoted as Mr., Ms., or Miss (even if he or she is a convicted criminal).

Grammar, punctuation, and capitalization can be tricky if you're not familiar with journalistic style. The *Associated Press Style Book* is a worthwhile investment for the person who is committed to writing news releases as professionally as possible. But we suggest that beginners hire a freelance copy editor to review their efforts. The name and phone number of a freelance copy editor can be obtained from a local newspaper or the department of journalism at a local college or university.

If you try to find one at the last moment, you may run into a crunch and decide to send it out without copyediting. Don't do this if you've never written a press release before. Remember, you have to convince only one or two people, an editor and possibly a reporter, that a story is newsworthy. But reporters and editors have been reading professionally prepared releases for years. To be taken seriously, your news release has to measure up to a standard. The quality of the writing, including grammar and style, and the neatness of the release, along with the news angle presented, will create an impression of credibility. As Will Rogers said, "You never get a second chance to make a good first impression," so do it right the first time, and every time.

Students of Many Cultures are Among Those Receiving Help in Entering Green Professions

LOS ANGELES, November 7 (1991)—The first 18 participants in a new program to serve community environmental needs and guide young women and people of color into conservation careers in national parks, forests and wildlife refuges were announced today by the national program director, Marta Cruz Kelly. Los Angeles is the first city to select students for the program, called the Conservation Career Development Program (CCDP). CCDP programs in San Francisco, Washington DC, and Newark, New Jersey, are also being launched.

CCDP is an educational program of the Student Conservation Association (SCA), a New Hampshire–based nonprofit organization that has been matching volunteers with conservation field opportunities in forests, parks and wilderness areas for over 35 years. Unlike SCA's volunteer programs, CCDP has year-round activities, involves paying a stipend to participants for summer field work and, though it does not exclude others, is designed specifically to meet the need for nonwhite and female professionals in conservation work.

Ms. Kelly said the program, which encompasses environmental education, mentoring, college preparation, field experience, leadership training and networking with conservation professionals, can provide up to six years of career development for high school and college-age participants, depending upon when they enter the program.

"A lifetime commitment to conserving the environment can begin for each of our participants," said Ms. Kelly. "These students will be training for careers in wildlife and resource management, forestry, planning, park and recreation administration, history and archaeology. Ours is the only program of its kind to focus primarily on helping women and multi-ethnics obtain important, skilled jobs in conservation."

The first group of CCDP participants from the Los Angeles area include students from Woodrow Wilson, Lincoln, Kennedy, Thomas Jefferson and Eaglerock high schools. Almost equally divided between male and female, the group ranges in age from 16 to 18. The annual selection of 24 young people from each of five cities has been set as a CCDP goal by 1993.

Participants bear no part of the cost of the program, which has been funded in Los Angeles by the Ahmanson Foundation, the Michael J. Connell Foundation, Millers Outpost, the James Irvine Foundation and the ARCO Foundation. Further information about the Los Angeles CCDP program may be obtained by calling 213-747-6798.

Epilogue: Business or Pleasure

Business has long contributed to the earth's environmental problems. Chemical and oil companies, the largest creators of pollution, were the worst offenders. Ironically, business is now the earth's salvation.

For decades business virtually ran amok. More stringent legislation and increasing public outcry have finally begun to convert business from predator to potential savior. While spending some $65 billion a year to comply with federal environmental regulations, business has finally begun to "get it" and has gone green, turning a spectacular financial obligation into a savvy marketing ploy along the way.

Gone, we hope, are the days when businesses could operate in any way they pleased for the most profit, oblivious to the alarming depletion of our natural resources and the contamination of the ground we depend on to produce our crops, the water we drink, and the very air we breathe. Gone, we hope, are the days when there were no government regulations or public scrutiny to divert business from its lethal lethargy, when there were just random objections by a few who dared to speak out but who were ignored or quickly silenced.

Now the focus is on how the world can continue to enjoy the same or greater comfort and luxury at considerably less cost to the planet. Only the relatively few diehard conservationists may be willing to make fewer demands on our resources by doing with less. Most people don't want to consume less; they want what they have but more efficiently. Certainly it's not in the best interest of business to promote across-the-board reductions in goods and services. Technologies must be developed to maintain lifestyles with more environmentally sound policies in place and with methods that actually pay off.

The idea of saving the planet while enhancing business and saving money is not new. Several years ago, former U.S. president George Bush was quoted as saying, "Successful economic development and environmental protection go hand in hand. You cannot have one without the other." This same sentiment has been expressed repeatedly since President Theodore Roosevelt addressed the Congress in 1903 decrying the waste of natural resources and the resultant threat to the country's prosperity.

The questions that remain unanswered are, Can we trust business to put its money where its professed conservation policies are? Will the new environmental broom keep sweeping with the same vigor through this decade and into the twenty-first century? Generations of plunder cannot be remedied by a few passes with an industrial-sized vacuum cleaner. Business must remain loyal to its promises and ever vigilant about its progress.

To ensure this loyalty and vigilance, consumers must continue to speak out both in voice and action. While government may need to adjust regulations to promote investments that can be justified both environmentally and economically, it cannot rely on strictly voluntary efforts. The squeeze on corporate America cannot be relaxed.

Environmental programs are still new enough as to be suspect. Speculation abounds on the reasons why a program is implemented—because it is cost efficient, mandated by law, or the trendy thing to do. But the reasons are not important. A company is not to be faulted because it recognizes that conservation is good business, chooses to be in the forefront of innovation, or is complying with legislative rule. Whatever the cause, the effect is what counts. The case studies chosen here address a range of companies that were spurred to action by government regulation, good business sense, public outcry, or just plain conscience; more than likely, a combination of all of the above.

Afterword

I doubt there are many challenges more complex—or more vital—than that of reconciling human economic activity with the natural environment. In the end, our planet's economic well-being depends on the continued health of its natural resources. We cannot maintain economies without maintaining ecology, and anything that depletes one will in time diminish the other.

This was the message that rang out clearly from last year's Earth Summit in Rio de Janeiro. No longer can we regard the costs borne by nature as "external" to the business calculus.

Seen in this light, clear-cutting the forest in the Amazon basin for short-term gain sacrifices not only an extraordinarily rich biological legacy but also the opportunity for the children and grandchildren of the Amazon rancher—and perhaps our children and grandchildren as well—to earn a livelihood from that forest, as well as discover new medicines and pest-resistant plants. The sediment washing from fields in Pennsylvania not only destroys the rich marshes of the Chesapeake Bay but also drains away the basic capital of agricultural livelihood, topsoil.

How long can this continue before farmers see their own income eroding? How long can a business that relies on extracted minerals survive with depleted supplies?

Whether we talk about topsoil, forests, water, or minerals, more and more we find that the loss of valued ecological resources stems from a wasteful and ultimately unsustainable economic activity. For that reason, businesses must develop a new environmental ethic for the long term.

In the global economy of the future, one of the defining elements of international competitiveness will be the environment. Which businesses will be most successful in adjusting to and incorporating environmental costs? Which businesses will address the environmental effects of manufacturing processes and sourcing raw materials? The answer to these questions will say a lot about which businesses come out on top in the global marketplace.

An even more fundamental question is: Which businesses will consider the ultimate effects of their products—both on nature and on society's consumption patterns? Far more fundamental than any single corporate initiative is a change in the very philosophy of business.

Aldo Leopold once wrote, "We abuse land because we regard it as a commodity belonging to us. When we see land as a community to which we belong, we may begin to use it with love and respect."

So until industry relinquishes its traditional "ownership" of natural capital and its fixation on short-term profits, it cannot truthfully speak of a "green" transformation. Until owners and managers remember that they, too, are citizens of the world, as dependent on that world's bounty as the rest of us, they cannot secure the future for themselves or for succeeding generations.

KATHRYN S. FULLER
World Wildlife Fund

RESOURCE GUIDE
AND BIBLIOGRAPHY

Organizations for Environment and Business Partnerships, Community Outreach Programs

Acid Rain Foundation
1410 Varsity Drive
Raleigh, NC 27606
919-828-9443
Strives to bring about a greater understanding of the acid rain problem.

African Wildlife Foundation
1717 Massachusetts Avenue, NW
Washington, DC 20036
202-265-8394
Works directly with Africans in both the public and private sectors in more than twenty-five countries to promote conservation, education, and wildlife management training.

Air and Waste Management Association
P.O. Box 2861
Pittsburgh, PA 15230
412-232-3444
Formerly Air Pollution Control Foundation, which was founded in 1907. Publishes the *International Journal of Air Pollution Control and Hazardous Waste Management*.

Air Pollution Action Network
Postbus 5627
N-1007 AP Amsterdam, Netherlands
International organization founded in 1985.

Air Resources Information Clearinghouse
Center for Environmental Information
46 Prince Street
Rochester, NY 14607
716-271-3550
Comprehensive reference and referral educational service on acid rain, ozone depletion, the greenhouse effect, etc.

Alaska Conservation Foundation
430 West Seventh Street, no. 215
Anchorage, AK 99501
907-276-1917

Alliance for Clean Energy
1901 North Fort Meyer Drive, 12th Floor
Arlington, VA 22209
703-841-1781
An alliance of low-sulphur coal producers, users, and transporters concerned about the acid rain problem.

The Alliance for Environmental Education
10751 Ambassador Drive, Suite 201
Manassas, VA 22110
703-335-1025
Serves as an advocate for a quality environment through education and communication, cooperation, and exchange among organizations.

Alliance for Responsible CFC Policy
1901 North Fort Meyer Drive, 12th Floor
Arlington, VA 22209
703-841-1781
Group composed of users and producers of chlorofluorocarbon chemicals.

Alliance to Save Energy
1725 K Street, NW, Suite 914
Washington, DC 20036
202-857-0666
Coalition of business, government, and consumer leaders who seek to increase the efficient use of energy.

Alternative Sources of Energy
107 South Central Avenue
Milaca, MN 56353
612-983-6892
Primarily concerned with windpower, hydropower, and photovoltaics promoted by the independent power production industry.

America the Beautiful Fund
Shoreham Building, Room 219
806 Fifteenth Street, NW
Washington, DC 20005
202-638-1649

American Council for an Energy Efficient Economy
1001 Connecticut Avenue, NW,
Suite 535
Washington, DC 20036
202-429-8873
Promotes the implementation of more energy-efficient and economical technologies and practices.

American Gas Association
1515 Wilson Boulevard
Arlington, VA 22209
703-841-8400
Alliance of natural, manufactured, and liquefied gas providers.

American Lung Association
1740 Broadway
New York, NY 10019-4374
212-315-8700
Involved in a variety of air pollution issues, particularly tobacco use.

American Petroleum Institute
1220 L Street, NW
Washington, DC 20005
202-682-8000
Cooperates with government and the environmental community to establish practices promoting energy use that is compatible with the environment.

American Rivers
801 Pennsylvania Avenue, SE, Suite 400
Washington, DC 20003
202-547-6900
Fax 202-543-6142
A nonprofit conservation organization leading the effort to protect and restore the nation's outstanding rivers and their environments.

American Society for Environmental Education
1592 Union Street, no. 426
San Francisco, CA 94108
415-931-7000

American Solar Energy Association
1667 K Street, NW, Suite 395
Washington, DC 20006
202-347-2000

Consists of distributors, retailers, engineers, and architects in the solar energy industry.

American Solar Energy Society
2400 Central Avenue, B-1
Boulder, CO 80301
303-443-3130
Professionals organized to promote solar energy through science and technology.

American Wind Energy Association
1730 North Lynn Street, Suite 610
Arlington, VA 22209
703-276-8334
Promotes the harnessing of wind energy as a renewable energy source.

Americans for Energy Independence
1629 K Street, NW, Suite 500
Washington, DC 20006
202-466-2105
Established to develop and utilize available domestic energy resources as an essential condition for economic health and security.

Americans for the Environment
1400 Sixteenth Street, NW
Washington, DC 20036
202-797-6665

Appliance Recycling Centers of America
654 University Avenue
St. Paul, MN 55104
612-291-1100
Recycles the freon in refrigeration and air-conditioning units.

Asia & Pacific Energy Planning Network
P.O. Box 12224
50770 Kuala Lumpur, Malaysia
60-32548088

Asia Pacific Confederation of Chemical Engineering
c/o Institution of Engineers
11 National Circuit
Barton 2600, Australia
61-62706555

253

**Asia-Pacific People's
Environmental Network**
Sahabat Alam Malaysia
42 Salween Road
100050 Penang, Malaysia
60-4375705

Asian Environmental Society
Vidhata House, 3d Floor, U-112
Vikasmarg, Shakarpur
Delhi, 110092 India
91-112223311

**Association of Local Air Pollution
Control Officials**
444 North Capitol Street, NW, Suite 306
Washington, DC 20001
202-624-7864
Publishes *Washington Update*, a newsletter
covering activities of the EPA.

Atlantic Center for Environment
39 South Main Street
Ipswich, MA 01938
617-356-0160

**Baltic Marine Environmental
Protection Commission**
Mannerheimintie 12A
SF-00100 Helsinki, Finland
358-0602366

**Biomass Energy Research
Association**
1825 K Street, NW, Suite 503
Washington, DC 20006
202-785-2856
Facilitates technology transfer,
information exchange, and education
in biomass energy research.

**Californians Against Waste
Foundation**
926 J Street, Suite 606
Sacramento, CA 95814
916-443-8317
Offers a guidebook for recycled paper.

**Center for Environmental
Information**
46 Prince Street
Rochester, NY 14607
716-271-3550

Provides timely, accurate, and
comprehensive information on
environmental issues through
publications, educational programs, and
information services.

Center for Our Common Future
Palais Wilson
52 rue des Paquis
1201 Geneva, Switzerland
41-227327117

Chesapeake Bay Foundation
162 Prince George Street
Annapolis, MD 21401
410-268-8816

**Citizen's Clearinghouse for
Hazardous Wastes**
P.O. Box 6806
Falls Church, VA 22040
703-237-2249

Clean Water Action Project
317 Pennsylvania Avenue, SE
Washington, DC 20003
202-457-1286

Clean Water Fund
317 Pennsylvania Avenue, SE, 3d Floor
Washington, DC 20005
202-457-0336

Climate Institute
324 Fourth Street, NE
Washington, DC 20002
202-547-0104
Researches global climate change.

**Coalition for Environmentally
Responsible Economies (CERES)**
711 Atlantic Avenue
Boston, MA 02111
617-451-9495

Commonwealth Forestry Association
c/o Oxford Forestry Institute
South Parks Road
Oxford OX1 3RB, United Kingdom
44-865275072

Community Environment Council
930 Miramonte Drive
Santa Barbara, CA 93109
805-963-0583

CONCAWE
(Oil Companies' European Organization
for Environmental Health Protection)
Madouplein 1
Brussels B-1030, Belgium
32-22203111

Concern
1794 Columbia Road, NW
Washington, DC 20009
202-328-8160
Provides environmental information to
individuals and groups and encourages
grass-roots participation.

**Conservation and Renewable Energy
Inquiry and Referral Service**
P.O. Box 8900
Silver Spring, MD 20907
800-523-2929
Acts as a clearinghouse for the U.S.
Department of Energy to aid in the
transfer of technology through the
dissemination of public information.

Conservation Education Association
RR 1, Box 53
Guthrie Center, IA 50115
515-747-8383

Conservation Foundation
1250 Twenty-fourth Street, NW
Washington, DC 20037
202-293-4800
Research and public education
organization founded in 1948.

Conservation Fund
1800 North Kent Street, no. 1120
Arlington, VA 22209
703-525-6300

**Conservation International
Foundation**
1015 Eighteenth Street, NW, no. 1000
Washington, DC 20036
202-429-5660

**Conservatree Consultants/
Conservatree Paper Company**
10 Lombard Street
San Francisco, CA 94111
415-433-1000, ext. 35

Offers a guidebook and workshops on
recycled paper issues.

Co-op America
2100 M Street, NW, no. 403
Washington, DC 20037
202-872-5307 or 800-424-2667

Council on Alternate Fuels
1225 I Street, NW, Suite 320
Washington, DC 20005
202-898-0711
Companies interested in the production
and development of synthetic fuels.

**Council on Plastics and Packaging
for the Environment**
1001 Connecticut Avenue, NW, no. 401
Washington, DC 20036
202-331-0099

The Cousteau Society
930 W. Twenty-first Street
Norfolk, VA 23517
804-627-1144
An international nonprofit organization
supported primarily by members and
dedicated to the protection and
improvement of the quality of life
through education by way of television,
lectures, and print media.

Cultural Survival
215 First Street
Cambridge, MA 02142
617-621-3818

Defenders of Wildlife
1244 Nineteenth Street, NW
Washington, DC 20036
202-659-9510
A national nonprofit organization whose
goal is to preserve, enhance, and protect
the national abundance and diversity of
wildlife.

EarthDay USA
P.O. Box 470
Peterborough, NH 03458
603-924-7720
Acts as a clearinghouse for Earth Day
activities and environmental
organizations.

255

Earthsave
706 Frederick Road
Santa Cruz, CA 95062
408-423-4069

Earthtrust
2500 Pali Highway
Honolulu, HI 04241
808-254-2866

Earthwatch
P.O. Box 403
680 Mt. Auburn Street
Watertown, MA 02172
617-926-8200
Sends volunteers to work with scientists
around the world who are researching
ways to save rainforests and endangered
species, preserve archaeological finds,
and study pollution effects.

Ecological Society of America
Public Affairs Office
2010 Massachusetts Avenue, NW,
no. 240
Washington, DC 20036
202-833-8773

**Emergency Earth Rescue
Administration**
1480 Hoyt Street, Suite 31
Lakewood, CO 80215
303-233-3548
Environmental rescue organization that
works to solve crises such as oil spills
and chemical spills as quickly as possible
with the least amount of environmental
damage.

Energy Conservation Coalition
1525 New Hampshire Avenue, NW
Washington, DC 20036
202-628-1400

Energy Research Institute
6850 Rattlesnake Hammock Road
Naples, FL 33962
813-793-1922
Individuals and companies interested in
alternative energy sources.

**Environment and Development of
Third World**
Boite Postale
Dakar 3370, Senegal
221-224229

**Environment and Energy Study
Institute**
122 C Street, NW, Suite 700
Washington, DC 20001-2109
202-628-1400

Environmental Action
625 Broadway
New York, NY 10012
212-677-1601

Environmental Action Foundation
1525 New Hampshire Avenue, NW
Washington, DC 20036
202-745-4870
Conducts technical and legal research in
solid waste issues, including source
reduction, underground storage tanks,
citizen suits, and corrective action.

Environmental Council
80 York Way
London N1 9AG, United Kingdom
44-712784736

Environmental Defense Fund
257 Park South
New York, NY 10010
212-505-2100
Dedicated to finding solutions to
environmental problems through the
combined efforts of scientists,
economists, and attorneys.

**Environmental Hazards Management
Institute**
P.O. Box 932
10 Newmarket Road
Durham, NH 03824
603-868-1547
Offers *Re-Source* newsletter on numerous
environmental issues.

Environmental Industry Council
1825 K Street, NW, no. 120
Washington, DC 20006
202-331-7706

Environmental Law Institute
1616 P Street, NW, no. 200
Washington, DC 20036
202-939-3800

Environmental Protection Agency Community Right-to-Know Hotline
800-535-0202

Environmental Protection Agency Pollution Prevention Clearinghouse and Hotline
800-424-9346

Environmental Resource Center
Crowder College
Neosho, MO 64850
417-457-3583

European Environmental Bureau
rue de la Victoire 26, Suite 12
B-1060 Brussels, Belgium
32-25390037

Freshwater Foundation
Spring Hill Center
725 County Road 6
Wayzata, MN 55391
612-449-0092

Friends of the Earth
218 D Street, SE
Washington, DC 20003
202-544-2600
Engages in lobbying, litigation, and dissemination of public information on the conservation, preservation, and rational use of the earth's resources.

Friends of the Everglades
202 Park Street
Miami, FL 33166
305-888-1230
Goal is ''to foster and facilitate through education, a harmonious coexistence between human and natural environment systems'' in the Everglades.

Friends of the River
909 Twelfth Street, no. 207
Sacramento, CA 95814
916-442-3155

Global ReLeaf/The American Forestry Association
P.O. Box 2000
Washington, DC 20013
202-667-3300
National tree-planting and tree awareness organization.

Global Tomorrow Coalition
1325 G Street, NW, Suite 915
Washington, DC 20005-3104
202-628-4016
Coalition of 115 organizations, with more than 8 million members, emphasizing global concern about environment and resources.

Green Cross Certification Company
1611 Telegraph Avenue, Suite 1111
Oakland, CA 94612-2113
510-832-1415

Green Seal
1250 Twenty-third Street, NW, Suite 275
Washington, DC 20037
202-331-7337

Greenpeace USA
1436 U Street, NW
Washington, DC 20009
202-462-1177
An international organization dedicated to protecting the natural environment. Campaigns against the slaughter of whales and seals, nuclear fuel processing, and indiscriminate abuse of resources around the world.

Inform
381 Park Avenue South
New York, NY 10016
212-689-4040
Conducts environmental research and publishes reports on practical actions for the preservation and conservation of natural resources and public health. Current research focuses on hazardous waste reduction, garbage management, urban air quality, and land and water conservation.

257

**Institute for Energy and
Environmental Research**
6935 Laurel Avenue
Takoma Park, MD 20912
301-270-5500

Institute for Environmental Auditing
1725 Duke Street, Suite 660
Alexandria, VA 22314
703-548-1906

**Institute for Environmental
Negotiation**
Campbell Hall, University of Virginia
Charlottesville, VA 22903
804-924-0311

**Institute for European
Environmental Policy**
Aloys-Schulte Strasse 6
D-5300 Bonn, Germany
49-228223810

**International Center for Solution of
Environmental Problems**
535 Lovett Boulevard
Houston, TX 77006
713-527-0135

International Energy Agency
2 rue Andre Pascal
F-75775 Paris Cedex 16, France
33-145248200

International Environmental Bureau
P.O. Box 301, Vollsveien 13B
1324, Lysaker Norway
47-2581800

**International Professional
Association for Environmental
Affairs**
31 rue Montoyer, Boite 1
B-1040 Brussels, Belgium
32-25136083

Jane Goodall Institute for Wildlife
P.O. Box 41720
Tucson, AZ 85717
602-325-1211

Provides ongoing support and expansion
of field research on wild chimpanzees
and studies of chimpanzees in captive
environments. Dedicated to publicizing
the unique status of chimpanzees to
ensure their preservation in the wild and
their physical well-being in captivity.

Keep America Beautiful
9 Broad Street, West
Stamford, CT 06902
203-323-8987

Kids for a Clean Environment
P.O. Box 158254
Nashville, TN 37215
800-952-3223

**Legal Environmental Assistance
Fund**
115 North Gadsen Street
Tallahassee, FL 32301
904-681-2591

**Municipal Solid Waste Management
Association**
1620 I Street, NW, 4th Floor
Washington, DC 20006
202-293-7330

National Arbor Day Foundation
100 Arbor Avenue
Nebraska City, NE 68410
402-474-5655
Sponsors public awareness for the
protection and conservation of trees
through Arbor Day, Tree City USA, etc.

National Audubon Society
950 Third Avenue
New York, NY 10022
212-832-3200
Aims to conserve plants and animals and
their habitats and to promote national
strategies for energy development and
use, stressing conservation and renewable resources and the wise use of land
and water. Seeks solutions for global
environmental problems. Local and state
regional offices.

National Coalition Against the Misuse of Pesticides
530 Seventh Street, SE
Washington, DC 20001
202-543-5450

National Environmental Development Association
1440 New York Avenue, NW, no. 300
Washington, DC 20005
202-638-1230

National Environmental Education Foundation
915 Fifteenth Street, NW, Suite 200
Washington, DC 20005
202-628-8200

National Hydropower Association
1133 Twenty-first Street, NW, Suite 500
Washington, DC 20036
202-331-7551
Hydrodevelopers, dam site owners, and manufacturers who promote the use of hydroelectric energy.

National Park Foundation
P.O. Box 57473
Washington, DC 20037
202-785-4500

National Parks and Conservation Association
1015 Thirty-first Street, NW, no. 400
Washington, DC 20007
202-223-6722

National Recycling Coalition
1101 Thirtieth Street, NW, Suite 305
Washington, DC 20007
202-625-6406

National Resources Council of America
801 Pennsylvania Avenue, SE, no. 410
Washington, DC 20003
202-547-7553

National Wildlife Federation
1400 Sixteenth Street, NW
Washington, DC 20036-2266
202-797-6800
Promotes the wise use of natural resources and protection of the global

environment through the distribution of periodicals and educational materials and participation in outdoor conservation programs.

National Wildlife Refuge Association
10824 Fox Hunt Lane
Potomac, MD 20854
301-983-1238

Natural Resources Council of America
1015 Thirty-first Street, NW
Washington, DC 20007
202-333-8495
Association of major national and regional organizations concerned with the sound management of natural resources in the public interest.

Nature Conservancy
1815 N. Lynn Street
Arlington, VA 22209
703-841-5300
An international nonprofit membership organization founded in 1917 and committed to preserving biological diversity. Manages a system of more than one thousand nature sanctuaries worldwide. Works with South and Central America to preserve rainforests.

North American Wildlife Foundation
102 Wilmot Road, no. 410
Deerfield, IL 60061
708-940-7776

North Atlantic Treaty Organization (NATO)
Auto route du Zaventem
B-1110 Brussels, Belgium
32-22410040

Office of Conservation and Renewable Energy
1000 Independence Avenue, SW
Washington, DC 20001
202-586-9220

259

**Organization for Economic
Cooperation and Development,
Environment Committee**
2 rue Andre Pascal
75775 Paris, France
33-145248200

**Organization for Economic
Cooperation and Development,
Nuclear Energy Agency**
38 boulevard Suchet
75016 Paris, France
33-145248200

Pacific Wildlife Project
P.O. Box 7673
Laguna Niguel, CA 92607
714-831-1178

Passive Solar Industries Council
2836 Duke Street
Alexandria, VA 22314
703-371-0357

People, Food and Land Foundation
35751 Oak Springs Drive
Tollhouse, CA 93667
209-855-3710
Small farmers concerned with low water
use, arid land crops, solar models, and
organic farming.

Physicians for Social Responsibility
1000 Sixteenth Street, NW, Suite 810
Washington, DC 20036
202-785-3777

Planet Drum Foundation
Box 31251
San Francisco, CA 94131
415-285-6556

Rails-to-Trails Conservancy
1400 Sixteenth Street, NW, Suite 300
Washington, DC 20036
202-797-5400
Establishes greenways for walking,
bicycling, horseback riding, cross-
country skiing, and wildlife habitation
by converting thousands of miles of
abandoned railway corridors for
public use.

Rainforest Action Network
450 Sansome Street, no. 700
San Francisco, CA 94111
415-398-4404
A nonprofit activist organization
dedicated to preserving the world's
rainforests.

Rainforest Alliance
270 Lafayette Street, Suite 512
New York, NY 10012
212-941-1900
Fax 212-941-4986
Dedicated to preserving the world's
tropical forests by promoting sound
alternatives to the activities that promote
deforestation.

Renew America
1400 Sixteenth Street, NW, Suite 710
Washington, DC 20036
202-232-2252
A nonprofit, tax-exempt national
organization created to promote a
sustainable society through the use of
renewable energy, resource
conservation, and sustainable
agriculture.

**Renewable Natural Resources
Foundation**
5430 Grosvenor Lane
Bethesda, MD 20814
301-493-9101

Resources for the Future
1616 P Street, NW
Washington, DC 20036
202-328-5000
Develops renewable resource projects
and provides information to local
groups.

Rocky Mountain Institute
1739 Snowmass Creek Road
Snowmass, CO 81654
303-927-3861
An information source on superinsulated
homes and other resource-efficient living.

Safe Energy Communication Council
1717 Massachusetts Avenue, SW
Washington, DC 20036
202-483-8491

Save the Bay
434 Smith Street
Providence, RI 03908
401-272-3540

Save the Dunes Council
444 Barker Road
Michigan City, IN 46360
219-879-3937
Dedicated to the preservation and protection of the Indiana Dunes for public use and enjoyment by working to minimize air, water, and waste pollution affecting the National Lakeshore and Northwest Indiana area.

Save-the-Redwoods League
114 Sansome Street, Room 605
San Francisco, CA 94104
415-362-2352
Fax 415-362-7017
Purchases redwood groves and watershed lands for protection in public parks; supports reforestation, research, and educational programs.

Sierra Club
730 Polk Street
San Francisco, CA 94109
415-776-2211
Founded in 1892, one of the largest and best-known environmental organizations in the world. Promotes conservation by influencing public policy and practicing the responsible use of the earth's ecosystems and resources.

Smithsonian Environmental Research Center
P.O. Box 28
Edgewater, MD 21037
301-261-4190

Soil and Water Conservation Society
7515 N.E. Ankeny Road
Ankeny, IA 50021-9764
515-289-2331
Advocates the conservation of soil, water, and related resources.

Solar Energy Research Institute
1617 Cole Boulevard
Golden, CO 80401
303-231-1000

Tree People
12601 Mulholland Drive
Beverly Hills, CA 90210
213-753-4600
Dedicated to the replanting of urban trees.

Trust for Public Land
116 New Montgomery Street, 4th Floor
San Francisco, CA 94105
415-495-4014
Dedicated to acquiring and preserving land in urban and rural areas for parks and gardens.

United Nations Environmental Programme
P.O. Box 30552
Nairobi, Kenya
254-2230800

U.S. Council for Energy Awareness
1776 I Street, NW, Suite 400
Washington, DC 20006
202-293-0770
Electric utilities manufacturers, industrial firms, research, and service organizations engaged in the development of nuclear energy.

U.S. Council on Environmental Quality
722 Jackson Place, NW
Washington, DC 20503
202-395-5750
Assists and advises the president on conditions, trends, and the quality of the environment.

U.S. Department of Energy
1000 Independence Avenue, SW
Washington, DC 20585
202-586-5000
or 202-586-8800 for Energy
Information Center
Central energy-data collection and
analysis arm of the federal government.

**U.S. Department of Energy
Conservation and Renewable Energy
Division**
1000 Independence Avenue, SW
Washington, DC 20585
202-586-9220

U.S. Department of the Interior
1849 C Street, NW
Washington, DC 20240
202-208-5048
The major federal agency responsible for
fish and wildlife, land management,
mining, national parks, and forests, and
Indian lands.

U.S. Energy Association
1620 I Street, NW, Suite 615
Washington, DC 20006
202-331-0415

Water Environment Federation
601 Wythe Street
Alexandria, VA 22314
703-684-2400

Water Pollution Control Federation
601 Wythe Street
Alexandria, VA 22314
703-684-2400

The Wilderness Society
1400 First Street NW, 10th Floor
Washington, DC 20005
202-842-3400
One of the oldest nonprofit membership
organizations dedicated to preserving
wilderness and wildlife; protecting
America's prime forests, parks, rivers,
and shorelines; and fostering an
American land ethic.

Wildlife Conservation International
Bronx Zoo
Bronx, NY 10460
212-220-6891
Fax 212-364-7963
An international organization committed
to preserving biological diversity and
resources by exploring and promoting
sustainable solutions.

Wildlife Society
5410 Grosvenor Lane
Bethesda, MD 20814
301-897-9770
Fax 301-530-2471
A nonprofit scientific and educational
organization dedicated to conserving and
sustaining wildlife productivity and
diversity through resource management
and education of wildlife professionals.

Windstar Foundation
2317 Snowmass Creek Road
Snowmass, CO 81654
303-542-7300
Publishers of *Recycling: 101 Practical Tips
for Home and Work* booklet.

World Environment Center
4198 Park Avenue, Suite 1403
New York, NY 10016
212-683-4700
Serves as a bridge between the
government and industry.

World Health Organization
Avenue Appia CH-1211
Geneva 27, Switzerland
Agency of the United Nations established
in 1948 to further international
cooperation for improved health
conditions worldwide.

World Resources Institute
1709 New York Avenue, NW, Suite 700
Washington, DC 20006
202-638-6300
Fax 202-638-0036
A policy research center that helps
governments, the private sector, and
environmental organizations address

issues of sustainable agriculture, energy, climate change, pollution, and economic incentives for sustainable development.

World Wildlife Fund
1250 Twenty-fourth Street, NW
Washington, DC 20037
202-293-4800
A private U.S. organization that works worldwide to protect endangered wildlife and wetlands, especially rainforests.

Worldwatch Institute
1776 Massachusetts Avenue, NW
Washington, DC 20036
202-452-1999
Publishes *State of the World Report*, focusing on ozone, food production, and alternative energy.

Industry Trade Groups

Aluminum Association
900 Nineteenth Street, NW, Suite 300
Washington, DC 20006
202-862-5100

Aluminum Recycling Association
1000 Sixteenth Street, NW, Suite 603
Washington, DC 20036
202-785-0951

American Paper Institute
260 Madison Avenue
New York, NY 10016
212-340-0600

American Petroleum Institute
1220 L Street, NW
Washington, DC 20005
202-682-8100

American Public Health
1015 Fifteenth Street, NW
Washington, DC 20005
202-789-5600

American Public Power Association
2301 M Street, NW
Washington, DC 20037
202-467-2900

American Public Transit Association
1201 New York Avenue, NW, no. 400
Washington, DC 20005
202-898-4000

Business Roundtable
1615 L Street, NW, no. 1350
Washington, DC 20036
202-872-1260

Can Manufacturers Institute
1625 Massachusetts Avenue, NW
Washington, DC 20036
202-232-4677

Center for Hazardous Materials Research
University of Pittsburgh Applied Research Center
320 William Pitt Way
Pittsburgh, PA 15238
412-826-5320

Center for Plastics Recycling Research
Rutgers University
Bldg. 3529, Busch Campus
Piscataway, NJ 08855

Clean Sites
1199 N. Fairfax Street, Suite 400
Alexandria, VA 22314
703-683-8522

Conservatree Paper Company
10 Lombard Street, no. 250
San Francisco, CA 94111
800-522-9200

Council for Solid Waste Solutions
1275 K Street, NW, Suite 400
Washington, DC 20005
202-371-5319

Council on Alternative Fuels
1225 I Street, NW, Suite 320
Washington, DC 20005
202-898-0711

Cross Pointe Paper Company
1295 Bandana Boulevard, N, Suite 335
St. Paul, MN 55108
800-543-3297

Earth Care Paper
P.O. Box 14140
Madison, WI 53714-0140
808-277-2900

Edison Electric Institute
701 Pennsylvania Avenue, NW
Washington, DC 20004-2696
202-508-5000

Electric Generation Association
2715 M Street, NW, no. 150
Washington, DC 20007
202-965-1134

Electric Power Research Institute
3412 Hillview Avenue
P.O. Box 10412
Palo Alto, CA 94303
415-855-2141

Environment Technology Export Council
7911 Herschel Avenue, Suite 300
La Jolla, CA 92037
619-456-1861

Federal Energy Regulatory Commission
825 N. Capitol Street
Washington, DC 20426
202-208-0200

Fertilizer Institute
501 Second Street, NW
Washington, DC 20002
202-675-8250

Flexible Packaging Association
1090 Vermont Avenue, NW, Suite 500
Washington, DC 20036
202-842-3880

Food Marketing Institute
800 Connecticut Avenue, NW
Washington, DC 20006
202-452-8444

Forest Products Research Society
2801 Marshall Court
Madison, WI 53705
608-231-1361

Georgia-Pacific Paper Company
Box 105605
Atlanta, GA 30348-5605
404-521-4000

Geosafe
Batelle Pacific Northwest Laboratories
4000 N.E. Forty-first Street
Seattle, WA 98105
206-525-3130
Glassification of hazardous waste that makes it safe for disposal.

Glass Packaging Institute
1627 K Street, NW, Suite 800
Washington, DC 20006
202-887-4850

Greenhouse Crisis Foundation
1130 Seventeenth Street, NW, Suite 630
Washington, DC 20036
202-466-2823

Gypsum Association
810 First Street, NW, Suite 510
Washington, DC 20002
202-289-5440

Hazardous Materials Controls Research Institute
7237 Hanover Parkway
Greenbelt, MD 20910
301-982-9500

Hazardous Waste Treatment Council
1440 New York Avenue, NW, Suite 310
Washington, DC 20005
202-783-0870

Institute of Scrap Recycling Industries
162 K Street, NW
Washington, DC 20006
202-466-4050

National Association for Plastic Container Recovery (NAPCOR)
4828 Parkway Plaza Boulevard, Suite 260
Charlotte, NC 28217
704-357-3250

National Association of Environmental Professionals
P.O. Box 15210
Alexandria, VA 22309
703-660-2364

National Association of Solvent Recyclers
1875 Connecticut Avenue, NW,
Suite 1200
Charlotte, NC 28217
704-357-3250

National Business Forms Association
433 East Monroe Avenue
Alexandria, VA 22301
703-836-6225

National Clean Air Coalition
801 Pennsylvania Avenue, SE
Washington, DC 20003
202-797-5436

National Coal Association
1130 Seventeenth Street, NW, 9th Floor
Washington, DC 20036
202-463-2625

National Cotton Council of America
1918 North Parkway
Memphis, TN 38112
901-532-9000

National Council of Paper Industry for Air and Stream Improvement
260 Madison Avenue
New York, NY 10016
212-532-9000

National Energy Foundation
5160 Wiley Post Way, Suite 200
Salt Lake City, UT 84116
801-539-1406

National Forest Products Association
1250 Connecticut Avenue, NW
Washington, DC 20026
202-463-2700

National Office Products Association
301 North Fairfax Street
Alexandria, VA 22314
703-549-9040

National Particleboard Association
18928 Premier Court
Gaithersburg, MD 20879
301-670-0604

National Petroleum Refiners Association
1899 L Street, NW, no. 1000
Washington, DC 20036
202-457-0480

National Propane Gas Association
1600 Eisenhower Lane, no. 100
Lisle, IL 60532
708-515-0600

National Recycling Coalition
1101 Thirtieth Street, NW, Suite 305
Washington, DC 20007
202-625-6406

National Resource Recovery Association
1620 I Street, NW, 4th Floor
Washington, DC 20006
202-293-7330

National Solid Waste Management Association
1730 Rhode Island Avenue, NW,
Suite 1000
Washington, DC 20036
202-659-4613

North American Association of Environmental Education
1255 Twenty-third Street, NW,
Suite 400
Washington, DC 20037
202-467-8754

Office of Environmental Safety and Health
1000 Independence Avenue, SW
Washington, DC 20585
202-586-6151

Paper Industry Management Association
2400 Oakton Street East, no. 100
Arlington Heights, IL 60005
708-956-0250

Paperboard Packaging Council
1101 Vermont Avenue, NW,
Suite 411
Washington, DC 20005
202-289-4400

**Plastic Bottle Information Bureau,
Plastic Bottle Institute**
1275 K Street, NW, Suite 400
Washington, DC 20005
202-371-5200

Printing Industries of America
100 Daingerfield Road
Alexandria, VA 22314
703-519-8100

Recoup
P.O. Box 577
Ogdensburg, NY 13669
800-267-0707
Lists fourteen thousand companies that
purchase recyclable materials in *American
Recycling Market* magazine.

Renewable Fuels Association
201 Massachusetts Avenue, NE, no. c4
Washington, DC 20002
202-289-3835

Society of Plastics Industry
1275 K Street, NW, Suite 400
Washington, DC 20005
202-371-5200

Solar Energy Industries Association
777 North Capitol Street, NE, Suite 805
Washington, DC 20002
202-408-0660

**Solid Waste Association of North
America**
8750 Georgia Avenue, Suite 140
Silver Spring, MD 20910
301-585-2898

**Textile Bag and Packaging
Association**
1024 Kinzie Avenue West
Chicago, IL 60622
312-921-3660

Timber Products Manufacturers
951 Third Avenue East
Spokane, WA 99202
509-535-4646

TOXNET
Specialized Information Services Division
National Library of Medicine
8600 Rockville Pike, Bldg. 38a
Bethesda, MD 20894
301-496-6531

Transportation Institute
5201 Auth Way
Camp Springs, MD 20746
301-423-3335

U.S. Chamber of Commerce
1615 H Street, NW
Washington, DC 20062
202-659-6000
National federation of business
organizations and companies. Has
committees on energy, environment,
and natural resources.

Magazines

American Forests
1516 P Street, NW
Washington, DC 20005

American Recycling Market
Recoup
P.O. Box 577
Ogdensburg, NY 13669

Animals
350 S. Huntington Avenue
Boston, MA 02130

Audubon
950 Third Avenue
New York, NY 10022

Buzzworm
P.O. Box 6853
Syracuse, NY 13217

The City Planet
4988 Venice Boulevard
Los Angeles, CA 90019

Consumer's Guide to Planet Earth
Schultz Communications
9412 Admiral Nimitz NE
Albuquerque, NM 87111

Co-op America Quarterly
Co-op America
1850 M Street, NW, Suite 700
Washington, DC 20036
202-872-5307

Defenders
Defenders of Wildlife
1244 Nineteenth Street, NW
Washington, DC 20036
202-659-9510

Design Spirit
438 Third Street
Brooklyn, NY 11215

E: The Environmental Magazine
Earth Action Network
P.O. Box 5098
Westport, CT 06881

Earth
Kalmbach Publishing Company
21027 Crossroads Circle
Waukesha, WI 53187

Earth Island Journal
Earth Island Institute
300 Broadway, Suite 28
San Francisco, CA 94133-3312

Earthwise Consumer
The Earthwise Consumer
P.O. Box 279
Forest Knolls, CA 94933

Ecologist
MIT Press
55 Hayward Street
Cambridge, MA 02142

EnviroEconomy
IFS Ltd.
Wolseley Business Park
Kempston, Bedford MK42 7PW,
United Kingdom
0234 853605

Environment Report
National Press Building
Washington, DC 20045
202-393-0031/202-393-1732

Environmental Action Magazine
Environmental Action
1525 New Hampshire Avenue, NW
Washington, DC 20036

Garbage
P.O. Box 56519
Boulder, CO 80322-6519
800-274-9909

In Business
P.O. Box 323
18 S. Seventh Street
Emmaus, PA 18049
215-967-4135

Packaging
1350 E. Touhy Avenue
P.O. Box 5080
Des Plaines, IL 60018-3303
708-635-8800

Packaging Digest
400 N. Michigan Avenue
Chicago, IL 60611-4104
312-222-2000

Pollution Abstracts
7200 Wisconsin Avenue
Bethesda, MD 20814-4811
301-961-5700

Pollution Engineering
1935 Shermer Road
Northbrook, IL 60062-5319
708-498-9846

Pollution Equipment News
650 Babcock Boulevard
Pittsburgh, PA 15237-5821
412-364-5366/412-364-5667

Preserve
Publisher's Service
P.O. Box 557
Smyrna, DE 19977

Recycling Times
1730 Rhode Island Avenue, NW,
no. 1000
Washington, DC 20036-3196
202-659-4613

Recycling Today
4012 Bridge Avenue
Cleveland, OH 44113-3320
216-961-4130

Resource Recovery Report
5313 Thirty-eighth Street, NW
Washington, DC 20015
202-298-6344

Resource Recycling
P.O. Box 10540
Portland, OR 97210-0540
503-227-1319

Reuse/Recycle
P.O. Box 3535
851 New Holland Avenue
Lancaster, PA 17604

Sierra
Sierra Club
730 Polk Street
San Francisco, CA 94109

Solid Waste Report
951 Pershing Drive
Silver Spring, MD 20910-4432
301-587-6300

Waste Age
170 Rhode Island Avenue. NW, no. 1000
Washington, DC 20036-3196
202-861-0708

Waste-to-Energy Report
1221 Avenue of the Americas
New York, NY 10020-1001
212-512-6310/212-512-4914

Wastetech News
131 Madison Street
Denver, CO 80206-5427
303-394-2905

Whole Earth
POINT
27 Gate Five Road
Sausalito, CA 94965

Wild Earth
Wild Earth
P.O. Box 492
Canton, NY 13617

Wildlife Conservation
New York Zoological Society
Bronx, NY 10460

WorldWatch
WorldWatch Institute
1776 Massachusetts Avenue, NW
Washington, DC 20036

Books

Biologic: Environmental Protection by Design
David Wann, 1990
Johnson Publishing Company
1880 S. Fifty-seventh Court
Boulder, CO 80301

The Earth Care Annual 1990
National Wildlife Federation, 1990
Editor: Russell Wild
Rodale Press
33 East Minor Street
Emmaus, PA 18098

Earth in the Balance
Al Gore, Jr., 1992
Houghton Mifflin Company
215 Park Avenue South
New York, NY 10003

*1992 Earth Journal Environmental Almanac
and Resource Directory*
Buzzworm Books, 1991
2305 Canyon Boulevard, Suite 206
Boulder, CO 80302

Ecopreneuring
Stephen J. Bennett, 1991
John Wiley & Sons
605 Third Avenue
New York, NY 10158-0012

*Environmental Address Book: How to Reach
the Environment's Greatest Champions and
Worst Offenders*
Michael Levine, 1991
Perigree Books
Putnam Publishing Group
200 Madison Avenue
New York, NY 10016

The 1993 Environmental Almanac
World Resources Institute, 1992
Houghton Mifflin Company
215 Park Avenue South
New York, NY 10003

Environmental Dividends
Compiled by the environmental
organization Inform, this book deals
predominantly with chemical companies
that have instituted environmentally
sound policies in their production of
materials and disposal of wastes.
Inform
381 Park Avenue South
New York, NY 10016
212-689-4040

Environmental Executive Directory
This extensive reference book was
published in November 1992 and
contains a wealth of information about
individuals, businesses, organizations—
both private and public—and media
sources that are involved directly in the
environmental industry. It serves as an
excellent guide for reaching key
environmental contacts in business,
government, and the media.
Carroll Publishing Company
1058 Thomas Jefferson Street, NW
Washington, DC 20007
202-333-8620

*Fifty Simple Things You Can Do to Save
the Earth*
Earth Works Group, 1989
Earth Works Press
Berkeley, CA

The Green Encyclopedia
Irene Franke and David Brownstone,
1992
Prentice-Hall General Reference
15 Columbus Circle
New York, NY 10023

*In Search of Environmental Excellence: Moving
Beyond Blame*
Bruce Piasecki and Peter Asmus, 1990
Simon & Schuster/Touchstone
Rockefeller Center
New York, NY 10020

Packaging for the Environment
E. Joseph Stillwell, R. Claire Canty, Peter
W. Kopf, Anthony M. Montrone, 1991
AMACOM Books
135 W. Fiftieth Street, 15th Floor
New York, NY 10020

*Readings for the Hurricane Island Outward
Bound School*
Editors: Alison Murray Kuller and Peter
O. Willauer, 1988
Hurricane Island Outward Bound Press,
Rockland, ME 04841

Addendum

The Laws That Govern

According to Paul Sorensen, director of corporate communications for Camp Dresser & McKee Inc. (CDM), an international environmental engineering firm, both the public and private sectors face a complex series of waste management alternatives.

"Every business and every state and local government sets its own priorities for managing waste effectively. It helps to create a hierarchy of priorities. In its simplest form, this hierarchy consists of four options," says Sorensen. "The most desirable alternative is waste reduction and waste minimization: Reduce what is produced and reduce the toxicity and contaminants of waste. Next, recycle—to recover whatever materials you can. A third option is energy recovery, or waste to energy, burning waste to generate energy." Landfills, he asserts, are viewed as a last resort, although there will always be a need for land disposal of some sort.

Legislative attempts to enforce the execution of these steps have resulted in a number of U.S. federal acts. Sorensen has helped us to define the legislation and to determine what implications each has for the business community, illustrated by the chart included here (asterisks represent amendments to original act).

LEGISLATION	YEAR ENACTED	DEFINITION
Federal Food, Drug and Cosmetic Act*	1938	established by FDA to regulate food and drug additives
*Delaney Clause	1958	prohibits sale of foods containing additives that cause cancer in humans or animals
Wilderness Act	1964	prohibits development of wilderness areas and establishes procedures for designation of new protected areas
National Environmental Policy Act	1969	declared a national environmental policy and created the Council on Environmental Quality
Clean Air Act (relegislated in 1977, 1990)	1970	formed the Environmental Protection Agency to oversee enforcement of air quality standards

LEGISLATION	YEAR ENACTED	DEFINITION
Federal Insecticide, Fungicide and Rodenticide Act (relegislated 1988)	1972	requires registration of all pesticides, applicant certification, and premarket testing
Clean Water Act (relegislated 1977, 1981, 1987)	1972	sets standards for wastewater treatment/sludge management; established effluent limitations and water quality standards
Endangered Species Act	1973	protects endangered or threatened species
Resource Conservation and Recovery Act (relegislated 1984)	1976	regulates the generation, transport, storage, treatment, and disposal of solid and hazardous waste
Toxic Substances Control Act	1976	gives EPA custody over assessing risks of chemicals and recordkeeping
Comprehensive Environmental Response, Compensation, and Liability Act**	1980	imposes liability on owners, transporters, and generators of hazardous waste; established fund to assist in cleanup costs (Superfund)
**Superfund Amendments and Reauthorization Act	1986	requires industry to publicly disclose chemicals and toxic hazards in their operations, in addition to other CERCLA provisions

In the estimation of Robert Marini, CEO of CDM, right now the Comprehensive Environmental Response, Compensation and Liability Act (CERCLA or Superfund) and RCRA have the greatest direct financial impact on industries. A firm may be held responsible for cleaning up a waste site if it owns or manages a contaminated property or generates hazardous waste or even transports or stores such material. If several businesses or industries share a site or facility, liability is jointly assumed, and if one party is unable to pay its share of the cleanup, the EPA can recover the remaining costs from the others. These parties can include previous owners and/or operators or any parties who have ever contracted to transport hazardous waste to that site or facility or who have inherited existing problems at the site.

"The Superfund is viewed largely as a result of the Love Canal disaster," says Sorensen. "Congress enacted CERCLA mainly to provide for the cleanup of abandoned toxic waste disposal sites. Of course, back in 1980, no one knew how bad the problem really was, and so Superfund has continued to expand its reach."

Understanding the Law

To better understand Superfund and the other laws listed in the chart, and the legal implications for the business community, we enlisted the advice of Mary B. Freeley, attorney with the law firm of Rackemann, Sawyer and Brewster in Boston. Her practice includes environmental, land use, and real estate litigation.

Through a combination of strict permitting requirements and effective enforcement tools, Congress has served up a virtual alphabet soup of environmental laws and regulations to address all varieties of discharges to our environment and to impose stringent compliance obligations on the industries that generate them. RCRA, CERCLA, SARA, CWA, and CAA, discussed briefly below, are but a few of the now-familiar acronyms for federal environmental statutes that establish minimum national standards for air and wastewater discharges and prescribe federal mandates for hazardous waste treatment, storage, and disposal. These statutes, and the environmental regulations promulgated under them, also create the administrative, civil, and criminal enforcement methods and penalty provisions that make compliance mandatory.

Apart from federal oversight, individual states have an increasing and significant impact on environmental compliance issues. In many instances, state requirements for the management of hazardous waste are far stricter than those contained in federal regulations.

The federal government's efforts to improve air and water quality have been implemented for more than two decades through a series of complex and comprehensive clean water and clean air legislative initiatives. The Clean Air Act of 1970 launched an ambitious national campaign to control air pollution by requiring the Environmental Protection Agency (EPA) to establish National Ambient Air Quality Standards (NAAQS) for a number of common pollutants: carbon monoxide, sulfur dioxide, nitrogen dioxide, ozone, particulates, and lead. These established standards, based on the protection of public health, establish ceilings for individual pollutant concentrations that should not be exceeded in the United States. NAAQS provide the basic foundation on which the federal air emission limitations and other regulatory controls are based. The Clean Air Act was substantially amended in 1990, adding provisions relating to the emission of toxic air pollutants, acid rain, and substances thought to affect the ozone layer.

Administrative enforcement actions and penalties and sanctions available to the EPA under the 1990 amendments have also been greatly expanded, dramatically increasing a company's exposure for noncompliance. Under the amendments, private citizens are authorized to seek civil penalties in citizen suits, and criminal enforcement provisions include stiff fines and imprisonment. Because of the increased severity of the enforcement sanctions, industries must plan an intelligent, effective air pollution control program in order to remain competitive.

The Clean Water Act (CWA) is the principal federal statute pertaining to water pollution control. Originally enacted as the Federal Water Pollution Control Act in 1972 and revised in 1977, the CWA creates a system of minimum national effluent limitations for each industry, water quality standards, a discharge permit program, and provisions for oil spills and toxic substances. In 1987 Congress substantially amended the CWA in an effort to improve water quality in areas where compliance with nationwide minimum discharge standards was insufficient to assure attainment of the CWA's water quality goals. Similar to the emission standards under the Clean Air Act, the effluent standards and criteria established under the CWA are legally enforceable against certain types of facilities with respect to discharges of pollutants into water streams.

Under the CWA, "best available technology" (BAT) effluent standards specify the amount of certain types of pollutants a particular type of facility may discharge through a "point source" (e.g., a pipe) into a navigable water. Ambient water quality standards under the CWA define the concentrations of acceptable surface water quality for certain types of uses.

Direct discharges to "waters of the United States" are regulated under the National Pollution Discharge Elimination System (NPDES) program. A NPDES permit establishes specific levels of performance the discharger must maintain and imposes a requirement to report failures to meet those levels to the appropriate regulatory agency. The EPA may also require the owner or operator of any point source to establish and maintain specific records, to make specified reports, to take samples or install monitoring devices, and to provide other information that the EPA deems necessary to ensure compliance. As with the Clean Air Act, significant penalties may be imposed under the Clean Water Act for the failure to report, the submission of false information, and the destruction of required information. In light of this exposure, the need for companies to implement well-funded and conscientious water pollution control compliance efforts is apparent.

In 1976 Congress passed landmark environmental legislation controlling the generation, transport, storage, treatment, and disposal of hazardous wastes. The cornerstone of the Resource Conservation and Recovery Act (RCRA) is waste minimization or pollution prevention. RCRA is designed to protect health and the environment on a national basis by establishing a cradle-to-grave regulatory program for present hazardous waste activities. To track hazardous materials from their generation to their ultimate disposition, RCRA requires the submission of detailed manifests to the EPA. RCRA also regulates underground storage tanks, land disposal restrictions, and cleanup of hazardous waste facilities. Violations of this act are subject to civil penalties of up to $25,000 for each violation. Criminal fines or imprisonment may be imposed for knowing violations.

Unlike RCRA, which was enacted as a *regulatory* program for current and new hazardous waste operations, the Comprehensive Environmental Response, Compensation and Liability Act, commonly known as CERCLA or the Federal Superfund Law, was designed as a comprehensive *response* and enforcement program for cleaning up those properties already contaminated with hazardous substances and for responding to spills of hazardous substances. CERCLA's scope is far broader than any of the other environmental statutes. CERCLA, and many of the state Superfund laws that were modeled after it or inspired by it, raised hazardous materials liability concerns to a new level of awareness. It radically changed many of the traditional principles of liability for the cleanup of releases or threatened releases of hazardous materials.

Enacted in 1980, CERCLA creates a revolving fund that can be tapped by the EPA and state and local governments to clean up hazardous waste sites (including those that have been abandoned) that have been listed by the EPA on its National Priorities List. Under CERCLA, current and former owners and operators of hazardous waste sites, as well as transporters and generators of the hazardous substances, collectively referred to as "potentially responsible parties" (PRPs), are made strictly, jointly, and severally liable for the cost of cleanup of hazardous substances released to the environment. This means that any one responsible party can be held liable for the entire cost of site investigation, cleanup, and other damages. The existence of this Superfund enables the government to initiate action to clean up a site where PRPs are not willing to undertake the work, are not available, or are insolvent.

With the enactment of the Superfund Amendments and Re-authorization Act of 1986 (SARA), the cost and complexity of hazardous waste liability defense and site cleanup under CERCLA increased, along with the number and pace of federal and state remedial action and cost recovery suits. These added costs, and the emergent division of legal authority governing the scope and extent of liability for potentially responsible parties' defense and cleanup obligations, pose a significant economic threat to companies that generate or dispose of hazardous waste. Further, under Title III of the SARA, also known as the Emergency Planning and Community Right-to-Know Act of 1986 (EPCRA), companies are required to identify the chemicals used in their operations and the possible toxic hazards they pose and to make that information available for public review.

The breadth and detail of information required of regulated industries under SARA create new challenges both from a public relations standpoint and from the perspective of effective risk management. Poor or inadequate waste management can have far-reaching consequences, including civil penalties, criminal indictments, citizen suits, and involvement in the cleanup of Superfund sites. In light of the increasing exposure to environmental liability, companies may perform environmental compliance audits simply to recognize areas where hazardous materials are being mismanaged to the extent that there has been or may be a release to the environment. Such evaluations are also routine prior to the acquisition or refinancing of businesses.

While directed at differing environmental pollutants, U.S. environmental statutes at their core share a common aim to effectuate public health concerns by preserving and improving the quality of the water we drink and the air we breathe. However, the sheer scope and complexity of these statutes (and of the numerous other state and federal laws not mentioned here) obscures this simple overarching principle and presents a compelling reason for businesses to implement aggressive programs to address their environmental compliance obligations. To the extent that current operators of a site or current proprietors of a business implement effective procedures to comply with the various environmental regulations that pertain to their operations, they will minimize or reduce the likelihood of bearing civil, criminal, and administrative penalties. Simply put, the impact of these environmental regulations on industry practice cannot be underestimated.

The Climate Is Right

In addition to the myriad programs that have been implemented by the Department of Energy, Department of Agriculture, and other United States agencies to prevent air pollution, the U.S. Environmental Protection Agency is expanding its efforts to reduce the risk of climate change by controlling greenhouse gas emissions such as carbon dioxide (CO_2) and methane (CH_4). Other types of air pollution that can be reduced significantly through this program include sulfur dioxide (SO_2)—a primary component of acid rain—and nitrogen oxides (NO_x), a contributor to both acid rain and smog.

Largely a voluntary effort, the program depends on widespread participation by companies and citizens to succeed. In this way the EPA is reaching out to the private sector to become its partner in embracing sound, cost-effective pollution opportunities and enhancing natural market forces to save energy, reduce pollution, and mitigate the risk of climate change. Early assistance and involvement is essential.

These new EPA programs provide mechanisms for improving energy efficiency leading to reduced fossil fuel use and lower carbon dioxide emissions and for capturing and using methane, a greenhouse gas. The key elements of EPA's voluntary green programs are the following:

1 Encourage consideration of energy efficiency for corporatewide purchasing. For example, departments responsible for purchasing equipment are urged to consider energy costs before making final decisions even though that department does not have to include electricity bills in its operating budget.

2 Identify energy-efficient products so that consumers can make educated purchasing decisions.

3 Promote mass purchases of energy-efficient technologies to drive down prices below those of their less energy-efficient alternatives.

4 Encourage industry to commercialize more resource-efficient technologies by demonstrating that these

products will sell. A viable market encourages manufacturers to get their products off the drawing board
quickly and onto store shelves.

5 Promote sensible utility regulation and legal frame-
works to encourage cost-effective investments in
energy conservation and methane-recovery programs. Fewer regulatory barriers can result in higher
profits for investors.

6 Promote the integration of environmental considerations into the design and planning of products and
services.

7 Expand international markets for resource-efficient
U.S. technologies. This not only creates additional
business opportunities for U.S. industry but also
helps to protect the global environment.

Go on Green

EPA's Green Lights Program is changing the way companies
light their offices and factories. Lighting accounts for over 20 percent
of total electricity consumption. Available technology can reduce this
by 50 to 70 percent and provide excellent investment opportunities.

By signing a partnership agreement with EPA, Green Lights
participants pledge to survey and upgrade 90 percent of all domestic
facilities with the most energy-efficient lighting systems that are profitable within five years. As of 30 September 1992, 651 "partners"
signed on. EPA projects a $7 billion to $15.8 billion reduction in the
nation's electricity bills by the year 2000. This estimate is based on
reported savings already achieved by such companies as Gillette and
Whirlpool.

Getting the job done is made easier with the EPA's technical
support from start to finish, including state-of-the-art software, information on financing, consumer reports of lighting products, and
networking through lighting manufacturers and management companies as well as utilities. EPA also provides opportunities for public
recognition through public-service ads, news articles, marketing materials, broadcast specials, and videotapes.

A Star Is Born

In 1992 computer systems were consuming 5 percent of all
commercial electricity. By the year 2000, a 5 percent increase is antic-

ipated. Because of this the EPA Energy Star Computer Program was born to create a market for energy-efficient desktop computers. Given that 30 to 40 percent of all computers are left on at night and over weekends and that they are active less than 20 percent of the time, even during the workday, the EPA is promoting the manufacture of personal computers that automatically "power down" when not in use. This could cut energy use in half and considerably reduce air pollution.

Within three months after it was launched in June 1992, the Energy Star Computer Program signed up 40 percent of all makers of personal computers and workstations sold in the United States. Each agreed to introduce personal computers that automatically reduce power when not in use. Consumers and businesses are urged to look for the Energy Star logo when purchasing new equipment.

Some Like It Hot

The cost for operating a heating, ventilation, and air-conditioning (HVAC) system could be reduced by 40 percent or more with the installation of a variable speed drive (VSD). VSDs adjust power based on the needs of the building occupants at any particular time or on weather circumstances.

To heat up demand for VSDs and to make them more afford-able, the EPA is providing the opportunity to participate in a group buy. Payback is realized within one to three years. EPA plans to ad-dress other green building technologies, such as solar thermal water heaters and amorphous core transformers.

Bugs Bunny Would Be Proud

Twenty percent of all residential electricity is consumed by refrigerators. To encourage the production of a more energy-efficient refrigerator, the EPA dangled a "Golden Carrot" to appliance manu-facturers. The gilded veggie, a multi-million-dollar pool, put together primarily by utility companies, provided rebate incentives to refriger-ator manufacturers for producing refrigerators 25 to 50 percent more energy efficient than the 1993 DOE performance standards. Whirl-pool became the recipient of a $30-million grant to build the largest number of the most efficient, chlorofluorocarbon-free refrigerators quickly and cheaply.

The environmentally superior refrigerator will be available to customers at a utility-subsidized price beginning 1994 or 1995. Annual savings in electricity payments are estimated at from $240 to $480 million, translating into an annual electric bill savings of 10 to 35 percent for an average household. Advanced heat pumps, residential central air conditioning, and clothes washers and driers are the next targets.

Support Your Local Utilities

As of July 1991, about a dozen states adopted comprehensive regulatory mechanisms to encourage conservation, touching off a positive move toward the relaxation and implementation of regulations that promise to make saving energy more profitable to utilities than selling it. Even though studies reveal that investment in energy efficiency is more cost effective than supply, regulations in most states continue to encourage investments in power plants and discourage investment in efficiency. The result has been an inefficient mix of resources, inflated costs, and unwarranted air pollution.

Under the Utility Reform Flagship Program, the EPA, the DOE, and other federal agencies are working to encourage more states to implement regulations that will prevent pollution while benefiting stockholders as well as rate payers. The basic premise is that utilities should be able to make as much money on energy saved as on energy sold when savings are properly verified. This philosophy was formally embraced in the 1990 Clean Air Act amendments, which provide incentives for utilities to reduce compliance costs through the use of renewable energy and energy efficiency.

Step on the Gas

Although a variety of proven technologies are available to recover and use methane, legal barriers and regulations discourage the harvest. Methane gas is produced by the decay of all organic matter and is principally concentrated around wetlands, cattle farms, and coal mines. Though created naturally, the accelerated release of methane into the air is a primary contributor to the greenhouse effect.

The principal legal question that has yet to be answered is, Who owns the gas emitted by coal mines? The EPA is working with the U.S. coal industry to get that question answered and documented as well as to identify the other barriers to methane recovery. The next step is to assist in lifting all of these stumbling blocks on both state and federal levels.

Recovery of methane from coal mines has major international implications. U.S. companies lead the world in the development of technologies to recover and use methane from coal seams, opening up opportunities for exports and international joint ventures. The EPA is organizing seminars, workshops, and conferences on coal-bed methane to showcase the achievements of U.S. companies and will continue these efforts in several countries, including the People's Republic of China, Russia, Ukraine, Poland, and the Czech and Slovak federal republics.

Green Nylons

The United States produces about one-third of the world's nylon in a manufacturing process that releases the greenhouse gas nitrous oxide (N_2O). These emissions can be reduced during the manufacturing process through the addition of a reductive furnace to adipic acid plants, the factories that produce nylon.

The EPA is working with major U.S. nylon manufacturers to expand the use of reductive furnaces. Developed now and expected to be fully commercialized by the mid-1990s, this technology recycles nitrous oxide, conserves energy, and saves on raw materials.

To Russia with Love

Russia is the largest natural gas producer in the world. About 6 percent of this gas is released into the atmosphere. In an attempt to reduce leakage to 2 percent, the EPA and GAZPROM (the Russian gas association) have established a working group of experts from both countries to increase the efficiency of the natural gas system in Russia by implementing projects using existing and profitable Western techniques and work practices.

Other projects include enhanced field maintenance, upstream refining of gas, leak detection and mapping, pipeline construction and rehabilitation, compressor upgrades, power generation, and improved measurement and control devices. The Russian Natural Gas Pipeline project could reduce methane emissions by 15 Tg, the equivalent of 90 million metric tons of carbon, while providing additional capital resources for new economic development projects in Russia and creating further export and investment opportunities for U.S. industry.

We Are the World

The United States was the first industrialized nation to become a signatory of the United Nations Framework Convention on Climate Change, drafted at the United Nations Conference on Environment and Development held in Rio de Janeiro, Brazil, in June 1992. Also signed by 153 other nations, the treaty calls on each to mitigate climate change by limiting its emissions of greenhouse gases.

Very quickly after the convention, the EPA launched its Climate Is Right voluntary programs. The United States is committed to the treaty's ultimate objective, which is to stabilize greenhouse gas concentrations in the atmosphere at a level that would prevent dangerous anthropogenic interference with the climate system. No one expects overnight results. In fact safe levels should be achieved within a time frame sufficient to allow ecosystems to adapt naturally to climate change, to ensure that food production is not threatened, and to enable economic development to proceed. The climate is right for action.